NARRATIVE WORLDS:

ESSAYS ON THE *NOUVELLE*

IN FIFTEENTH- AND SIXTEENTH-

CENTURY FRANCE

Medieval and Renaissance Texts and Studies

Volume 285

NARRATIVE WORLDS:

ESSAYS ON THE *NOUVELLE*

IN FIFTEENTH- AND SIXTEENTH-

CENTURY FRANCE

edited by

Gary Ferguson

and

David LaGuardia

© Copyright 2005
Arizona Board of Regents for Arizona State University

Library of Congress Cataloging-in-Publication Data

Narrative worlds : essays on the nouvelle in fifteenth- and sixteenth- century France / edited by Gary Ferguson and David LaGuardia.
  p. cm. — (Medieval and Renaissance Texts and Studies ; v. 285)
  Includes bibliographical references and index.
  ISBN 0-86698-328-7 (alk. paper)
  1. French fiction—To 1500--History and criticism. 2. French fiction--16th century—History and criticism. 3. Novelle—History and criticism. I. Ferguson, Gary, 1963- II. LaGuardia, David, 1963- III.
Medieval & Renaissance Texts & Studies (Series) ; v. 285.

PQ221.N37 2005
843'.209—dc22

2005004729

This book is made to last.
It is set in Garamond
smyth-sewn and printed on acid-free paper
to library specifications.

Printed in the United States of America

Cover Image:
Woodcut from *Les Cent nouvelles nouvelles*
(Paris: A. Vérard, 1486) Cliché Bibliothèque nationale de France, Pariss

CONTENTS

Acknowledgement   i

Introduction   1

"Une merveilleuse espece d'animal": Fable and Verisimilitude   17
in Bonaventure des Périers's *Nouvelles récréations et joyeux devis*
   Emily Thompson

Des Périers on Speed   35
   Tom Conley

Monkey Business: Imitation and the Status of the Text   59
in Du Fail's *Propos rustiques*
   Richard L. Regosin

Jeanne Flore and Erotic Desire: Feminism or Male Fantasy?   77
   Floyd Gray

History or Her Story? (Homo)sociality/sexuality   97
in Marguerite de Navarre's *Heptaméron* 12
   Gary Ferguson

Fictions of the Eyewitness   123
   John O'Brien

Exemplarity as Misogyny: Variations on the Tale   139
of the One-Eyed Cuckold
   David LaGuardia

Jacques Yver's *Le Printemps d'Yver*   159
and Trans-Gender Phantasmagoria
   Deborah N. Losse

Bibliography   173

Contributors   189

Index   191

Acknowledgement

Floyd Gray's essay "Jeanne Flore and Erotic Desire: Feminism or Male Fantasy?" was first published as part of the second chapter of the author's *Gender, Rhetoric, and Print Culture in French Renaissance Writing* (Cambridge: Cambridge University Press, 2000). It is reprinted here by kind permission of the publisher.

Introduction

Gary Ferguson and David LaGuardia

In terms of the volume of its production, the *nouvelle* represents one of the most important genres of the fifteenth and sixteenth centuries in France. With the possible exception of the *Heptaméron*, however, the critical literature devoted to it is rather sparse in comparison with the immense and continually growing body of work on Rabelais, Montaigne, and the poets of the Pléiade. The reasons for this neglect are no doubt manifold. The subject matter of the tales contained in the first collections in French—such as the anonymous *Cent nouvelles nouvelles* of 1462 and Philippe de Vigneulles's *Cent nouvelles nouvelles* of 1515—was perhaps considered too scabrous and vulgar to be addressed by the first scholars who read these texts from a critical point of view. While Rabelais frequently surpassed the vulgarity of these tales, his work might also be redeemed by the "seriousness" of its much-debated allegorical dimensions. Given its radically different point of view concerning the body's essential activities (as Bakhtin remarked, sex, eating, and scatology all belong to the same corporeal paradigm),[1] the *nouvelle* was not easily accepted by a generation of scholars (Paris, Bédier, Söderhjelm, even Auerbach) living in a context in which the more distasteful of these were rarely addressed in scholarly discourse.[2] The protagonists of the first *nouvelles* in French often indulge any and all of their bodily desires to extremes of scatological and sexual cruelty that remain difficult to accept to this day. A second reason for the neglect of the *nouvelle* no doubt

---

[1] See Mikhail Bakhtin, *Rabelais and His World*, trans. Hélène Iswolsky (Bloomington: Indiana University Press, 1984), 18–30.

[2] Cf. V. L. Saulnier's introduction to *La Nouvelle française à la Renaissance*, ed. Lionello Sozzi (Geneva and Paris: Slatkine, 1981): "Le conte de la Renaissance, le français comme l'italien, a longtemps souffert d'une fausse réputation. On y pressentait, principal et général, un goût des anecdotes égrillardes. Il n'y a pas si longtemps, l'*Heptaméron* lui-même, cette œuvre éminemment moralisante, apparaissait encore comme un recueil «gaulois». En certains cas, l'illustration graphique du texte ne fut pas faite pour décourager le contresens. On souhaite qu'il soit aujourd'hui dépassé" (vii).

concerns its mode of representation and character portrayal, which depend frequently on stereotypes. The *nouvellistes* returned again and again to a stock set of figures and themes (in addition to scatology, for example, adultery, cuckoldry, gluttony, larceny, and so on) that had little value or interest from the point of view of modern critics who required from fictional narratives both depth of character and at least the semblance of verisimilitude. This is a question to which we shall return below.

In spite of such objections, scholars did begin to examine the genre seriously at the end of the nineteenth century, focusing on two issues that have remained prominent in *nouvelle* scholarship to this day. The first was the task of defining the genre in relation to other types of narrative that were important during the Middle Ages and the Renaissance; the second was the necessity of delineating and explicating its historical and linguistic origins.[3] From these perspectives, one of the most complete and concise definitions of the genre was offered recently by Luciano Rossi:

> la nouvelle est une narration brève, généralement en prose (à la différence des fabliaus/fabliaux, des lais, des dits et des *novas* occitanes, qui sont en vers octosyllabiques). Elle présente des personnages humains (contrairement à la fable ésopique qui met en scène des animaux), mais généralement non historiques (à la différence de l'anecdote et de l'*exemplum*). Ses contenus sont vraisemblables (à la différence de ceux de la fable, qui sont fantaisistes). Le plus souvent elle est dépourvue de buts moraux ou de conclusions «moralistes» (contrairement à l'*exemplum*) ou alors, s'il y en a, ils sont présentés sous une forme ironique; par contre, elle développe souvent une perspective joyeusement grivoise.
>
> Le type de narration ainsi esquissé se réalise dans le choix entre différentes possibilités (récit «dénoué», ou intégré dans un «cadre»; écrit/oral, etc.). Né en Orient, il trouve au Moyen Age sa première réalisation en Italie, entre le XIII^c et le XIV^c siècles. Il s'affirmera plus tard en Espagne, aussi bien qu'au Portugal, puis en France. Ce-

---

[3] For a discussion of these early critical reactions to the *nouvelle*, see David LaGuardia, *The Iconography of Power: The French Nouvelle at the End of the Middle Ages* (Newark, DE: University of Delaware Press, 1999), chap. 1.

pendant, dans le reste de l'Europe, la concurrence avec les termes de conte, *cuento, conto* reste toujours très forte.[4]

In terms of its formal characteristics, then, the *nouvelle* is distinguished amidst a multiplicity of short narrative forms by its hybridity. While the genre may be a new one in its historical context, it still derives its formal meaning and characteristics from the place that it occupies in a series of generic intertexts. Thus, as recent scholarship has emphasized, the Renaissance tale must be defined as part of a system of narrative genres, all of which take their meaning from their relationships one to another.[5]

Just as the *nouvelle* is a complex genre that must be defined in relation to other types of narrative, so its origins are extremely difficult to describe in their entirety. Scholars such as Joseph Bédier, Janet Ferrier, and Roger Dubuis stressed its descent from native oral traditions and European narrative forms, notably the *lai*, the *fabliau*, and the romance.[6] Others, like Gaston Paris, sought to demonstrate the Oriental origin of much of the medieval

---

[4] Luciano Rossi, "Entre fabliau et facétie: La Nouvelle en France au XVe siècle," in *La Nouvelle de langue française aux frontières des autres genres, du Moyen Age à nos jours*, ed. Vincent Engel and Michel Guissard (Ottignies, Belgium: Editions Quorum, 1997), 28–39, here 30.

[5] Philippe de Lajarte expresses this conclusion in the following manner: "Rappelons-nous toutefois qu'il n'est de représentation historiquement juste d'un genre ou d'un type de discours littéraire que celle qui envisage ces derniers comme des éléments faisant partie d'un ensemble plus vaste—celui que constitue, à un moment donné de son histoire, la littérature considérée, précisément, comme un système de genres et de types de discours—et qui, par conséquent, inclut la représentation des rapports que ces genres ou ces types de discours entretiennent avec les autres genres ou les autres types de discours appartenant au même ensemble. Or, si on le considère de ce point de vue, le genre nouvellistique ou, pour mieux dire peut-être, le type de discours que constitue le récit bref apparaît, dans le champ littéraire du XVIe siècle, comme un élément susceptible d'entrer dans la composition d'une pluralité de genres qui, bien qu'appartenant à ce qu'on pourrait appeler une même constellation générique, n'ont pas tous—c'est là le fait essentiel sur lequel il faut d'entrée de jeu mettre l'accent—un contenu purement narratif": Philippe de Lajarte, "La Nouvelle aux frontières du commentaire et du dialogue dans L'*Heptaméron* de Marguerite de Navarre," in *La Nouvelle de langue française*, 77–113, here 78.

[6] See Joseph Bédier, *Les Fabliaux: Etudes de littérature populaire et d'histoire littéraire du Moyen Age*, 6th ed. (Paris: Champion, 1969); Janet M. Ferrier, *Forerunners of the French Novel: An Essay on the Development of the Nouvelle in the Late Middle Ages* (Manchester: Manchester University Press, 1954); Roger Dubuis, *Les* Cent nouvelles nouvelles *et la tradition de la nouvelle en France au Moyen Age* (Grenoble: Presses Universitaires de Grenoble, 1973).

narrative material that is exploited in its turn by the *nouvelle*, positing the transmission of Buddhist stories from India to Europe in Arabic or Latin translations, via the intermediation of the crusaders or through Moorish Spain.[7] The most recent attempts to unravel the beginnings of the Renaissance tale demonstrate that the possibility of completely sorting out and identifying its sources is remote. Rossi, for example, has written convincingly on the *nouvelle*'s relation to medieval translations of Justinian's *Novellae constitutiones*, a legal collection of the Byzantine emperor's new postcodification edicts in cases of everyday infractions, such as theft and adultery. Similarly, Alain Cullière explicated the relationship between a later *nouvelle* collection, Alexandre van den Bussche's *Premier Livre des procès tragiques* of 1575, and Seneca the Elder's rhetorical manual, the *Controversiae*.[8] As compelling as they are, these and the earlier attempts to locate the sources of the genre also point to a problem that is perhaps inherent in this search for origins. Since scholars have been able to locate the *nouvelle*'s analogues in narrative and even non-narrative forms that developed in the most disparate of linguistic and historical settings, it would appear that the more the *nouvelle*'s origins and sources are identified and explicated, the more proliferous and elusive they are revealed to be.

A third question which has been central to scholarship on the *nouvelle*, and which is of particular concern here, is that of the genre's "realism." Especially in the period preceding the posthumous publication of the *Heptaméron* in 1558, the characters of the *nouvelle* are conventional figures that lack complexity from a point of view that values realism and its typical representation of "deep" and "lifelike" characters. To a large degree, the *nouvelle*'s protagonists are evoked only by standard designations that imply stereotypical sets of attributes: the gluttonous monk, the greedy merchant, the drunken miller, the lascivious wife, the sexually predatory knight, the lazy clerk, and so on. "Real" people, who act rationally and logically, appear rarely in these texts; rather, we find character types that act according to established conventions and narrative patterns. Even so, for many scholars reading after the development of literary realism in the nineteenth century, the principal interest of the *nouvelle* lay in its being a precursor of the modern realist short story or the novel. It remained inferior to these later genres, however, to the extent that it disregarded verisimilitude and individuali-

---

[7] Gaston Paris, "Les Contes orientaux dans la littérature française du moyen âge," in *La Poésie du Moyen Age*, deuxième série (Paris: Hachette, 1895), 75–108, and idem, "Le Lai de l'épervier," *Romania* 7 (1878): 1–21.

[8] Rossi, "Entre fabliau et facétie," 30–34; Alain Cullière, "De la controverse à la nouvelle: Alexandre van den Bussche, lecteur de Sénèque," in *La Nouvelle de langue française*, 40–52.

zation of character. These scholars thus tended to identify and discuss appreciatively the *nouvelle*'s "modern" elements, while, on the other hand, depreciating those that were at odds with realist criteria. Such an approach characterizes, for example, the work of Werner Söderhjelm, who concludes that "cette marche vers un réalisme artistique et un subjectivisme approfondi est un signe que la Renaissance approche."[9] It also characterizes two important studies from the middle of the last century: Erich Auerbach's *Mimesis* (1953) and Janet Ferrier's *Forerunners of the French Novel* (1954).[10] Perhaps more than any other critic, Ferrier emphasized the lack of realism of so many of the *nouvelle* collections, with the notable exception of the *Heptaméron*. It is Marguerite de Navarre, for Ferrier, who breathes new life into the genre, making it a forerunner of the "novel of situation."[11]

The most important study of the *nouvelle* from the later decades of the twentieth century is perhaps Gabriel-A. Pérouse's monumental *Nouvelles françaises du XVIe siècle: Images de la vie du temps* (1977). As his title suggests, Pérouse reaffirms strongly the genre's association with realism, setting himself the daunting task "de relever tous les *realia*, d'analyser toutes les peintures de la société et du monde quotidien—quel que soit le milieu—dans tous les «contes» du XVIe siècle."[12] Pérouse pursues his ambition with patience and erudition, presenting numerous less-studied *nouvelle* collections as repositories of *realia* that afford images of the "real" lives of people living in fifteenth- and sixteenth-century France. While he does not deny that the process whereby experience of daily life is transformed into its literary representation involves a degree of distortion (if only that attributable to authorial bias, generic constraints, and so on), nevertheless, the critic's pri-

---

[9] Werner Söderhjelm, *La Nouvelle française au XVe siècle* (Paris: Champion, 1910; repr. Geneva: Slatkine Reprints, 1973), 229.

[10] Erich Auerbach, *Mimesis: The Representation of Reality in Western Literature*, trans. Willard R. Trask (Princeton: Princeton University Press, 1953), chaps. 9 and 10. Of the *Cent nouvelles nouvelles*, Auerbach writes: "Nothing is left . . . of the human, critical, and embracing perspective of the *Decameron*, of the multiplicity of its scenes and its reports of life. . . . the characterization . . . is purely 'creatural,' that is to say, not at all without life, and indeed quite true to life, but without any individualization. . . . The realism of the Franco-Burgundian culture of the fifteenth century is, then, narrow and medieval" (260–61). Of Boccaccio, however, Auerbach had earlier concluded: "His realism—which is free, rich, and assured in its mastery of phenomena, which is completely natural within the limits of the intermediate style—becomes weak and superficial as soon as the problematic or the tragic is touched upon" (231). For Ferrier, see n. 6 above.

[11] Ferrier, *Forerunners*, 5–6; cf. also 85–103.

[12] Gabriel-A. Pérouse, *Nouvelles françaises du XVIe siècle: Images de la vie du temps* (Geneva: Droz, 1977), 2; author's italics.

mary focus remains what he terms the collections' "*contenu documentaire*."[13] For Pérouse, the *nouvelles* constitute "une littérature narrative réaliste," revealing a culture and its "mentalités," in which "une société s'est complu à se dire elle-même."[14]

Scholarly literature on the *nouvelle* from the 1970s and 1980s tends to reflect similar critical concerns, viewing the genre as a "forerunner" of the modern novel and the first in European literature to attempt a "realistic" depiction of everyday life, devoid of magical figures and spiritual interventions (as Rossi remarked). This view of the genre as the birthplace of realism is evident, for example, in the work of Lionello Sozzi, as well as in that of Roger Dubuis on the *Cent nouvelles nouvelles*.[15]

Collections of *nouvelles* certainly reflect *something* of the reality of the everyday life of the period. There is much they can tell us about contemporary "mentalités" and "culture"; nevertheless, they do this, we would contend, not necessarily through a realistic portrayal of characters or actions. The pages of the *nouvelle* collections may be scoured for examples of contemporary *realia*; nevertheless, the differences between "daily life" and the obsessive narrative rehearsal of certain themes and certain sorts of plot, or between a literary "type" and any kind of socio-historical counterpart, seem to us fundamental and worthy of further and more probing examination. Narratives are generated according to conventions and rules that often have little to do with "reality";[16] frequently, for example, literary tradition and

---

[13] Pérouse, *Nouvelles françaises*, 8; author's italics.

[14] Pérouse, *Nouvelles françaises*, 492.

[15] According to Lionello Sozzi, in the *nouvelle* "l'étude désintéressée du réel commence à se faire jour": *La Nouvelle française de la Renaissance*, 2 vols. (Turin: G. Giappichelli, 1973–1977), 1:xvii, and, in general, xi–xxiii. While Roger Dubuis argues that "les *Cent Nouvelles nouvelles* sont loin d'être . . . le reflet du monde dans lequel vivaient l'auteur et ses lecteurs," he also contends that they nevertheless exemplify a certain literary realism: "Miroir fidèle de la réalité, mais aussi, et en même temps, tremplin de l'imagination la plus libre, le recueil illustre parfaitement une certaine conception du réalisme . . .": "Réalité et réalisme dans les «Cent nouvelles nouvelles»," in *La Nouvelle française à la Renaissance*, ed. Sozzi, 91–119, here 94–95, 118. A similar view is frequently implied in Dubuis's major study, referred to above, n. 6, on the *Cent nouvelles nouvelles*.

[16] Nabokov writes, in reference to the creation of *Lolita*: "It had taken me some forty years to invent Russia and Western Europe, and now I was faced by the task of inventing America. The obtaining of such local ingredients as would allow me to inject a modicum of average 'reality' (one of the few words which mean nothing without quotes) into the brew of individual fancy, proved at fifty a much more difficult process than it had been in the Europe of my youth when

intertextuality may be more critical determining factors: this is clearly one of the major implications of the many inquiries into the *nouvelle*'s sources. Given that the *nouvellistes* represent a world populated by cuckolds, gluttons, thieves, adulteresses, and philanderers, it might be suggested—provocatively—that they have as much to do with their contemporary reality as the soap operas and sitcoms of today have to do with our own world. A scholar attempting to know something about us five hundred years from now by viewing and cataloguing these televised narratives would derive a strangely distorted understanding of what "ordinary life" was like at the beginning of the twenty-first century. An understanding of everyday life in sixteenth-century France based upon a reading of the *nouvelle* collections might be equally far removed from what that life was like in actuality.

Nevertheless, reading at such a chronological remove, we do discover something essential about the period: we become familiar (as Pérouse recognized) with the types of stories and plots that fascinated large numbers of people—if we are to judge by the frequency of editions and re-editions of the *nouvelle* collections. By consistently repeating the same kinds of stories, the fifteenth- and sixteenth-century *nouvellistes* perhaps revealed something that was fundamental to their identities, if we define this concept in narrative terms, i.e., one's identity is essentially a story that one continually rehearses, modifies, and retells to oneself. The same could be said for the collective identity of a culture, which requires that stories be told and listened to constantly, producing a version of events that is an abstract accompaniment to the material world on which these stories comment.[17]

The characteristics we have outlined may seem to apply particularly to *nouvelles* of the earlier collections (as Ferrier argued); they are also relevant, however, to many of those of the later ones, including the *Heptaméron*. In relation to Marguerite's *nouvelles*, for example, Daniel Russell has argued that the coexistence of two very different conceptions of structuring character

---

receptiveness and retention were at their automatic best": Vladimir Nabokov, *Lolita* (New York: Vintage International, 1997), 312.

[17] In this respect, one of the most important contributions to recent scholarship on the *nouvelle* is the collection of essays on the *Heptaméron* edited by John D. Lyons and Mary B. McKinley, *Critical Tales: New Studies of the* Heptameron *and Early Modern Culture* (Philadelphia: University of Pennsylvania Press, 1993). In their introductory and concluding remarks, the editors note both that the *Heptaméron* "represents in microcosm the conflicts, tensions, and beliefs of early modern French society as viewed from one part of the court" and that it "prevents readers from falling into the world of the story and forgetting that they are confronted, not with a window on reality, but with verbal reports about the world" (ix, 263).

"highlights the transitional character of this society where there was no dominant, stable conception of the self, but where the model of medieval types was still feuding with the new ideal of the Renaissance individual."[18] Similarly, when Marguerite takes traditional tales, rewriting them so as to make them appear "new" and "true," such *nouvelles* do not thereby become realist narratives, any more than do Michel Tournier's modern rewritings of traditional myths and stories in our own time.[19]

The *nouvelle*'s traditional association by scholars with the development of realism and with verisimilitude or with a certain historical accuracy has no doubt been encouraged in part by the *nouvellistes*' own frequently repeated claim that their stories are "true." If, however, we examine this claim critically, and if we do not approach the *nouvelle* as proto-realist narrative, how else might we read its distorted, frequently hyperbolic, fictions—especially given the radically different perspective(s) from which we necessarily begin? The contributors to the present volume offer a number of possible responses to this question, sharing, most fundamentally, a concern to question in some way the *nouvelle*'s ready association with the "real." On the contrary, in the present essays a number of cognate binaries emerge which posit, for example, in critical relation, verisimilitude and fable, mimesis and parody, history and story, realism and fantasy. And in each case is revealed the extent to which the "truth" of the *nouvelle* is bound up with the fantastic, the phantasmic, the fictional.

Focusing on this central critical question, the essays nevertheless develop a broad range of critical and theoretical perspectives, drawing variously on the discourses and methodologies of history and literary history, psychoanalysis, narratology, post-structuralism, socio-criticism, feminism, and queer theory. Given such a variety of theoretical foundations, it is clear that not all the approaches adopted will necessarily be compatible with each other; that, indeed, they may lead to quite different readings and conclusions. Despite this diversity, however, a number of other common interests will also be seen to emerge. Issues of genre, intentionality, representation, and gender, for example, recur. As the essays reflect a plurality of theoretical approaches, so they deal also with a diverse group of primary texts, spanning a period of a little more than a century—from 1462, the date of the anonymous Burgundian *Cent nouvelles nouvelles*, to 1572, the date of the posthumous publication of Jacques Yver's *Printemps*. In addition to essays discussing these two collections, three studies deal, in whole or in part, with

---

[18] Daniel Russell, "Some Ways of Structuring Character in the *Heptameron*," in *Critical Tales*, 203–17, here 208.

[19] Cf., for example, many of the tales in Tournier's *Le Coq de bruyère* (Paris: Gallimard, 1978).

stories from the now canonical *Heptaméron* of Marguerite de Navarre, while two more examine Bonaventure des Périers's *Nouvelles récréations et joyeux devis*. One essay each is devoted to the rather less-studied collections of Noël du Fail, *Les Propos rustiques*, and Jeanne Flore, *Les Comptes amoureux*. The assembled critical voices thus speak individually yet also play off one another, like those of the *nouvelle* collections' own *devisants*.

In the first essay, Emily Thompson examines Bonaventure des Périers's *Nouvelles récréations et joyeux devis* in relation to the question of the genre of the *nouvelle* and its defining characteristics. Thompson provides a thorough overview of scholarly attempts to define the *nouvelle* based on historical and psychological realism, *vraisemblance*, or narrators' repeated claims to tell truthful stories. Reviewing the work of a number of critics, Thompson notes that "the tenacity of the debate has forced all scholars of the *nouvelle* to take a stance on the question of realism." Building in particular on the work of Lionello Sozzi and Gisèle Mathieu-Castellani, Thompson reexamines the issues involved, and particularly the ways in which the *conteurs* problematize the notion of "truth." She argues that the writers of the *nouvelles* were in fact attempting to redefine the narrative contract associated with the genre and "to create a new space for short fictional prose." Thompson examines the implied narrative contract set up between narrator(s) and reader(s) in the metadiscursive frames and commentaries of the *Nouvelles récréations* as well as of a number of other collections. Ending with a discussion of two of Des Périers's *nouvelles* that incorporate elements from the unrealistic genre of the fable, Thompson shows how the reader is meant to recognize both a given *nouvelle*'s intertextual relations with other literary genres and the *conteur*'s departures from the expectations thus generated. Elements of realism incorporated into the *nouvelle*, Thompson argues, function in a similar way, serving both to create and to undermine a sense of verisimilitude, and to produce a surprise which depends "both on an unusual story and on constant reminders of the social and literary conventions which it infringes." From this perspective, a talking monkey, a creature of fable, would not necessarily be out of place in a *nouvelle*—provided the reader recognized its hybrid literary nature and was amused.

Tom Conley also examines principally Des Périers's *Nouvelles récréations et joyeux devis*, but also offers some comparisons with another work sometimes attributed to the same author, the *Discours non plus melancholiques que divers*. Conley stresses the diverse nature of the sources on which Des Périers drew to produce his *nouvelles*. Medieval literary forms such as the *fabliau* and the bawdy tale are renewed and transformed by elements drawn from folklore, the Bible, humanist ideology, recent history, and everyday life. The *Nouvelles récréations* thus have a transitional quality typical of contemporary print culture as well as the plastic arts. Conley shows how Des Périers's works describe a French space, celebrating in the vernacular tongue the geography of a nation marked by variety and diversity. Des Périers thus betrays the figure of the ethnologist, the practitioner of everyday life, but most of all of the topographer. For Conley, the *Nouvelles récréations* and the *Discours* constitute a "'language-map' of a nation imagined united through a vernacular idiom. What the latter conveys is of a concurrent diversity made manifest by its own variegated nature. It is shown both to assure the presence of the hidden signature of a divine but forever secret origin and to give cause to a 'politics of language' or a new historical anthropology of a nation." A map is not a mirror, however (any more than Des Périers is a Stendhal).[20] The literary work as a cartographic object highlights its constructed nature, which corresponds not to a realistic representation of the world, but rather to its ideological projection into literary discourse, in the same way that a map projects a given ideological preconception of space and nation. Conley examines two cartographical characteristics of Des Périers's works in particular. First, the way in which at times the text's printed words "acquire a spatial or plotted look that makes them at once parts of pictural emblems and latent topographical sites of a book-map": repeated graphemes and words, puns, and the like, create visual and spatial patterns. The second characteristic concerns the collapse of duration or historical time, the plotting of movement within the stories and from one story to another, and particularly the creation of an impression of speed and of a world in acceleration. It may be, Conley suggests in conclusion, that it was precisely Des Périers's "ethics of speed," combined with a nationalism celebrating diversity, that religious authorities considered such a threat.

Concentrating on Noël du Fail's *Propos rustiques*, Richard L. Regosin returns to the questions of genre and realism raised by Thompson. The degree to which the *Propos* offer (or fail to offer) a realistic image of the historical and social world of Breton peasants has been the object of significant critical concern. At the same time, Du Fail has been haunted by Etienne Pasquier's charge that he was nothing more than a "monkey," a bad imitator, trying vainly to "ape" Rabelais. Even critics sympathetic to Du Fail have tended to be influenced by the comparison with Rabelais, seeing his work as sharing to some (lesser) degree in the qualities of *Gargantua* and *Pantagruel*. At what point, then, asks Regosin, does the difference between a text and its model become too great? At what point does an imitation become a "bad" imitation? The importance of such questions is

---

[20] Cf. Stendhal, *Le Rouge et le noir*, in *Romans et nouvelles* (Paris: Gallimard, 1952), 557.

clear in the light of the fact that imitation was a favored means of textual production throughout the Renaissance, and imitation always inevitably involves some degree of difference. It is in the figure of the ape as an emblem of parody that Regosin finds a way to answer these questions as they relate to Du Fail's work. Reading the *Propos rustiques* as a text of parodic disposition, Regosin highlights its indeterminate character and unstable, ultimately indefinable, intention. "Imitation can be a form of flattery or a form of mockery; parody does not always allow the reader to decide with any degree of certainty, it does not always announce its intention unequivocally. In fact, what parody does allow for is the unintentional reversal of intention, as when the imitation ends up mocking the mocker and the monkey makes a monkey of himself." So are the *Propos rustiques* a mocking imitation or a mock text? For Regosin, the *Propos* foreground precisely the question of imitation as central to the literary mode, revealing that all texts are part imitation, all writers part monkey. Noting the rich polysemy of the title—the *Propos* are not *nouvelles* but "propos" ("the matter of discourse, discourse itself, conversation, narrative, remarks and observations, intention")—Regosin concludes that "the *Propos rustiques* perform and parody the engendering of discourse in general. . . . the text self-consciously stages and mimics its own production."

Floyd Gray's essay on the *Comptes amoureux* of Jeanne Flore also concerns intertextuality, parody, irony, and the indeterminate intentionality of the work, revealing the plural ways in which so much of the text can be read. Do the *Comptes amoureux* express genuine feminist concerns or rather parody those concerns? Are they even misogynous? In the absence of conclusive information concerning the identity of the author(s), it is simply not possible to say for certain. As in the case of the *Propos rustiques*, the potentially parodic nature of the text opens up the possibility of multiple and contradictory significations and undercuts any attempt to define intention. Again like the *Propos rustiques*, moreover, the *Comptes* do not sit in a straightforward manner within the genre of the *nouvelle*, since the stories they recount are neither new nor recent but rather mythical, legendary, or at least old, often rewriting classical or canonical authors such as Virgil, Ovid, and Jean Lemaire de Belges. Flore's rewriting of the myth of Echo and Narcissus is examined in particular, and its problematic relation to a "feminist" viewpoint explored. For Gray, the discrepancy between the fanciful, dreamworld settings of the stories and the work's program for women's sexual equality is a signal to the reader of the text's ironic character, "suggesting that the author holds other views, alerting us therefore to the possibility of other readings and other meanings." As a result, the whole question of women's sexuality is placed in "a new and problematic context."

The issue of gender, raised by Gray, will be taken up, in varying degrees and in a variety of ways, by each of the remaining essays of the collection. Gary Ferguson focuses on the twelfth *nouvelle* of Marguerite de Navarre's *Heptaméron*, one of the earliest versions of the story of the murder of Alessandro de' Medici, the first Duke of Florence, by his cousin, friend and servant, Lorenzo (Musset's Lorenzaccio). Departing from traditional interpretations of the *nouvelle* as a historical tale, Ferguson builds on the work of Marie-Madeleine Fontaine to show how Marguerite's account differs radically from those of contemporary chroniclers in its selection and treatment of material. It is argued that, by casting Alessandro's murder in terms of a story of personal and familial honor played out among a triangle of protagonists (the duke, Lorenzo, and Lorenzo's sister), Marguerite not only avoids sensitive political topics; she is also able to explore issues of particular interest to her, issues that preoccupy the *Heptaméron* as a whole. Drawing on René Girard's notion of triangular desire and Eve Kosofsky Sedgwick's theories of homosociality, Ferguson examines the relationship between the duke and Lorenzo to show how the murder of the duke replaces the duke's intended rape of Lorenzo's sister, the murder mirroring and inverting, through the reversal of gender roles, the rape plot of an earlier *nouvelle*. In tale 12, therefore, the latent violence of male homosocial relations is played out between the two men without passing through the body of a woman. The sexually-charged rivalry between the duke and his servant is illuminated by reference to literary depictions of male rivalry within the courtly tradition, as well as to contemporary structures of homosexuality which eroticized the power distinctions between men within the social hierarchy. For Ferguson, Duke Alessandro's murder reads like a rape not only because it substitutes for the intended rape of the murderer's sister, but also because it inverts the roles of master and minion. *Heptaméron* 12's acute social critique thus depends less upon historical veracity—fidelity to a set of "facts," in any case doubtful and contested—than upon a strongly gendered narrative perspective that transforms "history" into "veritable histoire," *her* own "true story."

The relation of Marguerite de Navarre's *Heptaméron* to the questions of gender and the writing of history is also examined by John O'Brien, for whom "one of the most salient features of this work is that it asserts repeatedly the imbrication of truth and fiction." The scene in the first *nouvelle* of Saint-Aignan's wife witnessing her husband's plan for her destruction is seen as emblematic of women's limited access to knowledge and agency in male plots. Yet as an emblematic moment it is also inadequate, O'Brien argues, to account for the complexities of gender relations in early modern France, as the uneasy situation of the widow illustrates. Most contemporary male discourse concerning widowhood is motivated by widows' freedom from paternal and marital control, which is either celebrated as an excuse for male sexual license, or else becomes the object of regulation through moralizing admonitions to chastity. It is against this background that O'Brien reads a number of Marguerite's *nouvelles* as narratives of other possibilities. Despite the contrary moral judgements passed on their protagonists by the *devisants*, *nouvelles* 4 and 43 show two women (one a "vefve," the other a "damoiselle") who, in differing sets of sexually compromising circumstances, exercise control over the stories that will be told about them; thus they use fiction as a means of preserving reputation and status. In other *nouvelles*, the widow's story is written, albeit fleetingly, through an emblematic scene or a particularly telling use of metaphor. Focusing ultimately on the relationship between seeing and telling, witnessing, history, and fiction, O'Brien agues that such moments of intense symbolization belong to a form of women's historiography, one in the Herodotean mode, exploiting the resources of myths and stories—stories, here, of difference and speculation.

Issues of vision, storytelling, and power are also central to David LaGuardia's discussion of the story of the one-eyed cuckold, versions of which are found in both the Burgundian *Cent nouvelles nouvelles* and the *Heptaméron* (*nouvelle* 6). In order to examine the story's evolution from its misogynous origins in medieval exemplary literature, LaGuardia begins with the version of the tale found in Petrus Alfonsi's *Disciplina clericalis*. Freud's essay on "The Uncanny" supports the argument that the story betrays a fear of castration and of (female) sexuality. The "reality" that the tale represents is thus that of a "collective male fantasy that was the unconscious foundation of a quite conscious male domination of women." The phantasmic image of women, disseminated through the telling and retelling of this story, LaGuardia suggests, accompanies, indeed is perhaps virtually equivalent to, the transfer of power from one generation of men to another. He argues that "male power was disseminated for centuries through the telling of this story and others like it, which propagated and perpetuated misogynistic fantasy images of women and of female sexuality." In the versions of the tale that appear in the anonymous *Cent nouvelles nouvelles*, LaGuardia detects a different attitude towards the one-eyed cuckold on the part of the all-male, hierarchically differentiated narrators assembled at the court of the Duke of Burgundy. While the cuckold may still command respect and admiration on account of his physical stature and prowess, the narrators also take a perverse pleasure in his humiliation and mockery. Here the exemplary moral force of the tale is overturned by a transgressive, comic narrative discourse that valorizes adulterous sex and may figure the strengthening of homosocial bonds. Nevertheless, the comic tale, like the moral *exemplum*, is based on the fantasy image of the "over-sexed" woman, and both constitute "complementary sides of an ambivalent male imaginary." Only in the *Heptaméron*, by contrast, does the tale undergo radical revision. First, by altering the conclusion of the story, LaGuardia contends, Marguerite's narrator exposes the implausibility and artificiality of the conventional ending—reveals, that is, its entirely fictive nature. More fundamentally, the tale is recontextualized within a collection that simultaneously rewrites and rejects exemplary discourse: pursuing a twofold strategy of revision, the *Heptaméron* proposes new female examples, while at the same time questioning the very utility of the *exemplum* as a means of moral instruction, especially its relevance to the real lives of women.

Phantasm, in its various general meanings (illusion, delusion, counterfeit, fancy, specter), is also the subject of Deborah N. Losse's essay, which examines its role as a thematic and structuring principle of Jacques Yver's *Printemps d'Yver*. Frequently associated with the manifestation of erotic desire, phantasm is explored as it intersects with gender in the game of love. Phantasm may spring, for example, from ignorance of the opposite sex, from the frustration of unrequited passion, from the contemplation of a work of art; it may take the form of a mental vision, or even of a magical apparition. As a companion to desire, phantasm is capable of producing both negative and positive results: on the one hand, it may cause misjudgment and lead to error or social transgression; on the other hand, if accompanied by self-reflection which orders the unruly and chaotic impressions of the imagination and tests them against reality, it may help foster a discreet and faithful passion. Love associated with such reflection may be a moral virtue, leading to knowledge of self and ultimately of God. Thus, rather than containing realistic depictions of love, Yver's *nouvelles* reveal that their characters' conceptions are mediated by illusions and fantasies that suggest their author is "more intent on exploring the human capacity for imagination and self-reflection than on mirroring the details of the physical world about him." Indeed (like Des Périers's earlier *Nouvelles récréations*), *Le Printemps* is presented as a collection of stories offering the relief of fiction as a means of escape from the harsh realities of life in a time of war. Yet, for Losse, it is precisely in the tension found in the *nouvelles* between a desire for stability and a desire for change, between rational self-reflection and the disordered fantasies of the imagination, that the work is close to the outlook of later humanists like Montaigne and typical of its age. In the unsettling period of the civil wars, the *nouvelles* of *Le Printemps*, like the *Essais*, attest to the power of the chimerical products of the imagination and to the necessity of seeking to give these some kind of order, "les mettre en rolle."

The narrative trajectory we have traced here is only one among several that might have been proposed. Although we end with the latest work, chronologically speaking, we do not begin with the earliest. The arrangement of the essays reflects rather a filiation of critical concerns and topics. All of the contributors, however, suggest that the *nouvelle* is far from being a genre that offers a transparent account of reality, presented directly to the reader who seeks a kind of knowledge of the "real" life of fifteenth- and sixteenth-century France. Clearly, this is not to say that the *nouvelles* are devoid of relation to contemporary culture. In ways and to degrees that differ from one writer to another and from one tale to another, they may translate any number of social values, reinforcing or questioning orthodoxies; they may render any number of historical circumstances or social conditions. They may be places for rehearsing the familiar, as well as for examining principles or categories by testing their limits, for toying with possibilities, for imagining other ways, other worlds. They are, however, always stories. As a genre, the *nouvelle* is shaped by a myriad of literary or formal imperatives—narratological, intertextual, and so on. It is based as much if not more on an intimate knowledge of the vast body of sources and stories that were its foundation than on a conception of a true or accurate representation of the world. Thus, the *nouvellistes* were more self-conscious and critical than has generally been acknowledged in the past, frequently telling stories about the art of storytelling itself. Moreover, the ways in which the *nouvelles* structure and depict "reality" are determined as much by ideology and preconceptions of value as by the actual physical and historical characteristics of the objects that they represent.

Given the fundamental distance that separates the discourse of the *nouvelles* from the objects that they depict, it could be argued that the *nouvellistes* themselves were writing from a point of view determined by a certain kind of self-conscious irony, perhaps even skepticism. Becoming increasingly aware of the distance between their conceptions of the world and what could be construed as the world itself, writers of the century of Rabelais and Montaigne understood that "truth" and "reality" are concepts that are extraordinarily difficult to grasp, and that they might be approximated only within the countless variations of written discourse, engendering an incessant displacement towards other texts, stories, anecdotes, and examples. As Marguerite de Navarre's great contribution to the *nouvelle* literature reveals, any interpretation of the "true" and the "real," and any attempt at telling this truth, is a matter of one's perspective, one's voice, even—or especially—of one's body. While in no way claiming to exhaust the truth about this extraordinarily rich and complex genre, the following essays attempt to describe the *nouvelle* within this subtle and delicate literary and historical context. They address, in particular, one aspect of the *nouvelle*: its status as a non-mimetic, self-conscious, intertextual, ironic, perhaps even skeptical mode of writing. It is our hope that the perspectives they open will encourage further exploration along new paths of the early French *nouvelle*'s many and varied narrative worlds.

"Une merveilleuse espece d'animal": Fable and Verisimilitude in Bonaventure des Périers's *Nouvelles récréations et joyeux devis*

Emily Thompson

Astounded by his pet monkey's human likeness, the abbot in tale 88 of Bonaventure des Périers's *Nouvelles récréations et joyeux devis* calls it a "merveilleuse espece d'animal."[1] In the biased imagination of the proud pet owner, his monkey—part animal, part courtier—defies traditional categorization. The sixteenth-century *nouvelle* that relays the story of this hybrid creature to us also proves difficult to define. Its most important identifying characteristics, like the monkey's qualities, are often in the eye of the beholder. A completely satisfying, all-encompassing definition of the *nouvelle* genre defies even the most insightful and methodical of scholars, as Gisèle Mathieu-Castellani's study of the *nouvelle* and the problem of genre suggests.[2] The subject matter treated in the collections of *nouvelles* varies from the comic sexual situations of the *Cent nouvelles nouvelles* to the serious explorations of moral dilemmas in the *Heptaméron*. Nor do their structures or literary models appear to have much in common. The *Heptaméron*'s lengthy tales partially inspired by the *Decameron* scarcely resemble the one-page tales that the *Nouvelles récréations et joyeux devis* borrow from Poggio. Attempting to distinguish the *nouvelle* from other contemporary genres, many critics have proposed as possible criteria the *nouvelle*'s portrayal of a real historical *milieu* and its descriptions of realistic psychological situations.[3] Others

---

[1] Bonaventure des Périers, *Nouvelles récréations et joyeux devis*, ed. Krystyna Kasprzyk (Paris: Champion, 1980), 301. Subsequent references will be to this edition.

[2] Gisèle Mathieu-Castellani, "Pour une poétique de la nouvelle," *Canadian Review of Comparative Literature* 18 (1991): 167–78.

[3] Cf. Werner Söderhjelm, *La Nouvelle française au XVe siècle* (Paris: Champion, 1910; repr. Geneva: Slatkine, 1973), and Erich Auerbach, *Mimesis: The Representation*

have strongly rejected the association of verisimilitude with the *nouvelle*.[4] The tenacity of the debate has forced all scholars of the *nouvelle* to take a stance on the question of realism.

Within the *nouvelles* themselves, the recurrent promise of the narrators to tell truthful tales about their immediate and contemporary society also implies the importance of content. Without conflating a sixteenth-century notion of truthfulness and twentieth-century "realism," one can still recognize a shared assumption that such tales must be believable to the reader. For the narrators of the *nouvelles*, however, *vray* remains an unstable and ambiguous term; the narrators' forceful claims to historical truthfulness are tempered by the recurrence of implicit warnings not to interpret the tales as straightforward representations of the objective world. The narrators reveal themselves as inconsistent and forgetful, with a tendency to exaggerate and with a passion for jest. On occasion, they comment on the difficulty of telling entertaining stories that are also historically accurate.[5] Yet their warnings have gone unheeded by some of the more enthusiastic realist critics of our century, who see in the French *nouvelle* a historical portrait of sixteenth-century France. I would like to reorient the question of the realism of the *nouvelle* by suggesting that not their purported verisimilitude, but rather a constant *flouting* of this criterion unites the *nouvelles*. An analysis of Bonaventure des Périers's *Nouvelles récréations et joyeux devis* and of their use of fable, the anti-realistic genre par excellence, will demonstrate that realism does not define this particular collection. In conclusion, I hope to show that the characteristics that allow these tales to defy verisimilitude are shared by most *nouvelles* and thus supersede realism as an identifying factor for the *genre*.

First, it is useful to investigate further how twentieth-century critics of the *nouvelle* define realism. For W. Söderhjelm, the *nouvelle*'s realism lies in the descriptions of its setting, its portrayal "avec vérité" of "détails tirés de la vie bourgeoise."[6] The addition of specific geographic and historical references to the introductions of the tales constitutes one of the principal differences between the *nouvelle* and earlier forms of short fiction like the *fabliau* and the *exemplum*. However, as Roger Dubuis notes, in most cases these *effets de réel*

---

of Reality in Western Literature, trans. Willard R. Trask (Princeton: Princeton University Press, 1953).

[4] Janet Ferrier, *Forerunners of the French Novel: An Essay on the Development of the Nouvelle in the Late Middle Ages* (Manchester: Manchester University Press, 1954).

[5] Cf. Nicolas de Troyes, *Le Grand Parangon des nouvelles nouvelles* (choix), ed. Krystyna Kasprzyk (Paris: Librairie Nizet, 1970), 206. Subsequent references will be to this edition.

[6] Söderhjelm, *La Nouvelle*, 155.

"ne jou[ent] strictement aucun rôle dans l'histoire proprement dite."⁷ As a superficial extension of traditional stories, the historical and geographical elements fail to transform the plot in any substantial way.

Another characteristic, according to Söderhjelm, of what he terms "le réalisme artistique" lies in the *nouvelle*'s evocation of psychological phenomena.⁸ Comparing the *Decameron* to various *fabliaux*, Eric Auerbach, too, cites the more detailed psychological portraits of the characters as an example of the realism of the *nouvelle*. Though certainly more developed than in *fabliaux*, the depiction of characters in the *nouvelle* remains sketchy and caricatural. In the *Nouvelles récréations et joyeux devis*, for example, Des Périers distinguishes his characters essentially by their profession. Their intelligence, their vanity, and the motivations for their actions all stem from their social and professional status. An apprentice is impertinent, an abbot dull-witted, a fishwife sharp-tongued. The stereotypical categories of character types belie Auerbach's association of realism with individualization of character, setting, and plot. Although Auerbach claims that "the characterization of the personages, the local and social setting, are at once far more sharply individualized and more extensive" in the *nouvelle* than in the *fabliau*, Des Périers's narrator takes pains to deny the very notion of individuality in his stories.⁹ He reinforces the similarity between many of his tales, and between these and others with which the implied reader might be familiar, repeating on several occasions, "c'est tout un" (160, 305). As for the logical development of events within the *nouvelle* plots, it is perhaps more accurate to refer to a *predictable* development. Accompanying the stock characters are stock plots that reassure the reader, not by respecting his or her sense of reality, but by evoking a familiar literary universe.

Tzvetan Todorov addresses this connection between genre expectations and *vraisemblance*. For Todorov, the realism of a text is determined by the readers and "il y a autant de vraisemblables que de genres."¹⁰ Realism, then, is as much a structural concept as a semantic one, referring less to the relationship between a text and the world than to that between a text and similar texts. From such a perspective, the *nouvelle* could be considered *vraisemblable* simply by meeting generic expectations for short, comic prose.

---

⁷ Roger Dubuis, "Réalité et réalisme dans les «Cent nouvelles nouvelles»," in *La Nouvelle française à la Renaissance*, ed. Lionello Sozzi (Geneva and Paris: Slatkine, 1981), 91–119, here 96.

⁸ Söderhjelm, *La Nouvelle*, 225.

⁹ Auerbach, *Mimesis*, 186.

¹⁰ Tzvetan Todorov, "Introduction au vraisemblable," in idem, *Poétique de la prose* (Paris: Seuil, 1971), 92–99, here 94.

Sixteenth-century theoretical texts that offer definitions of short prose indicate that Renaissance readers also associated the *nouvelle* with referentiality to the historical context in which they lived. In his *Grand et vrai art de pleine rhetorique* (1521), Pierre Fabri offers an unusually detailed commentary on narrative, recommending that it aim at verisimilitude: "La narration doibt estre vray semblable ou possible, c'est a dire que [le] facteur doibt dire parolles et choses que les auditeurs puissent croire que il die verité."[11] He goes on to suggest ways of increasing the credibility of stories, including the extension of explanations and the specification of the times and places of events. Mary Jane Stearns Schenck recognizes just such a concern with increased verisimilitude in the development of the introductions to *nouvelles* that "provide some answers to the question of how and why the event occurred."[12] While she interprets this evolution as a distinctive feature of the *nouvelle* (as opposed to the *exemplum* and the *fabliau*), she finds it insufficient to convey the psychological motivations of the characters and to assure the coherence of the story, both of which are central to her definition of realism.

Given the scarcity of sixteenth-century theoretical discussions of the *nouvelle*, we are forced to consult the tales themselves for insight into what readerly expectations might have been. It is in the prologues and prefaces to the collections and in the metadiscursive remarks at the beginning and end of individual stories that Mathieu-Castellani finds four elements repeatedly associated with the *nouvelle*: stories are said to be "authentiques," "nouveaux" (recent), "nouveaux" (never before told or written), and "dignes d'être racontés."[13] Once again, the recurrence of these content-oriented characteristics in the presentations of the *nouvelle* suggests that, for the authors and their implied readers, the *nouvelle* could be defined and recognized primarily by the nature of its realistic content.

Recalling these traditional associations with simple prose narrative is not, however, the same as endorsing them. In fact, the narrators proceed to undermine their significance. Their commentary on the tales that follow serves more to unsettle the narratees than to guide them. Lionello Sozzi believes that the *conteurs* were attempting to redefine the narrative contract associated with their type of fiction and to free themselves from the constraints of older narrative forms.[14] The veracity claim, for example, was inherited in part from

---

[11] Pierre Fabri, *Grand et vrai art de pleine rhetorique* (Rouen: A. Héron, 1521), 67.

[12] Mary Jane Stearns Schenck, "Narrative Structure in the Exemplum, Fabliau, and the Nouvelle," *Romanic Review* 72 (1981): 367–82, here 380.

[13] Mathieu-Castellani, "Pour une poétique," 172.

[14] Lionello Sozzi, "L'Intention du conteur: Des textes introductifs aux recueils de nouvelles," in *L'Ecrivain face à son public en France et en Italie à la Renaissance*, ed. C. A. Fiorato and Jean-Claude Margolin (Paris: Vrin, 1989), 71–83, here 80.

the *fabliau* but had assumed new implications with the distancing of author from reader through the medium of printing. The frequency of the narrators' interventions and their obvious attempts to manipulate the narratees suggest a shift towards emphasizing the relationship between author and reader and the act of narration itself over traditional plots and exemplary historical accounts. Mathieu-Castellani proposes the alternation of narrative and of critical commentary on the narrative as "le trait structurel qui marque le plus fortement la poétique de la nouvelle au XVIe siècle."[15] Although readers continued to look to the *nouvelle* for its content, the *conteurs* were, in fact, attempting to create a new space for short fictional prose.

The two *conteurs* who most openly express their fictionalizing intentions are Philippe d'Alcripe in *La Nouvelle Fabrique des excellens traits de vérité* and Bonaventure des Périers in *Nouvelles récréations et joyeux devis*. Admitting that a *conteur*'s "truth" is but fiction from the start, D'Alcripe's narrator proposes truth as separate from authorial intention.[16] Des Périers's narrator makes a similar metadiscursive confession in the first *nouvelle* of the *Nouvelles récréations*: "J'ay voulu faindre quelques noms tout expres" (15). The French *conteurs* who continue to make traditional veracity claims are no less effective, however, at problematizing the notion of "truth." Nicolas de Troyes's narrator recognizes the limitations of his ability to tell the absolute truth in all of his tales, but continues to use indiscriminately the formulaic "vray est que . . ." (200), rendering it impossible to distinguish the fictional elements from those he claims are true. In this way he recalls Des Périers and D'Alcripe, treating truth as a kind of shared joke between him and his narratees. The narrators in all three collections anticipate skeptical narratees, eager to and capable of contesting the veracity claim. The inclusion of traditional appeals to the narratees' unconditional belief, accompanied by admissions of the fictional nature of at least some of the stories, could only function, therefore, as a joke between narrator and narratees. Rather than exploiting the implied readers' credulity with the veracity claims, then, the narrators seem instead to use them to unite narrator and narratee in a mutual recognition of the absurdity of the pretense of truthfulness.

In his *Cent nouvelles nouvelles*, Philippe de Vigneulles's narrator implies that the veracity claim functions as a kind of *captatio benevolentiae* and as an integral part of the oral storytelling tradition he clearly imitates.[17] None the

---

[15] Mathieu-Castellani, "Pour une poétique," 175.

[16] Philippe d'Alcripe, *La Nouvelle Fabrique des excellens traits de vérité* (Paris: Librairie Jannet, 1853), 8. For a similar treatment of truth and authorial intention, cf. the prologue of François Rabelais's *Gargantua*.

[17] Cf. Philippe de Vigneulles, *Les Cent nouvelles nouvelles*, ed. Charles H. Livingston (Geneva: Droz, 1972), 231.

less, refraining from overtly redefining his "truth" as different from an objective truth, Vigneulles conforms to conventions of verisimilitude and has his narrator introduce most of the tales with a generous dose of *effets de réel*.

Albeit more subtly, Marguerite de Navarre's *devisants* in the *Heptaméron* also arouse suspicion in their presentation of historical truth. The author herself appears as a minor reference embedded in the prologue and separated from her authorial persona by ten *devisants* with unfamiliar names. Their mediation suggests the distance between the historical Marguerite and the fictional one. The *devisants* also cite the future Henry II's fear that "gens de lettres" (with whom Marguerite would have been associated) deform historical truth with their rhetorical skills;[18] they thereby remind readers that the courtly anecdotes that inspired the *Heptaméron* have already undergone such a transformation. The recurring controversy among the *devisants* over interpretations of the tales they tell further problematizes the veracity claim. What "truth" seems to signify to these intradiegetic narrators is the serious or morally sound nature of their tales, irrespective of historical accuracy.

The admissions of unreliable narrators scarcely suffice to discredit the association of verisimilitude with the *nouvelle*. What remains to be determined is whether or not the authors of the *nouvelles* respected the contracts proposed by their narrators in the metadiscourse. I propose to compare the narrative contract as it appears in one of the prologues with the characteristics found in individual tales of the same collection in order to evaluate the importance of verisimilitude to the literary project of at least one *conteur*.

I have chosen to concentrate on the *Nouvelles récréations*, the collection that seems to oppose the truth/exemplarity/contemporaneity contract most strongly, evincing a constant struggle between the narratees' expectations and the narrator's provocative metadiscourse. As mentioned above, the narrator of the *Nouvelles récréations* resists the narratees' call for historical accuracy, admitting to having been "unscrupulous" when it comes to names and facts, but justifying his inaccuracies as intentional:

> j'ay voulu faindre quelques noms tout expres pour vous monstrer qu'il ne faut point plorer de tout cecy que je vous compte: Car peult estre qu'il n'est pas vray. Que me chault il, pourveu qu'il soit vray que vous y prenez plaisir? (16)

---

[18] Marguerite de Navarre, *L'Heptaméron*, ed. Michel François (Paris: Garnier, 1967), 9.

Following his startling disclaimer in the prologue, the narrator of the *Nouvelles récréations* continues to defy the expectations of the implied reader regarding the nature of the *nouvelle*. Not even the most subversive author, however, would want to risk alienating potential readers and/or rendering his or her short tales incomprehensible. A collection that met with considerable success during the sixteenth century and that has survived to represent the *nouvelle* in twentieth-century anthologies[19] must clearly share some narrative elements with the works of contemporary *conteurs*. Is the narrative contract in the *Nouvelles récréations* meant merely as a provocation, or does it challenge expectations that Des Périers judged irrelevant to the appreciation and the comprehension of the genre?

First let us outline the contract the narrator proposes. The characteristics that he assumes his narratees attribute to *nouvelles* fall into two categories: those related to content and those related to the process of reading itself. Apparently assuming that his implied readers look to him for detailed advice, the narrator addresses those still unsure of what to look for in a collection of stories. He denies any hidden meaning, "allegoricque, mistique, fantastique," or a level of difficulty requiring "vocabulaire [ou] commentaire" (15). The narrator also anticipates questions concerning the order in which the tales should be read. He leaves the answer entirely in the hands of the narratees; they can determine the order in which they would like to read the tales, for "quel ordre faut il garder quand il est question de rire?" (*loc. cit.*).

Just as the entertainment value of the *nouvelles* ostensibly replaces the commentary the narratees seek, so too must it outweigh traditional content in importance. As noted earlier, Des Périers denies the implied readers the promise of authenticity that he knows they expect. In accordance with his contemporaries, he has his narrator acknowledge the association between truth and the *nouvelle*, but proceeds to dismiss its importance to the appreciation of his collection. He denies a strict adherence to the correct names of characters and locations, and does not justify his stories by any claim to a moral or allegorized truth. At the same time, he implies that his stories may contain some truthful elements behind falsified names. The question of truth is left undecided, which suggests that the value of his tales lies elsewhere. In fact, the narrator presents his tales as an escape from reality, as a much deserved, though incongruous, comic break from the tragedy of war-ridden France: "pour vous donner moyen de tromper le temps, meslant des resjouissances parmy vos fasheries" (5). Choosing a verb ("tromper") that

---

[19] Cf., for example, *Conteurs français du XVIᵉ siècle*, ed. Pierre Jourda (Paris: Gallimard, 1965).

reiterates the distance he claims from referential truth, the narrator rejects the current historical climate as literary inspiration and defies the menace of death with laughter.

Two other characteristics often linked to collections of short stories in Renaissance France—the contemporaneity of the events and characters and the exemplary nature of the stories—receive far less attention in this narrator's metadiscursive comments. Although he occasionally alludes to contemporary historical and literary figures, Des Périers's narrator never insists on the recent nature of his tales. He also claims other "comptes" as sources for many of his tales, thereby admitting that he is not the first to tell (or perhaps even to write) the stories he relays. As for the didactic or historical merit of his stories, the narrator often admits ignorance as to the name of an admirable figure, or the outcome of a particular event. Indeed, he seems to prefer anecdotes featuring the unworthy: the foolish, the gullible, the criminal, the inept, the unsuccessful. Even here, the knowledge gleaned about the lives of these different marginal figures scarcely allows readers to enrich their understanding of sixteenth-century society. The characters are simply agents in a plot intended to amuse. The inconclusive outcomes of his stories likewise lack the moral clarity necessary for exemplary value.

The narrator does, however, recognize a potentially negative consequence of denying his tales any moral exemplarity. Such a claim would have helped certain narratees justify their interest in the *Nouvelles récréations*. As it is, he predicts that women narratees will be wary that his collection might contain stories of a sexual nature, inappropriate for a refined and chaste feminine readership. This suspicion suggests yet another expectation readers had of the *nouvelle*. Linked by their profane nature to the *fabliau* tradition, collections of tales in sixteenth-century France carried with them the lure and the taint of sexual topics. Yet the narrator tries once again to deny the implied readers their frame of reference: "Lisez hardiment, dames et damoyselles: il n'y ha rien qui ne soit honneste." In this case, however, he immediately mitigates his statement: "Mais si d'adventure il y en ha quelques unes d'entres vous qui soyent trop tendrettes . . ." (17). On the other hand, he argues in favor of stories inspired by local tradition or events. The local character of his tales covers several French regions and is therefore less restricted than Philippe de Vigneulles's stories centered around Metz. It never however extends beyond French borders:

> Et puis je ne suis point allé chercher mes comptes à Constantinople, à Florence, ny à Venise: ne si loing que cela. Car s'ilz sont telz que je les vous veulx donner, c'est à dire pour vous recreer n'ay je pas mieulx faict d'en prendre les

instrumens que nous avons à nostre porte, que non pas
les aller emprunter si loing? (16)

Clarifying their narrative contract in increasingly economic terms, the narrator tries to wean his narratees of their desire for literature that imitates Italian and Roman classics. According to James Woodrow Hassell, Des Périers did, in fact, use non-French sources, but his borrowings are limited to specific stories, subtly transformed. Hassell thus concludes that "the *Joyeux devis* was of predominantly French origin."[20]

In a short prologue, the narrator has listed several, sometimes mutually exclusive, expectations—an allegorical signification, a designated order in which to read, true tales, recent tales, morally sound tales, sexual stories, stories from Latin or Italian literature—and has deemed them all irrelevant, retaining only a preference for local settings and humorous subjects. If these characteristics typically associated with the *nouvelle* were not crucial to their essence, if readers did not need to believe that what they were reading reflected their reality literally or even allegorically, the question arises: what *does* make the *Nouvelles récréations* a collection of *nouvelles*?

By casting doubt on the validity of applying established criteria to his particular collection of tales, Des Périers's narrator openly renounces the traditional contract between narrator and narratee and therefore renounces realism (of both generic and absolute standards). Yet, while denying his narratees their familiar interpretative guidelines, he proposes a different approach to reading *nouvelles*. First and foremost, he insists that they accept laughter as the goal of his tales, and a specifically French humor as their content. Although the medieval *fabliau* and farce were clearly comic genres, the *nouvelle* can also claim the altogether more serious *exemplum* and *lai* as influences. Boccaccio and the *conteurs* who follow his model exploit comic elements, but they also retain a tragic tone in their stories, seen, for example, in the introduction of the *Decameron*, with its terrible portrait of Florence besieged by the plague. The two French collections called *Cent nouvelles nouvelles* also mix serious themes with light-hearted banter.[21] Marguerite de Navarre's *Heptaméron*, with which Des Périers might have been familiar,[22]

---

[20] James Woodrow Hassell, Jr., *Sources and Analogues of the* Nouvelles récréations et joyeux devis *of Bonaventure des Périers*, 2 vols. (Athens: University of Georgia Press, 1969), 2:161.

[21] Cf. Vigneulles, *Cent nouvelles*, and *Les Cent nouvelles nouvelles*, in *Conteurs français du XVIe siècle*, ed. Jourda, 1–358.

[22] Des Périers's collaboration with the Queen of Navarre as her *valet de chambre*, although predating the publication of the *Heptaméron* by at least twenty years, does not exclude the possibility of his having seen or copied parts of a collection,

again gives the upper hand to sobering social and moral questions. It is quite possible, then, that Des Périers's narrator had to convince his narratees that laughter was, on its own, a valid objective for writing *nouvelles*. Secondly, rejecting an elaborate guide to interpretation and listing the possible levels of exegesis only to deny that any of them are appropriate to his tales, he advises his narratees to adopt a personal, though superficial approach to reading them: "Telz les voyez, telz les prenez" (15).

Far from reducing his text to a cheap chuckle, the narrator is actually encouraging the narratees to read differently, critically. In certain frequently analyzed passages of Rabelais's *Gargantua*, the narrator, Alcofrybas, forces his narratees to respond critically to a similar hermeneutic ambiguity.[23] Here, too, the conflicting messages about the truth of the book and about its allegorical significance appear, initially, to put the narratees at a disadvantage. Alcofrybas's desperate bullying and repeated questioning of the narratees reveal, however, that the interpretative control actually shifts to the critical implied readers who will ultimately reach their own conclusions as to the meaning of the text. By liberating his narratees from the constraints of a fixed meaning and from the responsibility of reacting to "true" stories, the narrator in the *Nouvelles récréations* also urges them to rely on their own interpretative skills and to read his tales "telz les *voyez*" (15, my italics), in order to find meaning and/or entertainment.

The implied "vous" never unites the readership into a single interpreting body, for the narratees are presented as multiple from the outset. The singular, masculine "mon amy" (14) surreptitiously becomes "dames et damoyselles" (17). Both sets of narratees are given advice, both are pressed to read, but already their different concerns and reactions manifest themselves. While the "amy" needs instructions on how to laugh during these troubled times, the women are experts at laughter, albeit of the hidden variety. Both may wonder which tales to read and in what order, but the female narratees try to avoid the overtly sexual tales, while the male narratees fear a more subversive, allegorical menace.

The liberty that the narrator offers to his implied readers is, however, a limited one, and his hermeneutic advice is not to be taken quite so literally. Although he attempts to prevent his narratees from passively following a

---

believed by some to have been started long before the queen determined its final structure.

[23] For example, the prologue and chapters 6 and 9. For an eloquent synthesis of the critical polemics over these passages, see Terence Cave, Michel Jeanneret, and François Rigolot, "Sur la prétendue transparence de Rabelais," *Revue d'Histoire Littéraire de la France* 86 (1986): 709–16, and Gérard Defaux, "Sur la prétendue pluralité du prologue de 'Gargantua'," 716–22.

predetermined reading, he closely guides their assumptions and judgements. Through his bullying, his questioning, his prejudices, the narrator seeks to shape the narratees' judgments at every turn. The stories themselves provide a context that favors certain readings over others. Des Périers is unlikely to have believed in the possibility of a straightforward and immediate interpretation at a time when even the Humanists who most fervently promoted the powers of language to reflect the *res* alerted readers to the dangers and shortcomings of human language.[24] The complexity of the intertextuality in Des Périers's collection also bespeaks the impossibility of a literal "telz les voyez, telz les prenez" approach to reading. Indeed, he uses a shared literary culture to guide his readers in reading his sparse prose.

Des Périers relies on his readers' familiarity with related genres like the *fabliau*, fable, and *facetia*, as well as with proverbs and stock characters, to create the mood of the story that will follow. In order to provoke laughter and to accomplish what Dubuis rightly refers to as "l'âme de toute nouvelle: la surprise,"[25] the tales must remain relatively short and the characters and the setting be evoked in the briefest terms. By activating common schemata to flesh out the setting, Des Périers can concentrate on the moment of surprise, at which he suddenly departs from the expectations of the reader. It is this tension between reader expectations and narrative defiance, between the anxiety of influence and authorial innovation, that characterizes both the narrator's metadiscourse and the structure of the tales themselves. Des Périers introduces the tension in an exaggerated way in the prologue, thereby signaling the novelty of the tales to follow, tales that constitute a new type of distinctly French prose fiction.

Each tale can thus call into question a distinct characteristic of prose narrative; tales 29 and 87 specifically undermine that of its likeness to truth. The harmonious integration into the collection of two stories that so clearly defy both a twentieth-century notion of realism and the sixteenth-century association between the *nouvelle* and the veracity claim illustrates how little verisimilitude matters to the successful *nouvelle*. In these two tales, Des Périers merges the truth-affirming *nouvelle* with its direct opposite, the fable, a genre defined by Cicero, and then by Renaissance writers, as the very antithesis of truth, that which "oncques ne fut ne sera."[26] The rationalizing, emotive characters are animals, not humans, a fact that constantly reminds the reader of the tale's allegorical nature. Remaining consistent with his

---

[24] Cf. Marjorie O'Rourke Boyle, *Erasmus on Language and Method in Theology* (Toronto: University of Toronto Press, 1977), and Mary Jane Barnett, "Erasmus and the Hermeneutics of Linguistic Praxis," *Renaissance Quarterly* 49 (1996): 542–72.

[25] Dubuis, "Réalité," 111.

[26] Fabri, *Grand et vrai art*, 65. Cf. Cicero, *De inventione*, 1. 19. 27.

attitudes in the prologue, the narrator gives no explicit instructions on how to read the two animal fables mixed in with the more credible stories, but he supplies another tale, the eighty-eighth, that sketches a diegetic lesson in the reading of animal stories.

Tale 88 concerns an animal, but this one remains mute and is seen through the eyes of the human characters. The reader is privy only to their thoughts and words. The animal in question, a monkey, is the subject of a discussion between an abbot and an Italian gentleman who comment on the monkey's similarity to man and wonder if it would be possible to teach it to speak. The abbot, fascinated by the superficial resemblance between man and monkey, believes that the art of man can complement the work of nature, resulting in a talking monkey (or newly complete human). The Italian, motivated by the hope of monetary compensation, pretends to agree with the abbot, citing written examples of other animals learning to speak. The talking elephants and donkeys he evokes belong to the tradition of fables, but the abbot accepts them as scientific proof. The very way the abbot refers to the monkey indicates his inability to differentiate between fable and reality, for he sees in his domesticated pet a "*merveilleuse* espece d'animal" (301, my italics).

The Italian and the other guests at the abbot's table interpret the pet monkey as a synecdoche for the abbot and his favor. They mock the abbot's reading of the monkey with a lexicon reminiscent of that of the narrator in the prologue to the collection. The Italian ironically praises the way the abbot interprets the monkey; "Vous le prenez comme il le faut," he says. And, indeed, the abbot's interpretation resembles a literal reading of the dressed-up monkey and the fables it incarnates, "telz les voyez, telz les prenez." Like the narrator, the Italian directs attention to the narratee-abbot's credulity by insisting on the verb "croire." Although they share a certain vocabulary, the narrator and the Italian do not reach the same conclusions regarding the correct way of reading. While the narrator points out the abbot's laughable credulity, describing him as "acheminé à croire," he never lets the monkey's "education" come to a real test. The unfinished project neither disproves nor supports the abbot's "fantaisie." There is no final truth; the monkey remains the subject of multiple interpretations. Moreover, the abbot derives as much pleasure from his fantastic reading as the Italian profits from his self-interested one. A reference the narrator makes to a chess-playing monkey (most likely the one described in *Il Libro del cortegiano*) only increases the undecidability of the monkey tale. Rather than citing Castiglione, the narrator presents this particular race of monkeys as if it truly existed and could therefore lend credibility to the unusual talents of the abbot's monkey. Yet, in Castiglione's work, the narrator calls the story of the chess-playing monkey a "bugia" that is meant only to amuse his characters.[27] Elsewhere in the *Cortegiano* the characters liberate stories from the necessity of being true, recalling the spirit of the *Nouvelles récréations*:

> Or vedete come questa sorte de facezie ha dello ellegante e del buono, come si conviene ad uom di corte, o vero o finto che sia quello che si narra; perché in tal caso é liccito fingere quanto all'uomo piace senza colpa, e dicendo la verità adornarla con qualche bugietta, crescendo o diminuendo secondo i bisogno.[28]

In order to enjoy the animal story, then, it is not necessary to divorce fable from truth, as long as the reader is amused. The reader must, on the other hand, be aware of the tale's hybrid nature and mistake it neither for pure fiction nor for gospel truth, else he or she risks ridicule from other readers capable of identifying the different sources of the tale.[29] Nor should the reader seek advice on how to lead his own life in the literary elements presented by the tale. The abbot's scientific interpretation of fables recalls a husband's failed strategy in tale 16. This proud husband believes he can avoid cuckoldry by studying all the adulterous tricks presented in the *Decameron*. The Italian *novelle*, as he quickly discovers, make a poor marriage manual. Indifferent to moralistic ends, Des Périers actually wants to discourage belief in his tales, which could diminish their comic effect with distracting considerations of accuracy, identification, or application: "Riez seulement et ne vous chaille si ce fut Gaultier ou si ce fut Garguille" (15).

The narratees whose expectations no longer include historical truth or *vraisemblance* do not balk at the two animal fables in the collection. Like the

---

[27] Baldassare Castiglione, *Il Libro del cortegiano*, ed. Ghino Ghinassi (Florence: Sansoni, 1968), 143.

[28] Castiglione, *Cortegiano*, ed. Ghinassi, 136.

[29] The *conteurs* were not alone in exploring the ambiguous relationship between fable and truth. Boccaccio's *Genealogia Deorum Gentilium* was a model for many sixteenth-century writers who wished to contest the association of poets with liars. The analogy of biblical parables was frequently used to prove that a greater truth could be expressed by clearly unrealistic stories. In his "Preparation de voie à la lecture, et intelligence de la Metamorphose d'Ovide, et de tous Poëtes fabuleux," which forms the preface to *Les Trois Premiers Livres de la Métamorphose d'Ovide* (Lyons: G. Roville, 1556; ed. Jean-Claude Moisan with Marie-Claude Malenfant, Paris: H. Champion, 1997), Barthélemy Aneau touches on several of these questions in his defense of an allegorical reading of mythology. Pierre de Ronsard also feels it necessary to explain the distinction between poetry and history to his readers before starting the *Franciade*.

abbot, they are "acheminé[s] à croire" that animals can talk, if only for the time it takes to read the tales and to find amusement in them. The tales of talking animals share the structure and many of the topoi of the other tales, thereby aiding readers to assimilate them to the rest of the *Nouvelles récréations*. The narrator chooses to comment on his departure from the "realistic" tales only once. In tale 87, immediately preceding the monkey tale in the 1558 edition,[30] he explains why he has chosen to tell a tale about non-human characters: "C'est trop parlé de ces hommes et de ces femmes, Je vous veulx faire un compte d'oyseaux" (299). The birds none the less display the same credulity, fears, and penchant for deception as the men and women in the rest of the collection. The indication of difference collapses into a narrative sameness that simultaneously renders the fable more realistic and the surrounding tales less credible.

The bird fable is one of twenty-seven tales of two pages or less. It begins with the metadiegetic comment about storytelling quoted above and ends with one about the narratees' possible reaction to the story ("Si vous n'en riez, si n'en ploureray je pas" [300]). The tale relies heavily on a directly related dialogue with scant descriptions and no further narrative interventions. The story pits a mother bird against her young in a duel of wits. The fledglings, trying to demonstrate to their mother that they cannot yet fend for themselves, prove too smart for their own good. Countering their multiple, clever arguments, the mother responds: "sçavez vous bien tant? Or pourvoyez vous, si vous voulez" (300). As if the tale were not fabulous enough as a result of the attribution of speech to birds, their specific words and calculated rhetoric constitute the very core of the story. The narrator makes a point of emphasizing the tale's least believable elements.

Neither the thematic nor the structural characteristics of tale 87, however, startle the reader. Most of the stories in the *Nouvelles récréations* oppose two or more characters in a contest of intelligence and verbal prowess. Several of these contests (cf. *nouvelles* 5, 7, 20, 31, 58, 63, and 75) are played out in a similar attack/counter-attack form, where the character who has the final word wins the debate.

The unusual length of the other fable-like tale, tale 29, immediately serves as a narrative signal of its difference. Its six pages place it among the nine longest tales in the collection. Rather than insisting upon the animal nature of his protagonist, the narrator begins the tale by situating the story in a specific geographic setting. This detailed introduction, with its reference to a familiar place (le bas Maine), lends credibility to the tale that

---

[30] Although this is the first edition of the *Nouvelles récréations* known to us, it was a posthumous one and therefore the order of the tales does not necessarily correspond to that Des Périers would have chosen.

follows. Whereas in tale 87 the narrator attributes speech to the birds, here he credits the animal protagonist, a fox, only with thought. The fox can, none the less, speak different animal languages and understand the local human tongue. Like the monkey, this animal appears to want to talk, but it also experiences varied human emotions (fear, suspicion, jealousy, resentment) that the narrator elucidates in a detailed psychological portrait (by *nouvelle* or fable standards). The narrative dominates in this tale, with only one isolated reference on the part of the narrator to the act of narrating and with little direct discourse.

Other examples in the collection have a similar structure, and the fox shares many traits with his fellow protagonists in the *Nouvelles récréations*. Like them he is clever ("fin," "de bon esprit"), capable of adapting his language to different needs and situations, unrestricted by ethical considerations of truth or loyalty. He speaks "cagnesque" as well as the language of the foxes, and uses "rethoricque" to circumvent the suspicion of those he addresses. This linguistic flexibility gains him the sympathy of "des gens de bon esprit" who recognize his "bon entendement," much as the narrator often betrays his sympathy for the clever human rogues of the other tales. Neither his educated friends nor his intelligence and command of languages, however, can ultimately save him from the merciless system of justice, or from the wrath of the common crowd which sees only the evil ends to which he has used his gifts. His sad fate recalls that of the pickpocket in tale 81, where the narrator delights in the petty criminal's exploits before recounting his fatal encounter with an unfeeling and hypocritical member of the justice system. The narrator's comments in this latter tale apply directly to the situation in tale 29: "Car les regnards se trouvent tous à la fin chez le peletier" (288). Aided by the thematic and structural familiarity of tale 29, the readers require no additional commentary for the interpretation of the explicitly fabulous tale.

Despite their common treatment of abandonment, deception, and power relations expressed through linguistic mastery, the two animal fables have few structural features in common. Their length, representation of discourse, degree of narrative intervention, and type of conclusion place them at different ends of the spectrum of *Nouvelles récréations* tales. And yet, both find a place in the collection, complying with its internal logic. The reader is aided in his or her interpretation of them by their similarities both to other tales in the *Nouvelles récréations* and to literary patterns external to the collection and the genre. All of Des Périers's tales share elements with neighboring tales, but the areas of overlap differ from tale to tale. For example, the conclusion of one tale will recall a series of moralizing endings, whereas its characters will link it to another series of trickster tales. In like manner, the contrasting structural and narrative characteristics of the two fable-like tales each find echoes in other tales within the collection.

The intertextuality of each tale with other literary genres also renders them familiar to the reader. The fox character immediately recalls the *Roman de Renart*, as well as a number of Aesop's fables featuring crafty foxes who take on the community and the accepted code of morality. Likewise, the final maxim is typical of the fable's edifying intent. While the surprisingly moralistic conclusion ("Voila comment n'y ha finesse ne mechanceté qui ne soit punie en fin de compte" [139]) jars with the narrator's obvious sympathy for the immoral fox and certainly does not function simply as the fable's moral, its parodic force depends on familiarity with this type of storytelling. On the other hand, the bird fable ends with an open conclusion that departs from the typical fable moral. The narrator not only denies the narratees a neat didactic conclusion, but even suggests that he and they might not, need not, react in the same way to the birds' fate: "Si vous n'en riez, si n'en ploureray je pas" (300).

The key to understanding the internal logic of Des Périers's collection of *nouvelles* lies in this balance between literary references and formulaic writing on the one hand, and surprising departures from both readerly expectations and literary traditions on the other. Each tale represents a different combination of disparate elements from medieval *fabliaux*, *exempla*, and *contes merveilleux*, from ancient satires and comic texts, as well as from didactic fables. Each time readers are lulled into thinking they are in familiar territory, the narrator pulls the literary rug out from under their feet. The supposed realism of the *nouvelle* functions in a similar manner. The stories evoke ordinary life clearly enough to create a semblance of historical truthfulness, but the authenticity breaks down at unpredictable moments—with the narrator's frequent disclaimers on the one hand, and with fantastic elements introduced without commentary on the other. Thus a description of the life of an urban artisan co-exists with that of the innermost feelings of a fox-orator.

Des Périers's deconstruction of the veracity claim results in a collection in many ways unique. My comments regarding the *Nouvelles récréations* could be applied to Nicolas de Troyes's *Grand Parangon des nouvelles nouvelles*, where supernatural tales instead of fables are inserted into the collection. On the other hand, one would certainly have difficulty imagining the inclusion of an animal tale in the *Heptaméron*, even if these creatures, like the human characters, were to struggle with questions of love and honor. These contemporary collections, however, share the emphasis of the *Nouvelles récréations* on the act of narration itself. Although they sought their inspiration in varied places and perceived the function of the *nouvelle* collection differently, the *conteurs* share an interest in how to tell the story, how to keep the reader's attention, in what links the stories within the collection, and what style of discourse to favor. Only in a collection of short stories where the organization of the elements of a story must be tackled again and again, where the narrator can exploit the multiple prefaces and conclusions to address the narratees directly and repeatedly, can these kinds of questions be explored in depth. In rearranging characters and plots from familiar stories and in mixing the structural characteristics of different genres, the *conteurs* developed a new type of literature and alerted their readers to new ways of reading. The juxtaposition of traditional elements and new conclusions produces the surprise central to all *nouvelles*. Like the laughter in farce, this surprise depends both on an unusual story and on constant reminders of the social and literary conventions which it infringes.[31] The ordinary topics and settings that many critics have interpreted as proof of the *nouvelle*'s respect for verisimilitude, serve instead as "constant reminders of normal patterns of belief and expectation and are meant to emphasize that the nature of the action being projected on the backdrop of the normal world is incredible."[32] Although elements of reality and of generic verisimilitude certainly exist in the *nouvelle*, the moments that distinguish this genre from its models are those where both kinds of "reality" are overturned. The realistic elements of all these tales, then, function as do the talking animals in the *Nouvelles récréations*: they speak more about the expectations of readers (both in the sixteenth century and in ours) than about any retrievable historical reality.

---

[31] This is most obvious in comic tales, but the serious tales in the *Heptaméron*, for example, also rely on a tension between the exemplary and the extraordinary; while one *devisant* will present a story to demonstrate typical feminine behavior, another will insist that this story contradicts the reality of feminine behavior.

[32] Menachem Brinker, "Farce and the Poetics of the *Vraisemblable*," *Critical Inquiry* 9 (1983): 565–77, here 570.

Des Périers on Speed

Tom Conley

Bonaventure des Périers, a writer and a poet of the entourage of Marguerite de Navarre, does not figure prominently in the early modern French canon. He is best known for three literary works. One, a collection of facetious stories entitled *Nouvelles récréations et joyeux devis*, was written in the early 1540s, but only published in 1558, after the author's death (presumably by suicide) c. 1544. The fame of the tales might have been spurred by the effect of a libelous set of dialogues, entitled *Cymbalum mundi*, printed in 1538, whose reception in the hands of zealous religious authorities may have caused the author to take his own life. The great humanist printer, Jean de Tournes, printed a compact and handsome edition of the author's posthumous verse under the title, *Les Poésies du feu Bonaventure Des Périers* (1548). A general impression of these three works prompts most readers to associate Des Périers with the spirit of Humanism in France in the wake of Erasmus (who died in 1537) and the early Rabelais (whose *Pantagruel* and *Gargantua* appeared in the years 1532–1534). Writing in a moment in which reform was reduced to "silence" under the impact of resistance and repression exerted by Catholics in the aftermath of the "Affaire des Placards" (October 1534), Des Périers would be included among learned writers who craft works with a jagged and cutting edge. In one way, the writings are evidence of wit, agility, and illumination of the kind evinced in the *Adages* and the *Colloquies* of the Master of Rotterdam. But in another, with stylistic affinities with Rabelais and Clément Marot, the writings bring "agency" to contemporary and classical models of literature. Folklore, material drawn from the Bible, *realia* drawn from the foibles of everyday life, and recent history are combined and shaped to invent new political, aesthetic, and literary designs.

They are made manifest in all of the work, most directly and sensationally to be sure in the *Cymbalum mundi*, a strange composite of enigmas that has become a *locus classicus* for the interpretation of the origins of libertine views and atheism in sixteenth-century France. Des Périers's verse figures in the elegant innovations in typography launched by printers in Lyons after 1540. So too do the *Nouvelles* when they are printed by Robert Granjon in

1559 in the strange beauty of *civilité*, a font that is to be beheld as much as read. It can be asserted that all the writings play a role in the ferment of print culture in which, especially in the 1530s and 1540s, a mix of gothic and roman typographies attests to the extensively "transitional" condition of the new literary forms.[1] In a parallel fashion they confirm, too, what the plastic arts witness with a similar mix of decorative forms, where a flamboyant gothic idiom, prevailing throughout France for over a century, absorbs ornamental shapes, disinterred from the classical past, that are synthesized in persistently medieval spatial structures.[2] Flying buttresses are decorated with rosettes and pilaster strips, while vaults with tiercerons and liernes bear pendant bosses designed from architectural images seen in new editions of Vitruvius.

A permanent fusion of different idiolects also typifies Des Périers's work. In his poetry a mix of eclogue and blason puts the verse squarely in the frame of a "transitional" style that brings together classical genres with stylistic effects borrowed from *la grande rhétorique*. Such is the intermediate character of the *Nouvelles récréations*. They have been shown to refashion the earthy matter of the French *fabliau* and the bawdy tale (*Les Cent nouvelles nouvelles*) for the purpose of disseminating Humanistic ideology, but in their general aspect they attest to an experiment in matters of style. In the *Nouvelles récréations* a laconic narrative mobilizes in printed prose memories of

---

[1] Orthography, notes Susan Baddeley, preoccupied the minds of printers and pedagogues in Paris at the beginning of the 1530s. A significant work was the *Briefue doctrine pour deuement escripre selon la propriete du langaige Francoys*, first printed by Antoine Augereau, a humanist who would soon be burned at the stake in the aftermath of the "Affaire des Placards." The orthographic innovation, that included usage of the grave accent over the preposition à and the adverb là, might have been related to that of Olivétan (Pierre Robert), who published both *L'Instruction des enfans* (1533) and a translation of the Bible (1535) for which Des Périers was an active contributor. See S. Baddeley, *L'Orthographe française au temps de la réforme* (Geneva: Droz, 1993), 140–48.

[2] In the first chapter of his pathfinding *L'Art français du XVIe siècle: L'Invention du classicisme* (Paris: Flammarion, 1996), Henri Zerner shows that the coexistence of gothic and classical typographies throughout much of sixteenth-century France has as its analogue the extraordinary assimilation of classical decorative idiolects into gothic monuments. The moment of coextension of such vastly different shapes could be compared, too, to that of Des Périers's work, where the medieval earth of the *fabliau* and *conte grivois* becomes the vehicle for dialogues in the style of Lucian, humanistic *facéties*, adages, "bons mots," and Erasmian satire. Such is Lionello Sozzi's hypothesis concerning the relation that Des Périers's stories hold with Poggio Bracciolini's *Liber facetiarum* and other humanistic sources: *Les Contes de Bonaventure des Périers: Contribution à l'étude de la nouvelle française de la Renaissance* (Turin: Giappichelli, 1965).

the rhymed stories performed by Jean Bodel, the earthy after-dinner prose of the signature of the court of Charles the Bold, and even drolleries of *miséricorde* sculptures on chairs and church pews that had long offered comic images of everyday life. They conflate the Erasmian adage with fables of Aesopic signature. The tales bring a new consciousness of French space, developed in humanistic dictionaries and *itineraria* by Charles de Bovelles and Geofroy Tory, into new and striking toponymical designs.[3] They also translate idioms by putting different ways of speaking and naming into a new and unified orthographic and narrative matrix.

The effects of the *Nouvelles récréations* are especially salient when the collection and a fourth work, probably of Des Périers's signature, the *Discours non plus melancoliques que divers* (Poitiers: Enguilbert de Marnef, 1557), are juxtaposed. Although the *Discours* do not carry Des Périers's name (and perhaps for the same causes related to heresy that marked the *Cymbalum mundi*), the opuscule displays traces of the author's signature. It is written under the sign of *brevitas*, and is terse to the point of offering schematic renderings of dialogue, in which diagrammatic sentences concatenate into narratives that seem patterned on equations of reciprocals. Like the *Nouvelles récréations*, the work uses the concept and practice of the *facétie* and the *propos de table* to promote a consciousness of the history of the relations of language to geographical space. It attends to local and practical knowledges so as to promote the idea of a narrator who, as author, is merely a collector and assembler of materials whose "diversity" attests to the signs of the divinity of their creator. An intermediary between the world at large and the languages that are brought forward to make a printed *catalogue raisonné* of fragments taken from an infinite totality of words and things, the narrator betrays the figure of an ethnologist or, in the context of our world, the practitioner of everyday life who finds in anodyne and innocuous—if not even trivial—observation the raw materials with which to build greater ideological programs.

In the reading that follows, I should like to juxtapose the *Nouvelles récréations* and the *Discours non plus melancoliques que divers* in order to see if there

---

[3] An implicit geography inhabits Tory's *Itinerarium provinciarum omnium Antonini Augusti* (Paris: Henri Estienne, 1512) and Bovelles's *Liber de differentia vulgarium linguarum et gallici sermonis varietate* (Paris: Robert Estienne, 1533). They are linguistic guides that provide toponyms for virtual stories. Frank Lestringant calls the *récit toponymique* that which affixes a comic narrative to a place name in order to offer a discursive etymology that calls into question (and often confirms) what is understood in the etymology of place names: "Rabelais et le récit toponymique," repr. in idem, *Ecrire le monde à la Renaissance* (Caen: Editions Paradigme, 1993), 109–28. Stories serve to "memorize a passage, depositing into the thickness of the local signifier the traces of a way of doing things [*d'un faire*]" (127, my translation).

can be discerned the construction of a linguistic space that belongs to France, a vernacular France said to owe its identity to the relation of French to a mixed heritage of Greco-Roman and other origins. The reader witnesses signs of a "combat" waged for the cause of French in the midst of another no less noble but equally rich idiom, geography. With a consciousness of French comes the savor of places that, when they are imagined in cartographical and grammatical designs, spatialize the study of language and nation.[4] The new spatial consciousness that is gained from these two works is seen *accelerating* the transmission of knowledge. Geographical representations of France spatialize its history, hence giving it to be studied by the mind's eye. The narrator of these works is a figure who sees and who observes language and local culture. One of the salient traits of the author of the *Discours* is his anonymity. His namelessness owes to the fact that he must belong to France (he writes in French and is aware of other idioms spoken in the milieus) but remain everywhere and nowhere. He is daimonic in that he is an *other* bearing the identity of a French *author*. The persona of the author of both the *Discours* and the *Nouvelles récréations* is constructed to mirror that of the ordinary people who listen and learn about life wherever they may go. Projected is the image of a roving philologist, a rootless observer forever on the road, an errant soul of good will, a Pauline traveler, but also a nomadic ethnographer who records popular ways of expressing and doing things. The author is conceived no less as a geographer who coordinates spatial consciousness with the advancement of French ways of speaking and doing.

There results in both pieces of writing what has elsewhere been called, in respect to Rabelais's toponymical tales, a "language-map" of a nation imagined united through a vernacular idiom.[5] What the latter conveys is of a concurrent diversity made manifest by its own variegated nature. It is shown both to assure the presence of the hidden signature of a divine but forever secret origin and to give cause to a "politics of language" or a new historical anthropology of a nation. One of the virtues of Des Périers's opuscules, above and beyond the volatile mix of tones at once authoritative, ironic, and conversational, resides in the way their own printed discourse

---

[4] The "combat" for the French language is the topic of Claude Longeon's anthology of texts, *Les Premiers Combats pour la langue française* (Paris: Livre de Poche Classique, 1989). The mosaic of selections comprises a narrative telling of an increased consciousness of the strength and virtue of vernacular French in both literary and economic spheres.

[5] Terence Cave, "Travelers and Others: Cultural Connections in the Works of Rabelais," in *François Rabelais: Critical Assessments*, ed. Jean-Claude Carron (Baltimore: Johns Hopkins University Press, 1995), 39–56, here 47–48.

acquires cartographical measure. Now and again the words describing the chosen events and phenomena themselves acquire a spatial or plotted look that makes them at once parts of pictural emblems and latent topographical sites of a book-map. Another, which stands at the center of this inquiry, concerns the way that the consciousness evinced in the narratives about idiolects and ways of living in different regions betrays a collapse of duration or historical time. The work is aware of the impact of its dissemination throughout francophone France. It implies that it is an open-ended summary or a fairly comprehensive "image" of various topographies, but also that its printed form is bringing continuity and regularity to the cultural differences it describes. Its impression of speed—the brevity of its narratives, its terse aura of laconic style, the geometrical lines of its sentences, its pragmatic ethic, and its praise of wit and *brevitas* in all action—aligns it with the new ideology of print culture and endows it with a "politics of language."[6]

Through the twenty-one chapters of the *Discours*, it can be observed more broadly, in the context of the religious reform, that there exists in the work a concurrent effort to equate translation of sacred texts into the vernacular with a cartographical impulse, in which is plotted (or imposed) a new configuration of the nation.[7] The narrator travels as might a Pauline

---

[6] Michel de Certeau, Dominique Julia, and Jacques Revel have noted in *Une Politique de la langue: Enquête sur le rapport de l'Abbé Grégoire* (Paris: Gallimard, 1975) that the erstwhile Abbé's *questionnaire* of 1793, sent to regional magistrates throughout post-Revolutionary France, intended to impose the vernacular idiom, like a decimal system, as the official language of the nation. It sought to leave Latin to the clergy and, by eradicating the "routines" of regional ways of speaking, to nationalize the pedagogy of French. The by-product of its colonial policy (ironically, of an intramural or internecine character) was, of course, the startling and enthusing discovery of myriad differences and practices within the nation. An ethnography came as an accident of the inquiry. In their sequel to the study, "La Beauté du mort," in *La Culture au pluriel*, ed. Luce Giard (Paris: Seuil, 1994), 46–68, the same authors show how Charles Nisard's invention of "popular culture" in the 1850s amounts to formalization of Grégoire's discovery. A monument or a scientific object replaces that which elicited what was taken to be a dangerously erotic fascination with alterities residing within French borders. It is important to look at Des Périers's writings in conjunction with what these historians map out for the years 1793–1850. Born in the prose are the same politics of language and incipient anthropology of the French kingdom, but without a project of assimilation yet being apparent.

[7] Beyond the transgression inherent in the project of a vernacular edition of sacred writings, there is also an unwritten but vital dimension that touches on geography. French Bibles that ensued and that were issued from Geneva often carried maps of the Holy Land for the purpose of teaching the reader principles of European cartography. Catherine Delano Smith, in *Maps in Bibles* (Geneva: Droz,

voyager who obtains through displacement a sense of concurrently sacred and local (but never really profane) space. The geographical persona comes, perhaps, as a by-product of the iconography of Evangelical reform that marked the first two decades of the reign of François I (from 1515 up to the aftermath of the "Affaire des Placards"). Surely the return to Pauline writings carried the bonus of the geographical implication of the saintly author's peregrinations, that were indeed the topic of maps of Europe that depicted the course of his travels.[8] The *Discours* and the *Nouvelles récréations* share a penchant to anchor language in a constructed imagination of geographical space. They evince what historians of print culture and of the growth of cartography in the middle years of the sixteenth century might together call a nascent impulse to situate local history within greater spatial pictures.

Like Rabelais, Des Périers is a cartographer. He produces not concepts but *images* of ambient life in and about the matrices of printed letters. Each image is a verbal picture destined to affect the reader or the listener by the uncommon character of its own description.[9] In the *Nouvelles récréations* many of the tales become sketches or quick, quasi-photographic "takes" in the way they "signify" more than they mean: by way of litotes and the condensed diction of poetic prose, they establish in a flash an entire social space and the contradictions and conflicts that define the conditions of possibility for the transmission of printed writing. Both the *Nouvelles* and the *Discours* appear conscious of the effects that print might exert on what they give to be an older or traditional society. The work must thus put forward several cultural "speeds" within its units of narrative. In the differences it inaugurates, each story underscores a perception of places whence, in the greater fragmentary mass (but never a sum) of tales, some common barriers of exchange are implied.

1992), provides an exhaustive list of schematic maps inserted in sixteenth-century Bibles.

[8] A surviving fragment of a map of the travels of Saint Paul by Peter Apian (in the Liechtenstein Collection of the Houghton Library at Harvard University) is illustrated and studied in Robert Karrow, Jr., *Sixteenth Century Mapmakers and their Maps* (Chicago: The Speculum Press for the Newberry Library, 1993), 55–56 and 624–25.

[9] In *Rabelais* (Paris: Les Editeurs Français Réunis, 1955), a work anticipating his *La Production de l'espace* (Paris: Anthropos, 1971), Henri Lefebvre notes repeatedly that Rabelais and Leonardo da Vinci are "artistes autant que savants" who "ne séparèrent pas le savoir de l'émotion, ni l'image du concept, ni la pensée de la saisie sensible des objets" (111). A simultaneous creation and perception of space is witnessed in the articulation of the image.

A Monk on the Run

In story 58, "Du moyne qui respondoit tout par monossyllabes rymez," a field of social contradiction is given through that of the spatial and philological counterpoint. The entire tale is as compact and portative as the whole collection.

Nouvelle LVIII

Du moyne qui respondoit tout
par monossyllabes rymez

> Quelque moyne, passant pays, arriva en une hostellerie sus l'heure du soupper. L'hoste le fit asseoir avec les autres qui avoyent desjà bien commencé, et mon moine, pour les attaindre, se met à bauffrer d'un tel appetit comme s'il n'eust veu de trois jours pain. Le galant s'estoit mis en pourpoint, pour mieux s'en acquiter; ce que voyant l'un de ceux qui estoyent à table, luy demandoit force choses: qui ne luy faisoit pas plaisir, car il estoit empesché à remplir sa poche. Mais, affin de ne perdre gueres de temps, il respondoit tout par monossyllables rymez; et croy bien qu'il avoit apprins ce langage de plus longue main, car il estoit fort habile. Les demandes et les responses, c'estoyent. L'autre luy demande: «Quel habit portez-vous? — Fort. — Combien estes-vous de moines? — Trop. — Quel pain mangez-vous? — Bis. — Quel vin bevez-vous? — Gris. — Quelle chair mangez-vous? — Beuf. — Combien avez-vous de novices? — Neuf. — Que vous semble de ce vin? — Bon. — Vous n'en bevez pas de tel? — Non. — Et que mangez-vous les vendredy? — Oeufs. — Combien en avez-vous chascun? — Deux.» Ainsi, ce pendant, il ne perdoit pas un coup de dent; et si satisfaisoit aux demandes laconicquement. S'il disoit ses matines aussi courtes, c'estoit un bon pillier d'eglise.[10]

An *other* arrives in a place that is at once secular and ecclesial, an inn or *hostellerie*, where a *hoste* places the monk "with the others." The narrator, here

---

[10] Bonaventure des Périers, *Contes ou Nouvelles récréations et joyeux devis, suivis du Cymbalum mundi*, ed. P. L. Jacob (Paris: Garnier, n. d.), 158–59. Subsequent references will be to this edition.

connoted as an *autre* who cannot be pigeonholed as a figure residing in the inn or being of similar passage, is both *in* and *out* of the space of the community produced by the alimentary communion. The narrator underscores a distance from the subject of the event through the irony of typographical proximity to the monk. The formula, "mon moine," simple in aspect, signals how the possessive adjective carries a sign of a will to be dispossessed both of the monk and of his attributes. The "gallant" man is said to "lower his frock" in order better to be stripped of its worth. But it also connotes alacrity in the signifying chain of letters and words. "*Pain*," what the monk had not seen, leads to "pour*point*," the substantive that anticipates "*pour mieux s'en acquiter*," the very definition of the act of being dispossessed.[11] A locution is given a narrative design that tends to be literalized in the shape of both an emblem and a rebus. "Mon moi. . .ne" suggests that the self of the narrator acquires its sense of place by being figurally distant from what is given to be the physical proximity of the genitive adjective to its noun. Yet the monk becomes the narrator's money, his *moyen*, that will result from the performative effect of the telling. He is the "not-I" that makes him exemplary of what his inquisitive shadow, the *je*, can never be, even though his habits pertain to a tradition of signs foreign to one of representation or transcription ("et croy bien qu'il avoit apprins ce langage de plus longue main").

The situation of question-and-answer stages the inquiry of an ethnologist in the field asking questions of his informants. We are begged to behold and visualize what passes in the space of the exchange. The monk eats as if he had not seen bread for *three* days, and it is *one* of the interlocutors at the table who notes his rapacity. He might be seen as the male equivalent of the madwoman known in the tradition of the rebus as the first *dévoreuse d'hommes*: "Follement je vis . . ."[12] But in the end *we* are asked to visualize the

---

[11] In his *Dictionarie of the French and English Tongues* (1611), Randle Cotgrave notes that "mis en pourpoint" designates "turnd into his dublet, made not worth a groat; robd or deprived of, despoyled or stript out of, all he hath" (Columbia, SC: University of South Carolina Press, 1950).

[12] Cf. Geofroy Tory, *Champ fleury* (Paris: G. Tory and G. de Gourmont, 1529): "Les Deuises qui ne sont faictes par lettres significatives, sont faictes dimages qui signifient la fantasie de son Autheur, & cela est appelle ung Resbuz au quel on a resue, & faict on resuer les autres. Telz images sont ou hommes, ou femmes, bestes, oyseaux, poissons & autres choses corporelles & materielles, desquelles choses ie voy ung Resbuz de quatre versets & lignes en francois estre moult bien inuente, car toutes les dictions desdites quatre lignes sont paintes en diuers Images, & y a en substance. On me tient fol, faisant folle folye. / Ainsi ie vis, puis ainsi ie folye. / Fol entre folz, coquard entre mains vis, / On me maintient, car follement ie vis" (fol. xlii v). The figure of the monk at the table is painted with similar colors and

difference between a scene in an inn and a language lesson that pivots on an uncommon adverb, *laconicquement*, the least laconic and most learned of all of the words uttered and printed in the story. The adverb of five syllables, the most extravagant sign in the midst of many monosyllables, uses what is long—such as the figure of the frock or *pourpoint*—to denote things short. By antithesis the final image of the monk at dinner-time performing terse *matines* brings the reader's eye to the emblem of the "bon pillier d'eglise," the metaphor of the monk who uses speed to make the most of his carnal or acquisitive ways, the pier or pillar of the church here connoted to be its finest pilferer.[13]

Concatenations

The figures in the tale, like the tale itself, move across space as might a traveling salesman through the countryside. Other tales tend to be situated. The twenty-third, "De maistre Pierre Faifeu, qui eut des botes qui ne luy cousterent rien, et de Copieux de la Flesche en Anjou," has as its locale the city of Angers. The narration marks the capital of the Anjou as a point on a road, where travel moves with the speed of a flying arrow. The movement related in the tale reflects the disposition and the style of the preceding stories. The sense of its passage in a cultural and physical geography depends on its relation to the stories that immediately precede and follow. In the nineteenth, a good cobbler named Blondeau spends his life and labors in Paris, where he uses wit and guile to solve two perplexing situations that had cast him into melancholy. The twentieth takes to the road by succinctly relating an episode in the lives of three students who come to Paris to learn Latin. After finding better training in carnal pleasures, the prodigal sons, en route to their father's home, find themselves in an obliging situation. They are mistakenly apprehended as the criminals at the scene of a murder on a

---

thus stands as a verbal image. See also Jean Céard and Jean-Claude Margolin, *Rébus de la Renaissance: Des Images qui parlent*, 2 vols. (Paris: Maisonneuve et Larose, 1986), 2:267–68.

[13] The tale has often been compared to the episode of Brother Fredon in the *Cinquiesme Livre*, attributed to Rabelais (chap. 28), the sheer length betraying a different motivation. Closer to Des Périers is the rhymed dialogue in Etienne Tabourot's *Bigarrures et touches* (Paris: Jean Richer, 1603), fol. 148r–v. Tabourot disavows the work of Des Périers in the preface to the poem: "Je n'ay point veu de vous François monosyllabes à la fin, si ce n'est qu'on en pourroit faire infinis, & fort aysément. Veu qu'au cinquiesme livre, attribué à l'inimitable Rabelais, il y a bien des grosses de Frere Fredon, qui ne respondoit que par monosyllabes. De ces responses j'ay mis en vers ce peu qui s'ensuyt, pour exemple . . ."

road leading through a forest. The three young men are almost hanged for misusing the shards of Latin that they mime like the monkey who had been Blondeau's victim in the nineteenth tale. The twenty-first also begins in Paris and takes its cue from the same conundrum of translation, when a youth uses mime and wit to execute with ingenuity what the three young men of the preceding story had almost botched. The twenty-second tale inverts the situation of overbearing priests holding authority over children by dint of their Latin by offering the tableau of a rustic priest from Le Mans who studs his recital of mass with "Jesus" to camouflage his ignorance of the learned idiom.

The episodes concatenate and rebound from one tale to the other. The story of Faifeu is consequently given to be understood taking place on a road where language circulates to and from Paris and Angers, the same path on which, perhaps, had traveled the three brothers of the twentieth tale, from the site of Blondeau's world along the Seine. The plays on words, the misprisions and mistaken idioms or malapropisms amount to comic markers or signs strewn along a passage or network of highways that the twenty-third tale takes care to elaborate in its story of a trickster. A variant of Villon and Panurge, Faifeu evades both his creditors and the enraged victims of his pranks.

Three types of concatenation define the itineraries within and across the microsum—a sort of microcosm—comprising the five stories. One includes the virtual linkage of sites chosen for the locale of the narratives, that can be inferred to give some privilege to Paris but only in contrast to the provinces connected to it. In this instance, from the two anecdotes in the nineteenth tale of Blondeau's nonchalant "habitus" in the mantle of an artisan living in a local albeit central community, the narration moves to Le Mans. It then proceeds to Angers, implying a vector drawn along a southwesterly axis. The nineteenth and twentieth tales lead from Paris to two areas, the fatherland (where Latin is spoken) and the motherland (the French countryside and the maternal, vernacular idiom of French). The same spatial configuration is held in the twenty-first tale, in which, in an undesignated area of France, another son returns to his father and his priest where, at home and hearth, he undergoes a language lesson that, were it not for fate or wit that mark both tales in the unit (19 and 20), would have put or fixed the players in their place. The bumpkin priest of the twenty-second tale that takes place in Le Mans is affiliated with the students of the two preceding stories who had encountered and resisted clerical culture with varying degrees of success. The placement of this tale in the Maine is marked by the contiguous physical geography of the Anjou in which Faifeu travels in the twenty-third, with the cultural difference given by the way his character arches back in its recall of the Parisian milieu of Blondeau.

A second concatenation is the road itself, on which two of the stories (the twentieth and the twenty-third), as it were, "take place." That of the three brothers who "believed they were being hanged for their Latin" occurs on the road, in passage, *passant pays*, or in concurrent translation of language and place. Their ways of living are at once admonished and praised for the way they *spend* time in movement and in adolescent invention. "Trois freres de bonne maison avoyent longuement demeuré à Paris, mais ilz avoyent perdu tout leur temps à courir, à jouer et à folastrer. Advint que leur pere les manda tous trois pour s'en venir . . ." (71–72). If time is wasted, implies the formulation, it is done in the interest of movement and of economy so laconic that each of the three brothers predicates one of the three activities (running, playing, frolicking) in a sentence whose geometry seems to be the form of its content. Each is said to learn "one word" of Latin for their worldly *provision* as they prepare to return to the dominion of "their father." The tension of the joke turns on the contrast of the "Latin" centers, identified by "Paris" and "Father," to the road, where their appeal to the natural, fluvial language of "Mother," French itself, keeps them from being sent to the gallows ("les povres gens eussent esté penduz à credit, n'eust esté que, quand ilz veirent que c'estoit à bon escient, ilz commencerent à parler le latin de leur mere et à dire qu'ilz estoyent" [72]). The sense of passage is underscored by the narrator's parting shot, fired in response to a hypothetical question concerning the successful apprehension of the real criminals, that states, "What do I know, my friend, I wasn't there" (" — Et qu'en sçay-je? mon amy, je n'y estois pas"). With the narrator's insistence on not having been at the roadside, the end of the story becomes something of a lesson stressing what it means to "be" in narrative and geographical space, in passage, in an indefinite past. The peregrinations of the three youths anticipate the context of those of the more accomplished thief, Faifeu, who happens to share some of the traits that Blondeau had worn in the anecdotes of his own life and deeds.

A third element of intranarrative linkage is found in the reincarnation of figures and situations. In the nineteenth tale Blondeau has the aspect of a sacred being of reformed ideology. He lives by good will and good wits, and he knows how to exchange material for physical wealth quickly and for the benefit of the community. His character aligns him with the sacred clown, such as Marot's Jean Serre celebrated in a crowning epitaph in the *Adolescence clémentine*, who brought pleasure to his audiences.[14] Like Serre,

---

[14] His epitaph is as follows:
Cy dessoubz gist et loge en serre
Ce très gentil fallot Jehan Serre,
Qui tout plaisir alloit suyvant

Blondeau is awarded a poem for his tombstone that refers directly to the genre for which the author of the *Adolescence* had been known.[15] Pierre Faifeu of the twenty-third story becomes a variant of any of a number of characters in Marot's world. To the contrary of Blondeau, who is eternized in the manner of Jean Serre, Faifeu is satirized in the manner of the ballad the poet wrote to describe the dubious merits of Brother Lubin, who had been a thief in the cloak of a prelate.[16] He is a trickster, worthy of comparison to *personae* in the works of Villon and Rabelais:

> Pour mettre, comme un homme habille,
> Le bien d'aultruy avec le sien,
> Et vous laisser sans croix ne pille,
> Maistre Pierre le faisoit bien. (79)

The invention of the verse connects the one figure, Blondeau, to his inverse. It signals how and where the work is populated with tricksters who scurry through the world of the tales. The epitaphs attributed to them assure them of having sped through life but, no less, of leaving the trace of a way of living consonant with the shape and tenor of the poems dedicated to them. They share traits with other figures—such as the benevolent inebriate

---

Et grand joueur en son vivant,
Non pas joueur de dez ne quilles,
Mais de belles Farces gentilles . . .
(Clément Marot, *Œuvres complètes*, ed. B. Saint-Marc, 2 vols. [Paris: Garnier [1911]], 1:444).

[15] It is also worth citing:
Ci-dessoubz gist en ce tombeau
Un savetier nommé Blondeau,
Qui en son temps rien n'amassa,
Et puis après il trespassa.
Marriz en furent les voisins,
Car il enseignoit les bons vins. (71)

[16] Marot's Lubin is another personage who lives on speed:
Pour courir en poste à la ville,
Vingt foys, cent foys, ne sçay combien;
Pour faire quelque chose vile
Frere Lubin le fera bien;
Mais d'avoir honneste entretien,
Ou mener vie salutaire
C'est à faire à un bon chrestien,
Frere Lubin ne le peult faire.
(*Œuvres complètes*, 1:307).

Janicot (tale 77 [199–203]), reminiscent of the drunken clarity of the Socrates eternized in the prologue of *Gargantua*, but by the form of their presentation as "passed masters" or as figures of wit gone by (all wit being explosion and spark that illuminate and extinguish). The figures whose lives and ways bear the narrator's admiration have commonly borrowed identities. They are familiar but mercurial in the way they are amalgams of popular characters that circulate in the margins of printed matter.[17] By extension, the tales are implied to become, for the good fortune of Des Périers's editors, his own epitaph. Insofar as the author needs to be dead to validate the transaction of transmitting his work to the reader, a sense of the fragility of the contents is heightened.[18]

Time of the Essence

A fourth concatenating agent, also one in which speed is shown to be a paramount virtue, punctuates the recurring descriptions of a world in acceleration. Taking part in a broader thematics of the explosion of intellectual energy that, unpredictably but with immediacy, gives to a subject an illuminating vision, certain words recur in order to disappear. They resemble marks of measure or also, in the alchemy of the wit of the *Nouvelles récréations*, catalytic agents that move the discourse ahead. They confer on the text a sense of place and movement in the physical and geographical world. Exemplary is *incontinent*, in its adverbial form meaning roughly "incontinently, instantly, immediately, presently, suddainely, forthwith, out of hand, as soone as may be" (Cotgrave). It has the value of an emblem, of a word-image, or a component of a *festina lente* that compounds rapidity and probity. It appears thus in the story of the neighboring monkey that ferrets through

---

[17] Most noteworthy is Pierre Faifeu himself, a renegade of Charles Bourdigné's *La Légende joyeuse de maistre Pierre Faifeu* (1532), re-edited by Francis Valette in a critical edition (Geneva: Droz, 1972).

[18] Jean-Claude Arnould argues that the reformed printer plays on the death of the author in order to valorize his own role as the figure responsible for the circulation, in 1559, of the Erasmian material of earlier vintage. Granjon "a donc compris que la vocation même des récits, et *a fortiori* de ceux de Bonaventure, n'était pas d'exister de manière statique et définitive, mais de devenir les objets d'une circulation et d'un échange permanents, que viendront confirmer les emprunts et les amplifications postérieures": "L'«Auteur» invisible: Les *Nouvelles récréations et joyeux devis de feu Bonaventure des Périers*, de Robert Granjon," in *Conteurs et romanciers de la Renaissance: Mélanges offerts à Gabriel-André Pérouse*, ed. James Dauphiné and Béatrice Périgot (Paris: Honoré Champion, 1997), 27–37, here 36. No matter what Granjon's economic and ideological motives may have been in the publication of the edition in "civilité" typography, rapidity of the circulation of information is extolled.

Blondeau's tools and wares when the cobbler is away from his bench. Harassed, Blondeau uses simian tactics to outwit the simian:

> A l'une des fois Blondeau aguisa un trenchet et le fit couper comme un rasoir, et puis, à l'heure qu'il veid ce singe en aguet, il commença à se mettre ce trenchet contre la gorge et le mener et ramener comme s'il se fust voulu egosiller. Et quant il eut fait cela assez longuement pour le faire adviser à ce singe, il s'en part de la boutique et s'en va disner. Ce singe ne faillit pas *incontinent* à descendre, car il vouloit s'esbatre à ce nouveau passe-temps, qu'il n'avoit point encores veu faire. Il vint prendre ce trenchet et tout *incontinent* se le met contre la gorge, en le menant et ramenant comme il avoit veu faire à Blondeau. (71, my italics)

Blondeau takes his time to eat and drink while the monkey kills himself by suddenly falling prey to his own mimetic habits. In the following tale, when the police arraign the three adolescents for being the brigands they are not, the first brother comes forward. "*Incontinent* le plus grand, à qui l'honneur appartenoit de parler le premier, va dire: «Nos tres clerici»" (72, my italics). The next tale makes suddenness the order that brings together the stern father, the pretentious priest, and the ingenious son, but in such a way that the word accelerates and carries local time and history into a story that begins in an aura of folklore:

> Un laboureur riche et aisé, après avoir tenu son filz quelques années à Paris, le manda querir, par le conseil de son curé. Quand il fut venu, le pere, qui estoit jà vieux, fut joyeux de le veoir, et ne faillit à envoyer *incontinent* querir monsieur le curé à disner, pour luy faire feste de son filz. (73, my italics)

The adverb activates, it catalyzes, but it also draws attention to the immediacy of its own place in both the implied geography of France and the syntax of the sentence itself. As was the case in the preceding story, reference to speed is placed adjacent to the ease and pleasure of the dinner-table, the site where the narrative would most likely be reiterated. *Incontinent* does not recur in the story of the priest who failed to make his way through the Latin of his missal because the situation calls for its opposite, a condition prompting the narrator to summarize: "Il disoit cet evangile si pesamment et vous y trouvoit tant de motz nouveaux et si longs à eppeler, qu'il estoit contraint d'en laisser la moitié, et vous disoit à tous coups *Jesus*, encores qu'il n'y fust point" (77).[19] At the dinner-table, the *locus amoenus* of many of the narratives, the joke of the tale turns on the exchange of "Monsieur" for "Jesus," words that can be grasped immediately and incontinently, over food and wine, with legerdemain, contrary to what is stated *si pesamment* in the situation inverting the paradigm of the twenty-first tale.

By contrast, *incontinent* describes the suddenness of Faifeu's actions. He acts impulsively, on the spur of the moment, but always in ways that lead him by diverse means to a speedy exit. Hurrying to leave Angers, he packs off in order not to die with his boots on:

> Il se trouva une fois entre toutes si pressé de partir de la ville d'Angiers, qu'il n'eut pas loisir de prendre des botes. Comment! des botes? Il n'eut pas le loisir de faire seller son cheval, car on le suivoit un peu de près. Mais il estoit si accort et si inventif, qu'*incontinent* qu'il fut à deux jetz d'arc de la ville, trouva façon d'avoir une jument d'un povre homme qui s'en retournoit dessus en son village, luy disant qu'il s'en alloit par là et qu'il la laisseroit à sa femme en passant. (79, my italics)

Incontinence acquires a manifold inflection—and Faifeu gallops off from Angers to La Flèche—with the implied comparison to Marot and Villon sustained from the quatrain two sentences above. In *Le Testament*, "Angiers" had rich proverbial innuendo: in one popular inflection, the proper name was associated with sexual and procreative congress.[20] In this tale incontinence of

---

[19] A scabrous undertone is obvious: in the weakened deixis the *il* of "encores qu'il n'y fust point" can refer to the bumbling priest who has not found the rhythm of his reading, to "Monsieur," who does not follow the conversation, and to Jesus, who was not present either.

[20] A current meaning of *engier* was "to produce, to multiply, to furnish with flora and fauna, and to gratify." As Cotgrave later put it: "*Enger*. To produce, or make to grow; to store, furnish, or fill with th'increase, or kind of; also, to grow, increase, extend, or spred itselfe abroad." David Kuhn notes *à propos* "Angiers" in the *Lais*: "Villon nous explique qu'il va 'a Angiers': encore une équivoque usuelle, sur 'ongier' *foutre*, et sur 'engier' *augmenter*": *La Poétique de François Villon* (Paris: Armand Colin, 1967), 109, 133–34, n. 15. Des Périers's Faifeu resemble le horseman noted in some lines Kuhn cites from the contemporary of Charles Bourdigné, Roger de Collerye:
Tout soudain chaussa ses houseaulx
Puis après monta à cheval,
Et en courant à mont, à val,

bodily generation and expulsion gives way to acceleration. Half-dressed, Faifeu makes quick tracks but is at "the distance of two arrow shots" (memories of Brother Lubin notwithstanding) from the city, or geographically, en route to La Flèche, where he arrives "tout mouillé et tout mal en point" (79), after having fashioned for himself from remnants of straw a flimsy pair of boots. The local cobblers of the town mock him for his appearance. After coming to his senses ("quand il fut un petit revenu auprès du feu" [80]), he tricks the men who mocked him, obtaining one of a pair of boots from two different cobblers. In each exchange he accepts one of the shoes and returns the other. "*Incontinent* qu'il fut departy, maistre Pierre envoye par un autre valet querir un autre cordouannier . . ." (81, my italics). The second arrives with the boots and is sent off to redesign the one that doesn't fit what he reports to be his swollen leg. "*Incontinent* que le cordouannier s'en fut allé, maistre Pierre reprend sa bote de la jambe droite et monte à cheval sus sa jument et va vie avec ses botes, et des esperons, lesquelz il avoit acheptez, car il n'avoit pas loisir de tromper tant de gens à un coup; et de picquer!" (82, my italics).

Speed, haste, and action are Faifeu's essence. The best trickster, merchant, or thief is the self-contained but dispossessed individual who acts adroitly, quickly, decisively. He moves with alacrity and style. As in Rabelais in the celebrated episode where the narrator spends several months in the mouth of his master Pantagruel, *incontinent* has a geographical or spatial inflection that makes both the printed characters and the personage travel at a mercurial speed and, no less, in a world that expands its borders within the frame of the printed narrative. For the author of *Pantagruel*, *incontinent* was marked with speed vital to procreation, to bodily dilation, and to a world expanding in a flash from a local to a global perspective. "Ainsi que Pantagruel avecques toute sa bande entrerent es terres des Dipsodes, tout le monde en estoit joyeux, et incontinent se rendirent à luy, et de leur franc vouloir luy apporterent les clefz de toutes les villes où il alloit . . ."[21] In the chapter relating the narrator's discovery of another world in Pantagruel's mouth the literally incontinent perspective of the episode is marked in the confusion of cities, lands, continents, and worlds contained pell-mell in each other ("sa bande en*trer*ent es *terres* des Dipsodes, *tout* le *monde* en estoit joyeux, et in*continent* se rendirent . . .").

Pour éviter les grans dangers,
Cuydant arriver à Angiers
Il vint coucher à Carcassonne.
(Kuhn, *La Poétique*, 134)

[21] François Rabelais, *Œuvres complètes*, ed. Mireille Huchon, Bibliothèque de la Pléiade (Paris: Gallimard, 1994), 330.

In Des Périers, by contrast, the narration tends to the svelte or minimal description with a resulting spatial inflection tending to topography more than cosmography. Faifeu has to rely on the speed, wit, and energy that mark, ironically, the hidden homily of the collection. Sudden, self-contained, alert and reasoned action is extolled through the vectors of Faifeu's travels in the Anjou. The topography is synthesized into the literal character of the place names (from Angers to La Flèche) when the personage is suddenly assimilated into the secret figure of the author absconded from the text. Faifeu is first described through allusion to Marot's Frère Lubin and the trickster of *Le Grant Testament*. But the narrator adds "et trouvoit fort bon le proverbe qui dit que tous les biens sont communs et qu'il n'y ha que maniere de les avoir" (79). The trick is to discern the best way to trick, "dextrement et d'une si gentille façon" (79), so that speed and self-evacuation become a major attribute of style.

Here and elsewhere what is deemed "good" or *bon* acquires capital value. Like a *bon mot*, a well-chosen proverb adjudicates dilemmas of means and ends.[22] It is good, it guides, it authorizes action. It allows chance to dictate means of executing what is needed to obtain profit or salvation. In this tale Faifeu makes "good" things happen at moments marked as opportune by the same adjective. He will settle accounts left unpaid after the locals of La Flèche mocked him for the style of his makeshift shoes:

> Quand [Faifeu] fut un petit revenu auprès du feu, il commence à songer comment il auroit sa revenche de ses Copieux qui luy avoyent ainsi fait la bien venue. Si luy souvint d'un *bon moyen* que le temps et la nécessité luy presentoyent, pour se venger des cordouanniers, en attendant que Dieu luy donnast son recours contre les autres. Ce fut qu'ayant faute de botes de cuir, il imagina une invention de se faire boter par les cordouanniers à leurs despens. (80, my italics)

He concocts his plan by telling the host of the inn that he had left so quickly that he never had leisure enough "de se houser ny esperonner" (81). The host (who, like the figure in the tale of the monosyllabic monk, carries a strong religious dimension in being related to the sign of Christ) is

---

[22] In a celebrated article on the Erasmian inflection of the joke or "good word" in Des Périers, Henri Weber notes how much the explosive wit of the story becomes the money of humanism: "La Facétie et le bon mot du Pogge à Des Périers," in *Humanism in France at the End of the Middle Ages and in the Early Renaissance*, ed. A. H. T. Levi (Manchester: Manchester University Press, 1970), 82–105.

seduced into inviting one of the local shoemakers to pay a visit to the traveler who carries among his effects neither boots nor spurs. "«Pour Dieu, ce dit maistre Pierre, envoyez m'en querir un, mon hoste.» Ce qu'il fit. Il en vient un, lequel, de *bonne aventure*, estoit l'un de ceux qui l'avoyent ainsi bien lardé à sa venue" (81, my italics).

On the Tracks of the Name

In a world where sudden action and decision count, and where speedy connections are essential for success, a quirk of fate, chance, or *bonne aventure* brings the malicious shoemaker to the inn. The locution figures in a matrix not only of things good but also of the departed author's given name. *Bonaventure* thus is affiliated with Faifeu, the man who burns his way through life. In the context, Faifeu's revenge constitutes a "good means" or a golden rule of doing unto others as others do unto oneself. A fastidious exercise would be taken up in accumulating variations on *par aventure, bon moyen, bonne invention*, and words of *bonté* that stud the style of the environing tales. On these occasions, either by design, incontinence, or sheer suddenness, the ends of the book are folded into the geography of its style. "En l'eglise Saint-Hilaire de Poitiers y eut jadis un chantre qui servoit de basse-contre, lequel, parce qu'il estoit *bon* compagnon et qu'il beuvoit bien . . . , estoit bien venu entre les chanoines, qui l'appeloyent bien souvent à disner et à soupper" (13). "Au pays d'Anjou y eut jadis un gentilhomme qui estoit riche et de *bonne* maison, mais il estoit un peu suget à ses *bons* plaisirs" (19). "En la ville de Poytiers y avoit un gentilhomme de bien riche maison et de *bon* cueur, homme de *bonne* entreprinse; mais il avoit un grandissime deffault naturel, qui estoit de la langue . . ." (136). "Telles *adventures* sont *bonnes* à ces jeunes gens, pour leur faire rasseoir un peu leur cholere; entre lesquelles est la rencontre d'un Poytevin, quand on va par pays" (186). Here and elsewhere unexpected connections that tie the proper name to the common effect of good action and good fate become the emblem of the virtue of speed itself.

A latent cartography of an author who has the good fortune of bearing godspeed—*bonaventure*—becomes foreground and background to the tales of actions and foibles of human behavior in a network of towns, roads, and cities loosely grouped together in the vernacular idiom of the *Nouvelles récréations*. The late (*feu*) author of the book is melded into its contents at the level where the printed characters spell out an exemplary style of vernacular prose. That style is of the same temper as the action and pragmatism. It is something of a mystified rationalism that works, literally, as it was seen in the tale of Faifeu, on the spur and fate of the moment.

Grammar and Geography

In the *Nouvelles récréations* the name of the author reverberates through the literal character of the tales. The accumulation of ninety stories of tricksters, foibles of local practices, and jokes based on misprisions or translations of patois offers an early geography of French identity. The first tale of the collection, underscoring its own efficacy as both a narrative and a preamble, that is, a *preambulation* about the space that the collection is creating, announces that its author will provide "a way of fooling time" ("moyen de tromper le temps" [5]), a formula that might be construed both to potentiate and waste currency. The book is conceived to be a time-machine, a work using spatial form to alert its reader to fugacity. The inaugural topos of the *carpe diem* is aimed, it seems, to chisel into the words of counsel the vanishing name of the author. "Bien vivre et se resjouir. Une trop grande patience vous consume; un taire vous tient gehenné; un conseil vous trompe; une diete vous desseiche; un amy vous abandonne. Et, pour cela, vous faut-il *desesperer*?" (6, my italics).

To enhance the pleasure obtained through speed, the reader is advised not to read from beginning to end but to open the book anywhere. Wherever the eye happens to look or the ear to hear, little doubt will be cast about the *space* of the creation. Implied is that the events narrated, however much their origins can be disputed, are resolutely French and belong to the geography of contemporary *Gallia*. Des Périers's twofold allusion to given provinces as "cartiers" endows the text with the aura of French cartography. "«Oh! cecy ne fut pas faict en ce cartier-là! — Je l'avoys desjà ouy compter! — Cela fut faict en nostre pays.» Riez seulement, et ne vous chaille si ce fut Gaultier, ou si ce fut Garguille. Ne vous souciez point si ce fut à Tours en Berry, ou à Bourges en Tourayne" (7), the place-names being nothing more than matter for debate. Implied is that the story is universal in character, but that its occurrence is on French soil. The demonic trait extolled in the passage is one that traces a line of division between *exempla* of total social facts drawn from a general encyclopaedia or spatial compendium of human exchange and differently inflected spaces that belong to France and France alone. A geography lesson is concurrent with that of decision and action. "Et puis je ne suis point allé chercher mes Comptes à Constantinople, à Florence, ny à Venise, ne si loing que cela" (6). The concatenation runs from East to West, from the antonomasia of a *conte* in Constantinople, to what arches toward France.

Discours non plus melancoliques . . . qui appartiennent à nostre France

In 1557 the Poitevin printer Enguilbert de Marnef issued a modest work entitled *Discours non plus melancoliques que divers, de choses mesmement qui appartiennent à nostre France: & a la fin La maniere de bien & justement entoucher les Lucs & Guiternes*. A short work counting less than one hundred pages, it is a *mélange*, an opuscule lumping together various historical and archeological trivia before ending with an illustrated chapter on the playing and maintenance of stringed musical instruments. The work does not carry the name of a single author. It celebrates its own mixed origins. In his preface to the reader, the printer announces that in his city he has sought the good company of wise men for whom letters have contributed to the mores of man. "Tu croiras donques aisément, que Dieu m'a fait cete grace, que j'ai aquis en ceste ville la connoissance & amitié de prou de gens savans de maintes nations: plusieurs desquels ne m'ont rien celé, qui fust en leurs coffres & estudes. Ainsi ay recouvré les discours, dont est fait ce livre, & maints autres escrits, & labeurs divers de plusieurs . . . aucunesfois des aucteurs mesmes, aucunesfois d'autres que des auteurs, qui avoient cela retiré des auteurs, ou en quelque sorte leur estoit venu entre les mains, sans savoir rien des aucteurs."[23]

The author-function is assimilated into the space that the work creates through an accumulation of comparative facts of grammar and geography. The first chapter treats of "historians who seek the origins of the Gauls and the French," while the second provides a historical grid for the names of the days of the week with a discussion and a table with nine representative languages. Chapter three takes up the historical etymology of *Africa*. Chapter four brings us back to the story of the Gallic Hercules, while chapter five takes up French grammarians. The sixth chapter treats of the names of the Rivers Saône and Rhône. In the seventh, discussion turns to accents and "la mode qu'on prononce aujourduy le Grec & Latin." A pattern is quickly established of movement to and from language and French space.

Emerging from the design of the book is a variant of a *politics of language* or an anthropology of French ways of speaking and doing. Unlike the future project of the French Revolution that would impose one idiom in order to make reason and common sense the administrative backbone of the nation, the *Discours*, like the *Nouvelles récréations*, admit that variety and difference constitute national unity. The work inaugurates an ethnology of

---

[23] [Bonaventure des Périers], *Discours non plus melancoliques que divers, de choses mesmement qui appartiennent à nostre France: & a la fin La maniere de bien & justement entoucher les Lucs & Guiternes* (Poitiers: Enguilbert de Marnef, 1557) [Houghton Library *FC.P3625.557d], fol. 1v. Subsequent references will be to this edition.

France, in which spatial and linguistic differences attest to a health of diversity. It clearly follows the Pauline ethic of seeking in the natural world the signs of divine creation, but in doing so it pulls its reader in and through spaces that are changed by the effect of the discourse itself.

Prior to developing a more extensive analysis of the traits that link the work to Des Périers's *Œuvre* (as Charles Nodier has done),[24] we can observe, first, that the apparent "author" of the work is a roving and somewhat demonic ethnographer and, second, that the mass of his reported data yields a spatialization of language and human activity. The work can be classified as an early model of descriptive geography in a vernacular idiom.[25]

---

[24] Nodier's appreciation, rich and detailed, merits quotation: "*Le Cymbalum mundi* de Desperriers a été réimprimé trois fois de 1711 à 1753, mais plutôt par égard pour sa rareté que pour son mérite, et de médiocres vignettes de Bernard Picart lui ont valu la plus grande partie de son succès. Aujourd'hui qu'il est regardé par les gens de goût comme une des productions les plus piquantes de notre littérature de la renaissance, il faut en donner aux amateurs une édition chaste et fidèle, avec des notes courtes et rares, qui ne sauront être à mon avis trop exemptes de vaines hypothèses et d'ambitieuse philologie. Mais ne faut-il pas aussi remettre en lumière cet excellent écrivain tout entier, ou du moins tels de ses ouvrages qui n'ont jamais été reproduits, comme ces charmants *Discours non plus melancoliques que divers*, dont ce titre de mauvais goût pourrait bien avoir différé la célébrité? Je conviendrai, si l'on veut, qu'ils ne lui appartiennent pas exclusivement, et qu'il faut en rendre quelques chapitres à Nicolas Denisot et à Jacques Pelletier, les amis de Bonaventure, et ses collaborateurs présumés dans le joli livre des *Contes* ou *Nouvelles récréations*; mais cette question, fort difficile à résoudre aujourd'hui, ne demande qu'un *avant-propos* de quatre lignes, et le reste de ces ingénieux mélanges qui ont servi de modèle, suivant moi, à l'admirable auteur des *Essais*, n'exige pas une note d'explication ou d'éclaircissement; car il est peut-être impossible de citer dans toute la littérature de cette époque (1557), un seul texte de langue dont le style soit plus correct, plus clair, plus élégant, plus souple, et plus soutenu. J'ajouterai qu'ils empruntent de leurs sujets mêmes un attrait inexprimable qui en rendroit la réimpression fort bien entendue au milieu des études de notre temps, puisqu'ils sont presque entièrement consacrés à l'examen de ces questions d'histoire et de langage dont il est à la mode de s'occuper maintenant. Ces matières difficiles n'ont jamais été abordées avec plus de grâce et de légèreté dans une discussion d'ailleurs forte et solide, et je ne connois point d'exemple d'une alliance plus heureuse de la mordante causticité de Rabelais avec le scepticisme grave et profond de Montaigne. C'est un de ces ouvrages substantiels et savoureux, si rares en tout pays, qui nourrissent l'intelligence en faisant sourire l'esprit": *Des Auteurs du seizième siècle qu'il convient de réimprimer* (Paris: Techener, 1835), 7–8.

[25] Numa Broc has noted that in the Renaissance "descriptive" geography overtakes its "mathematical" counterpart with the growth of the new genre of "universal cosmography" inaugurated by Boemus and Sebastian Münster. "The modern

It is stuffed with *varia* that on occasion are developed into narrative pictures. In one vignette the figure of the author is glimpsed as an inquisitive foreigner in his own land, as an avatar, perhaps, of the chubby homunculus who wanders through the maps and descriptions of the *Guide Michelin.* In the ninth chapter, entitled "D'ou viennent les noms de Regle, Esquerre, Compas, Plomb, & Niveau," the narrator is suddenly seen ambulating about the country:

> Je me trouuay un jour en un astelier, entre grand nombre de massons, lesquels interrogai volontiers, & mis en propos des choses de leur mestier. Entre eus y avoit un petit Normant avancé en aage plus que nul autre de la compagnie, qui sur tous me satisfaisoit a ce que leur demandois. Et finalement sans autrement lesser sa besogne, me pria d'ouir une rime (vous scavés qu'a Rouan on ne parle autrement qu'en Rime) de l'office, & de toutes les choses, ou pour le moins de la plus grand'part de ce qu'il faut qu'un masson aie, laquelle il me dit qu'il avoit faite luy mesme en l'an disseptiesme de son aage: de laquelle je retins ces deux vers
>
> Aie Regle, Esquerre, & Compas,
> Plomb & Niveau n'oblie pas.
>
> Despuis ne ma fois souvenu de ceste rimasserie, que n'aie pensé, dont sont sortis ces noms Regle, Esquerre, Compas, Plomb, Niveau, ainsi que sont autres de nostre Gaule, qui arrachent tout notre langage du Roman, & du Grec, sans oblier l'Ebrieu. (fols. 33v–34r).

Whereas the masons of Rouen, who might be the "native informants" of the dialogue, speak a language of nature—that is, jargon or poetry that attaches craft to the world itself—the narrator is consigned to commit the knowledge to memory. He transcribes the material before reflecting on the historical geography of language that reaches back to Roman, Greek, and Hebraic idioms.

---

reader is struck by the apparent disorder, the continual digressions, the impression of all-things-being-equal, the absence of a thematic thread. . . . However, the readers of the Renaissance enjoyed this confused encyclopedism whence have emerged most of our 'human sciences'": *La Géographie de la Renaissance (1420–1620)* (Paris: Bibliothèque Nationale, 1980), 81, my translation. Mathematical geography becomes progressively restricted to specialists while descriptive geography takes a new lead (86). Des Périers would be a "descriptive topographer" of similar kind.

The effect of his labors, given in the form of the content of the *Discours*, is one that collapses differences of time and geography into the slim space of the volume. Inferred is that the work will provide, in the instantaneity of its form, a historical sweep of French practices. Lexicography is an exercise in historical geography. The scheme of the chapters given to alternate remarks on place with those of usage see fuller development in cosmographies and compendia affiliated with Sebastian Münster and François de Belleforest, but here, in a stenographic form that resembles the quick and laconic "takes" on local culture in the *Nouvelles récréations*, the particularities and historical singularities of French are embedded in space. In the passage that follows, the fact of the cohabitation of three languages in the Guyenne is less important than the ethnographic eye that discerns the qualities of the region:

> Des langages desquels est composé nostre François, & des etymologies d'aucuns mots François, Chap. 17.
>
> Quant les Romains ont esté seigneurs de ce païs, ils y ont semé leur Latin: mais d'ou nous vient ce Grec? Je n'en sçay rien, fors qu'en la Gaule Narbonoise, qui s'appelle aujourdhuy Prouence, Languedoc, sont venus jadis demourer force Grecs, & ont là basty plusieurs villes, desquelles l'une est Marseilhe, comme vous diront Strabon, Justin, & autres: en laquelle ville de Marseilhe on parloi[t] jadis trois langues, la Greque, Latine, & Gauloise, ce dit saint Jerome au proesme du segond livre de ses commentaires sur l'epistre *ad Galatas*, là ou il dit aussi davantage, que la Guienne se disoit anciennement estre pareilhement de nation greque. Les histoires anciennes sont perdues, qui parloient de ceste origine de Guiennois, mais cela suffit, qu'on voit par cet aucteur, qu'ils sont sortis de la Grece. Ainsy y a eu jadis trois langues en la Guienne, comme en Marseilhe, & ainsi voit on que nostre Gaule peut avoir prins beaucoup de mots de ces Grecs icy. (fols. 70v–71r)

Like the author who is other, or the sources of the book that are mixed in one source or another, the Guyenne becomes specifically French (at least according to the title of the chapter) when it can be discerned that the linguistic landscape is of diverse origin, and that the alterity the traveler discovers in passing is of substantial historical depth. The narrator doesn't know whence originate the Greek origins of France, but he can count on Strabo to surmise that former historians, "ces aucteurs," came from Greece. To be sure, France is being constructed as a linguistic, geographical, and historical object, but only by way of the mobile and self-estranging observer can it be glimpsed at once as a physical entity and as a spatial and historical abstraction. The perception of the country depends on the speed and mobility of the ever-curious and rootless traveler.

Parting Shots

An anthropology is born in the descriptive narratives of both the *Discours* and the *Nouvelles récréations et joyeux devis*. By and large the former work has the appearance of a notebook or a compendium of data that informs the more finished project of the merry tales of the latter. The *Joyeux devis* borrow their narrative elements from sources that have been amply documented, but for purposes not entirely to mold folklore to the shape of a laconic tale. One of them is geographic, and for that reason the book considers history and the state of being in contemporary France in spatial terms. In both works an ethics of speed is given through the impression that their printed medium offers to the eye of the reader a compendium of spatial and lexical differences that both define and remain within the fluid boundaries of France. The works are written to celebrate a variety of ways of living and perceiving different spaces, but they are also descriptive cartographies that in their future reception will attest to a latent nationalism that celebrates spiritual and temporal diversity. It may be that in the 1540s the speed by which the narrator and readers "commute" from one area to the next posed for authorities of religious control a seductive threat. The wit and wile, the *vitesse* of Des Périers's work, like others of similar attitude, had to be throttled. The errant narrator, a literal heretic, could not be allowed to travel at will. Like characters seen in the stories, the reputed and late author of these works probably knew all along the way that speed kills.

Monkey Business: Imitation and the Status of the Text in Du Fail's *Propos rustiques*

Richard L. Regosin

> "Un conte attire l'autre"
> (Sixteenth-century proverb)

Eight years after the publication of Noël du Fail's *Propos rustiques* in 1547, Etienne Pasquier wrote disparagingly about the author and his text, comparing them unfavorably to Rabelais and to *Gargantua* and *Pantagruel*. Attributing to Du Fail the audacious desire to imitate Rabelais, Pasquier mocked what he considered to be the writer's inevitable failure:

> Il n'y a celuy de nous qui ne sçache combien le docte Rabelais en folastrant sagement sur son Gargantua et son Pantagruel, gaigna de grace parmy le peuple. Il se trouva par après, deux singes qui se persuaderent d'en pouvoir faire tout autant, l'un sous le nom de Leon l'Adulfy en ses *Propos rustiques* . . . Mais autant y profita l'un que l'autre: s'estant la memoire de ces deux livres perduz.[1]

The folly of the imitator was to imagine that he could equal the achievement of Rabelais in blending the serious and the comic, that he too could master the oxymoronic "folastrer sagement." In attempting to reach the heights of writing that conferred "grace," Du Fail had only succeeded in lowering himself to the level of the beast; he had, literally, made a monkey of himself. The price of this audacity and the resultant self-debasement, Pasquier says sarcastically, is that the work has been all but forgotten.

---

[1] The quotation from Pasquier is cited in Noël du Fail, *Propos rustiques*, ed. Gabriel-André Pérouse and Roger Dubuis (Geneva: Droz, 1994), 17, n. 17. In this essay I will be referring to this edition.

Pasquier's claim in 1554 that the *Propos rustiques* had been completely lost from public memory was made with a measure of bad faith since there had been at least five editions prior to that time.[2] The text did, however, drop almost completely from sight from the end of the sixteenth century until a renewal of interest produced two important editions in the late nineteenth century. And although in the twentieth century the *Propos rustiques* have been included in the prestigious *Pléiade* collection (*Conteurs du XVIe siècle*) and in Droz's "Textes littéraires français" series (in the Pérouse/Dubuis edition I am using), it remains for the most part a work little known or read. Pasquier thus was only premature when he relegated Du Fail's work to obscurity, but was he correct in attributing its fate to the fact that it imitates Rabelais? Imitation in itself cannot, in fact, have been the culprit, given the place it occupied for both the theory and practice of writing—and aesthetics in general—in the Renaissance. What Pasquier criticizes in this case is the failure of imitation to produce a legitimate simulacrum, the failure of the writer to "pouvoir faire tout autant." What he indicts is the unacceptable difference between the model and the copy, the scandalous gap that transforms a man into an ape.

Pasquier's commentary implies that Du Fail takes himself for what he is not, overreaches, and exposes himself as the parodic counterpart of Rabelais. But it reminds us at the same time that imitation itself is always a form of "aping" and that every writer is thus always part ape. Imitation is by definition derivative, and thus necessarily secondary, since it can never be that which it aspires to reproduce, the model itself. Plato reminds us of this paradox in the *Cratylus* when he has Socrates ask the following question: if a god were to make the image of Cratylus into the exact duplicate of Cratylus himself, if he were to copy all Cratylus's qualities and place them in another form, would this be Cratylus and the image of Cratylus or would there be two Cratyluses? The answer, that there would be two Cratyluses, discloses the truth of imitation: if the image expresses in every point the entire reality (of the model), it is no longer an image. Do you not perceive, Socrates concludes, that images are very far from having qualities that are the exact counterpart of the realities they represent? (*Cratylus* 432b–433a). Pasquier's characterization of Du Fail goes to the heart of the issue of imitation: when is "very far" too far?; what are, in fact, the limitations of a difference that is both necessary and inevitable? When is the gap between model and copy too wide, so that imitation betrays its representative function, that is, betrays both its model and itself? At what point in this spatial metaphor of

---

[2] For the editions of the *Propos rustiques*, see ed. Pérouse and Dubuis, 31–32.

difference does excessive distance produce a "bad" imitation? When does Du Fail become nothing more than a "singe"?

I raise these questions in part because Pasquier's damning review continues to haunt Du Fail, as if he were always to remain in some sense a Rabelais "manqué," or Rabelais's monkey. Recent criticism has sought to confront this issue, but its conclusions cannot entirely rescue the writer from the failure inherent in imitation.³ The emphasis on imitating Rabelais has allowed Du Fail to bask in borrowed light, thus enhancing the worth of various aspects of his work by association. Its festive ambiguity, its depiction of the peasant world, its mixture of nature and culture, and its portrayal of Panurge-like characters are, the claim goes, original variations on Rabelaisian material. From this perspective, Du Fail could be considered as having been able to some degree to "faire tout autant," to have produced a text that, in effect, is not "too far" from its model. In this view, he is not so much "manqué" as minor, a Rabelais in a minor key. But at the same time Du Fail always comes up short since he will always pale by comparison; he will never entirely escape the label of "ape" because the *Propos rustiques* will never be more than an image of *Gargantua* or *Pantagruel*.

Rabelais's monkey or a clever simulator? A literary achievement or a servile copy? The question of imitation raises the issue of precisely what one reads when one reads Du Fail. And this issue has broad pertinence because it appears to extend significantly beyond the problem of Rabelais to other structural, thematic, and rhetorical aspects of the *Propos rustiques*. Is the work a realistic image of the historical and social world of the Breton peasants, as the text seems to claim? Is it a reckless (or careless) mixture of fact and fantasy, an unreliable recording, as some have claimed? Or is it an example of literature's necessary transformation of reality? Are the *Propos rustiques* an encomium of rural life imitated from classical sources, or the satiric presentation of country bumpkins? The text's assembled speakers each holding forth recalls Boccaccio's framing device, but the work shows no other traces of the *Decameron*'s influence. Is the composite structure—juxtaposing narrative, portrait, and description in episodic and non-linear segments—an integral, and meaningful, textual element, or the unsatisfactory, and gratuitous, effect of the writer's inexperience? Does the writing express a nostalgia for the past derived from utopian literature, or does it in fact parody that nostalgia? And finally, what generic association can be

---

³ See especially the classic study by E. Philipot, *La Vie et l'œuvre littéraire de Noël Du Fail* (Paris: Champion, 1914); G.-A. Pérouse, "Le Dessein des *Propos rustiques*," in *Etudes seiziémistes offertes à Monsieur le Professeur V.-L. Saulnier par plusieurs de ses anciens doctorants*, intro. Robert Aulotte (Geneva: Droz, 1980), 137–50; and the collection of articles in *Noël du Fail, Ecrivain*, ed. C. Magnien-Simonin (Paris: J. Vrin, 1991).

made to elucidate the question of what is being read? The *Propos rustiques* are not novellas; the "contes" they relate are not only or even primarily narratives. They are, by their own claim, "propos," a title that covers a broad semantic range that only contributes to its problematic siting: the matter of discourse, discourse itself, conversation, narrative, remarks and observations, intention. How does one speak, we might ask, of the nature and status of this work that for all intents and purposes defies definition and classification, either by design or by default, and that seemingly eludes the determination of coherent meaning?[4]

Here I want to return to Pasquier's striking image of Rabelais's monkey. What Pasquier's derogatory epithet discloses as a suggestive alternative reading is that the indeterminate character of Du Fail's *Propos rustiques* is due to its parodic disposition, the monkey standing as a conventional emblem for the imitative function that lies at the heart of parody. Like the ape, parody both resembles and differs from its model; it is both itself and the other simultaneously. Parody is a sign of respect and an act of aggression, and its critical force can either be directed against the model or turn inadvertently, unintentionally, against the imitator. From its site beside the model (as a preposition, the Greek *para* had the sense "by the side of"), parody becomes the para-site that draws from and lives off its model, that copies, mirrors, borrows and incorporates aspects and elements from prior literary works that it in fact reveres, that mimics them in spite of itself, sometimes to the detriment of its model and often to its own. This complementary, oppositional, and oxymoronic relation is contained as well in the prefix *para* which, in Greek composition, had such cognate adverbial meanings as "amiss, faulty, irregular, disordered, improper, wrong." It also expressed, in terms richly suggestive for my reading, "subsidiary relation, alteration, perversion, simulation."[5]

This range of *para*doxical meanings speaks directly to the varying ways in which readers have characterized the *Propos rustiques*, from Pasquier's judgment of the work as simian "simulation" or as a "perversion," to the modern criticism that the sequence of chapters is "disordered" and the transitions "faulty." Even the rehabilitative perspective takes the work as having a "subsidiary relation," as minor to Rabelais's major league work, as I indicated earlier. I want to suggest that what "parody" allows us to see is that Du Fail's text is, in fact, all of these things, that from alongside its

---

[4] Philipot asks, "A quel genre appartient ce petit livre? C'est ce qu'on ne saurait dire au juste" (*La Vie*, 95). Pérouse refers to "cette œuvre inclassable" (*Propos rustiques*, ed. Pérouse and Dubuis, 9).

[5] *The Oxford English Dictionary*, Compact Edition, 2 vols. (New York: Oxford University Press, 1971), 2:2070.

model texts it sings its song (from the Greek *ôidê*, song) both in apposition and in opposition, simulating and altering as it carries out its monkey business.[6] Imitation can be a form of flattery or a form of mockery; parody does not always allow the reader to decide with any degree of certainty: it does not always announce its intention unequivocally. In fact, what parody does allow for is the unintentional reversal of intention, as when the imitation ends up mocking the mocker and the monkey makes a monkey of himself. But even these performances, what we might call "bad" performances like the ones that Pasquier said are "too far" from their models, cannot always be securely labeled as "bad" because parody, by definition, is also a performance so bad as to be the equivalent of intentional (and successful) mockery. The "equivalent" of intentional mockery, however, is not the same as "intentional mockery," and this means that intention itself is not a reliable indicator of the parodic because it is not always possible to determine what, in fact, was intended. Moreover, parody can be either intentional or unintentional; it can be destructive or self-destructive, or both at once. Are the *Propos rustiques* a parody of other texts in the sense that they successfully mimic (and thus mock) them, or do they become a mock text themselves, a parody of textuality that succeeds only in revealing the limits of imitation and its own limitations? Parody subverts intention because it

---

[6] There are at least two schools of thought concerning the definition and use of the term "parody." There are those who seek to narrow and restrict meaning and application and those who prefer to extend usage, often as widely as possible. My own preference, for rhetorical purposes in this paper, is to exploit the polysemous nature of the term. Recent useful works on parody include Margaret Rose, *Parody: Ancient, Modern, and Post-modern* (Cambridge: Cambridge University Press, 1993); Linda Hutcheon, *A Theory of Parody* (New York: Methuen, 1985); *Le Singe à la porte: Vers une théorie de la parodie*, textes rassemblés et édités par Groupar (New York: Peter Lang, 1984); Gérard Genette, *Palimpsestes: La Littérature au second degré* (Paris: Seuil, 1982). It should be added that parody has become a ubiquitous term in modern criticism; one finds it referred to and discussed by the Russian formalists, by reception theorists, and by structuralist and post-structuralist critics, most often as an aspect of intertextuality (Rose's chapters 3 and 4, and her extensive bibliography, can serve as a helpful guide through this vast critical corpus). To speak of a Renaissance text as parodic is immediately to evoke the writings of Mikhail Bakhtin and to recall the concept of "double-voicedness" that characterizes his notion of parody. In a general way, the appropriation of the languages of others—languages that are social, cultural, and literary—in the *Propos rustiques*, and the uneasy and often conflictual relation they have with each other, resonate with Bakhtin's concept of parody. See especially the essays in *The Dialogic Imagination: Four Essays*, trans. Caryl Emerson and Michael Holquist, ed. Michael Holquist (Austin: University of Texas Press, 1981).

reveals that the same or similar forms and phrases can be inhabited by dissimilar motives; moreover, it disperses the unity of the subject on which intention itself is founded by proliferating other possible subjects of the parodied discourse. Diderot embodied this essential indeterminacy in the character of Rameau's nephew, the ultimate parodist, the parasite who both adores and despises his hosts, at the same time a mimic of genius and a mediocre actor, priceless and worthless. In our own time, and in a different medium, parody functions similarly: the stage performances of the cult comedian Andy Kaufman (also of *Taxi* fame) were said to be so "bad" that they were good; one could not tell whether he was simply a bad comedian or a brilliant parodist of the (bad) comedian.

What do the *Propos rustiques* intend and what occurs beyond, or alongside, their intentions? On the unstable ground that parody thus provides, the intention and status of the text remain necessarily unsettled. But in the process of carrying out their monkey business, the *Propos rustiques* expose the play of imitation itself as central to the literary mode, their shamelessly imitative performance revealing that the originals, the mirrored texts, are themselves imitations, simulations, as if the parodic text were also a mirror in which we cannot help seeing that all men are monkeys as well. Although I began my discussion with Pasquier's image of Rabelais's monkey, we can now recognize that, however much Du Fail might have borrowed or copied from Rabelais, the issue of the status of the *Propos rustiques* is not ultimately about "Rabelais" in any exclusive or even dominant way. What "imitating" Rabelais opens up is the question of imitation itself, the problematic, parodic relation between a text and its models, that is, the irrepressible repetition that motivates writing and makes a monkey of textuality. "Un conte attire l'autre," as I quoted in the epigraph, "one tale drawes on another," in Cotgrave's words;[7] it draws on others to which it has been attracted, just as it attracts and induces those that follow and that "imitate" in their turn. Taking imitation as a figure of the generative nature of writing, I want to extend the trope to propose that the *Propos rustiques* perform and parody the engendering of discourse in general. Under the sign of the writer-imitator of the liminary sonnet ("contrefaire," "feindre" [37]) and in the name of "propos" (a subject of discourse, discourse itself, conversation, narrative, observation, intention), the text self-consciously stages and mimics its own production. Du Fail, we might say, is his own monkey.

---

[7] Randle Cotgrave, *A Dictionarie of the French and English Tongues* (Amsterdam: Theatrum Orbis Terrarum; New York: Da Capo Press, 1971).

From alongside the main body of the text, in the "para"-text that is the title page, the author's signature on the *Propos rustiques* inscribes the name as mask and draws the reader's attention to the parodic double voice that will inhabit the text. We read not Noël du Fail but Maistre Leon Ladulfi, the anagrammatic *alter ego* whose feigned presence introduces difference and alterity. "Feigned" because the ploy of the anagram is obvious, because the mask is intended to reveal as well as to conceal, and yet "present" in a real sense because Ladulfi does in fact alter things by his appearance—he doubles, repeats, and thus fragments simultaneously; he disperses the unity of the writing subject whose now-shared discourse circulates in the void between "I" and the "other I." Although he speaks directly to the reader only in the prefatory "Au lecteur" and in the opening chapter where he sets the scene for the interlocutors of the "propos," Ladulfi confounds his voice with that of Du Fail and in the process confounds those readers who rely on an integral writing subject to establish the integrity of the text and on a monologic discourse to safeguard its meaning. How can one hear (read) the voice of authorial authority if it is inhabited by other voices? How is the "Au lecteur," where the author-narrator proposes in grandiloquent prose to "faire un brief et sommaire Discours du nom et imposition d'iceluy [the name 'rustiques']" (38), to be understood if there is interference from a ludicrous comic discourse on life and lovemaking among their primitive ancestors? The clarity of what sounds like an encomium of the past and of rural life inspired by classical antecedents and filled with erudite references is muddled by parodic, subversive laughter reminiscent of Rabelais. Is this a serious outside that contains subversive ludic play on the inside? Or is the surface itself comic, as the rest of the text will attest, as if only an artifice containing a serious message within? The inside/outside model, however, is as unstable as parody itself, and in chiasmic reversal turns inside out and outside in, like the anagram of the author's name where Du Fail and Ladulfi are each inside the other. And like their voices that cannot be confidently and permanently separated out and secured, for they speak, like ventriloquists, from within each other. As one often wonders in the case of ventriloquists, who precisely is the ventriloquist and who the "dummy"; does Du Fail speak for Ladulfi, or is it the other way around?

The uncertainty that has dominated critical discussion over the actual presence of Du Fail in his text and the supposed realism of the *Propos rustiques* attests to the relevance of these questions. Ladulfi claims in the "Au lecteur" that "les Propos d'aucuns Rustiques nous sont en main" (38) and in the succeeding chapter describes how this came about: "les ouy jazer et deviser privément de leur affaires Rustiques, desquels ay fait, par heures rompues et de relaiz, un brief discours" (50). The narrator's words have traditionally been taken for those of the author, and Du Fail has been pictured, upon his return to Brittany as a young man, listening to the peasants' conversations and recording them after the fact. This has traditionally given the *Propos rustiques* the status of an anthropological document, and only recently have critics followed the lead of Philipot in stressing the literariness of the text rather than its referential nature.[8] What has not yet been sufficiently recognized is that the source of this confusion lies precisely in the confusion of Du Fail and Ladulfi that the writing willingly exploits. Both "authors" are implicated in the parodic imitation of peasant conversation that the *Propos rustiques* perform. In the liminary sonnet dedicated to "L'Autheur," and which praises him for being wise enough to imitate the fool ("badin") in a natural way, the reader must acknowledge that the mimic of the fool, the mimic who "becomes" the fool, is simultaneously and confusedly the double-voiced anagrammatic author of the title page, both wise and foolish.

Through this confusion, and collusion, the natural conversations that the author pretends to witness and to record are doubled, mediated, and transformed by the transcription. The imitation of peasant speech does its own turn, frames itself in a setting and structure that are already literary topoi, loses its regional dialectal character, acquires erudition, and in the name of truth, authenticity, and an innate grace that the "propos" allegedly possess, denies the rhetoric and adornment that inform both its matter and its movement. Aware of his task and of his activity, the author self-consciously simulates authorial demeanor. Having read *Gargantua*, he mimes Alcofribas, imitating that other "badin" who was wise enough to share *his* name with Rabelais. He too seeks inspiration and strength in the septembral nectar, he also sweats and strains to produce his discourse as if laboring and as if he were also in labor, and like his model he engenders a loquacious text that threatens to run on endlessly: "après avoir ahanné long temps, resvant et devinant ce que je devois dire, estois contraint boire deux ou trois voltes" (50; "ahaner": "labourer la terre," "faire un grand effort," "souffrir"). In the fictive format that mirrors his own production, in which both he and his characters generate "propos," where both can be said to "jazer et deviser" about rustic life, the conditions prevail that allow and encourage language's uninhibited flow, like the wine that lessens reserve and loosens the tongue. The scene is set on a festival day where leisure removes temporal limitations and opens space for unconstrained discourse (53). The banquet-like atmosphere provides that conventional moment when food and words enhance

---

[8] See especially Nicole Cazauran, "La Première Manière de Noël Du Fail," in *Noël du Fail, Écrivain*, ed. Magnien-Simonin, 35–47; see also Pérouse, "Le Dessein."

each other, when the mouth both introduces and produces.⁹ The interlocutors are of the older generation; representing the collective memory, they are the bearers of communal lore and, most importantly, they are prone to prolixity. There is history to recount, in effect a history to be created through recounting, as the speakers represent themselves to themselves through the events and characters of the past. While the speakers appear to constitute their own audience and thus in a sense to make their discourse self-generating by talking to themselves, there is also a larger audience that listens (overhears?)—their peers, the youth of the village, the inhabitants of the larger community—and whose presence also constitutes the call to speak. As each speaker thus responds to the call and holds forth in his turn, the word circulates in a round that can turn without end.

The "propos" recall past generations and depict a less corrupt, more idyllic world, but one that remains remarkably like the present, at least in one essential regard: it too was filled with talk. The old men to whom Ladulfi listens tell stories about the earlier generation which, in its turn, told tales about the storytellers of *its* past. But the seriousness of this discourse is vitiated; whether as history or as encomium of the past, it is undermined from within by that other ever-present voice of mimicry and mockery. As one of Ladulfi's four "preudes gens" tells his story, he evokes a scene that mirrors his own situation and his own storytelling in a ludic *mise en abyme*: "et au soir, aux raiz de la Lune, jazans librement ensemble sur quelque bagatelle, rians à pleine gorge, contans des nidz d'antan et neiges de l'année passée; et revenans des champs, chacun avoit son mot de gueule pour gaudir l'un l'autre et raconter des contes en la journée faits" (52). Like their predecessors, Anselme and his three old cronies are also "jazans librement ensemble"; the onomatopoetic "jaser" will suggest later to Ronsard the endless croaking of frogs, just as earlier the "jaseur" evoked for Rabelais the indefatigable babbler: "grands jaseurs et beaulx bailleurs de balivernes," as he put it with alliterative wit.¹⁰ G.-A. Pérouse suggests that this is "radotage," "bavardage sénile," the drivel of the old, and he is, in part, correct; but more is at stake here than the comedic effect of senile prattle repeated from generation to generation.¹¹ What more appropriate (stock) character

---

⁹ See M. Jeanneret whose subtitle to *Des Mets et des mots* (Paris: J. Corti, 1987) resonates suggestively for a reading of Du Fail: "Banquets et propos de table à la Renaissance."

¹⁰ François Rabelais, *Gargantua*, ed. Jacques Boulenger (Paris: Gallimard, 1955), 77. The definition of "jaser" and the literary allusions are from the *Dictionnaire du moyen français*, ed. A. J. Greimas and T. M. Keane (Paris: Larousse, 1992), 368.

¹¹ In his introduction to the *Propos rustiques*, Pérouse asks, "La trame même de leurs *Propos* ne nous est-elle pas explicitement présentée comme pur radotage?"

to populate a text that takes discourse as its subject than the garrulous *senex* who speaks to forestall death, for whom the breath that produces language is also the breath that sustains life? What more appropriate moment for lived experience to become the matter for a book and sexual impotence to generate a potent discourse (89)? *Propos rustiques* are about "bavardage" itself, its generation, imitation, motivation (what makes it move), and particularly its inclination to run on, to prolong itself as it transforms, renews, repeats, and degrades itself. The "propos" of each generation evoked in the work reprise and parody the discursive activity that preceded at the same time that they contaminate what is to follow, including and especially the discourse of Ladulfi himself.

Ladulfi's discourse begins with his withdrawal to the countryside to finish some business, although in effect the discourse has already begun in a variety of modes: with his signature on the title page, with the liminary sonnet addressed "à l'autheur," with his disquisition "au lecteur" on the name "rustique" that is both the invocation to the reader and his evocation through the punned apostrophe "O lecteur." But business ("negoce," from Latin *negotium*, work) gives way to leisure (*otium*)—both the author's as he strolls through the neighboring villages and that of the peasant festival in which the "propos" take place—before later becoming the "work" (we recall "ahaner") that repeats and transforms "propos" into *Propos*, the double and duplicitous text that is simultaneously oral and written, the peasants' and the author's, Du Fail's and Ladulfi's. From the outset it is clear that as long as there is leisure time there will be discourse. "Mais puisque nous avons du loysir, et jour suffisamment, je vous prie, avec le reste de la compagnie, de poursuyvre le propos encommencé," one of the cronies says to Anselme when he stops talking (53). Once underway, the discourse must respond to the call, the plea ("prier"), to continue. Only the end of the day puts an end to storytelling that is, in itself, inexhaustible. This is, of course, a convention of the storytelling genre, a reversal of the situation of Sheherazade who ends her story with the end of the night, and it characterizes the *Decameron* as well as the *Heptaméron*, avatars of the *Thousand and One Nights* as performances of endless tales. Only what is exterior to discourse (the bells ringing for vespers in the *Heptaméron* as another, and higher, calling, for example) can bring things to a close, but this close is never more than an interruption, a hiatus, because discourse itself does not produce a

---

(22). In a note to the text on p. 122, he explains Anselme's inclination to talk without being invited in these terms: "Le bavardage sénile est un des traits comiques les plus constants des *Propos rustiques*."

logical or necessary conclusion. Here in the *Propos rustiques*, the higher call comes from the wife of Lubin who expects him home when the day is over (147).

When Lubin announces his intention to leave at nightfall he signals what should be the "end," the breakup of the group, the dispersion of the raconteurs and of the audience as well. Because Ladulfi records only one day's stories, there is no need for a plague to run its course or for floodwaters to subside in order finally to put an end to things. The end, however, is never quite final, nor does it come about easily, as if the discourse had difficulty shutting down. When Lubin says, "Il est temps faire fin à noz propos" (154) and announces that he is leaving, the others take his cue ("Quoy voyant, tout le reste se retira"); the verb tense indicates that everyone has left, that the day has come to a close, that silence reigns. But discourse always produces a surplus that must be postponed to another day ("remettant le surplus à la prochaine feste"), and in fact no one has yet departed. Even as the audience is leaving ("avant que partir"), the "surplus" that was ostensibly deferred continues to overflow: it cannot entirely be put off to the next day or the next festival because discourse cannot contain itself, it spills out so that the call to "faire fin à noz propos" actually calls forth more "propos." Huguet himself is already leaving, but from his horse he addresses the departing audience with "propos" about serving God, maintaining emotional equilibrium, remaining detached from worldly things. Speaking perhaps to their backs as they move off, he rants on: "Faites donques grand chere . . . riez, jazez, voltigez, gaudissez, beuvez d'autant, entretenez les Dames, triomphez, penadez, ballez, gambadez, poussez le Dets . . ." and on and on. Is anyone listening? Does it matter? Does discourse need a call from outside itself or even an audience to motivate itself? This outpouring is followed by an indistinct jumble of unidentified voices that bid farewell, that order wood for roofing, that still have something to say ("Escoutez!"), until finally someone declines to speak when the opening is provided: "Si vous ne vouliez dire . . . ?" "Nenny, non! . . ." The ellipsis at the very end indicates that even this closure is also an opening, that the opening is always provided, or perhaps, that discourse always provides its own opening, generates itself from within regardless of what obtains on the outside. Even saying no to discourse cannot ultimately suppress or stifle its inevitable surplus: there is always more to be said.

The interlocutors' "propos" begin to tell stories by returning to the past, idealizing what has preceded in order to denigrate the present (as the old, nostalgically, are wont to do), creating a common history that recounts the loss of innocence with the passage of time, as I said earlier; but the return to the past by the aged speakers is in fact what produces the storyteller himself. People imagine the storyteller as someone who has come from afar, Benjamin says, but they enjoy no less listening to the man who has stayed at home, and who knows the local tales and traditions.[12] There are, he adds, two archaic types of storytellers, the resident tiller of the soil and the trading seaman, although storytelling in its full historical breadth is inconceivable without the intimate interpenetration of the two; the lore of faraway places combines with the lore of the past. We might adapt this observation to say that, in this case, the storyteller resides at the intersection of time and space, where the lore of the past is already that of a faraway place. When the old tillers of the soil in the *Propos rustiques* create the gap between past and present to begin their "propos," they establish at the outset the necessary difference that is the condition for storytelling. After Anselme has made his point that times have changed, Pasquier remarks: "Mon compere, vous dites toute verité, et me semble proprement estre en un nouveau monde" (53). The storyteller in this case speaks about the "old world" that he has seen, as distant from the present as Brittany is from what will also be called a "nouveau monde," that recently discovered faraway world that will also produce endless tales.

The analogy is not far-fetched. When Huguet responds to the call immediately thereafter to talk about the banquets he had known in the past ("dix ou douze se leverent pour le prier leur dire la façon des banquets de son temps" [54]), he describes a moment when one of the older peasants of that earlier generation in his turn heeds a call to speak: "Lors, quelcun des plus vieux (à la request de ses coëvaux) commençoit à harenguer les jeunes gens, où avoit telle audience que ha celuy qui, estant venu de quelque païs estrange, veult conter quelque nouveauté" (60). The storyteller always in some sense comes from a strange and foreign country even when he comes from his own, and especially when his tales tell of a remote and distant past. Here Benjamin's venerable tiller of the soil speaks to the young, bringing them "news" from that other, older world. It should not escape us that these "propos" all bear the mark of novelty and mark themselves in this regard as parallel to the novella. From alongside or beyond (*para-*, as I insisted earlier), the *Propos rustiques* are the novella's distorted and distorting mirror: they imitate its frame, mimic its orality, simulate its claims to be both new and true, mock its exemplarity, and parody its means of production.[13]

---

[12] Walter Benjamin, "The Storyteller," in idem, *Illuminations*, trans. Harry Zohn, ed. Hannah Arendt (New York: Schocken Books, 1968), 83–109.

[13] In *La Conversation conteuse: Les Nouvelles de Marguerite de Navarre* (Paris: Presses Universitaires de France, 1992), Gisèle Mathieu-Castellani attributes four characteristics to the novella: "la relation de faits et d'événements (1) authentiques et authentifiés par un témoin digne de foi; (2) nouveaux, c'est-à-dire survenus récemment,

The epigraph, "Un conte attire l'autre," that I evoked earlier to represent the mimetic relation of text and model also suggests that within a text like the *Propos rustiques* the stories draw on each other, are drawn to or from each other in apparently tireless generation. The popular maxim rings true, but while discourse is apparently self-generating, and seemingly inexhaustible, the production of "propos" suggests that it is not entirely spontaneous nor wholly motivated from within. Discourse, it would appear, also needs to be prompted, and moved along, from outside—primed, we might say, to get it going, and then lured on (the French verb "amorcer" indicates that to prime is already to lure). Leisure time, as we saw, is a prime, as is the natural inclination to verbosity of the old, and also the call to speak, the invitation or the plea that elicits speech. Ten or twelve people rose to request, beg, beseech ("prier") Huguet to talk about the banquet, and he acquiesced, after having primed himself with wine. How could he have done otherwise: "A quoy s'accorda facilement le bon Huguet qui après avoir beu une fois de vin . . . commença à dire" (54). The frame which requires that the word circulate, that each speaker hold forth in his turn, is another mechanism that keeps discourse on the move. And there is competition among the speakers, a fact that emerges from the story within a story that is the description of the "banquet rustique," that assures that the speakers will, in fact, take their turns, after having sought their inspiration in wine, of course: "Tellement faisoient-ilz, lesquelz, après avoir beu de mesmes et à toutes restes, le tout sans hazard, commençoyent à jazer librement du fait d'agriculture, et à qui mieux mieux" (55).[14] When discourse wanders off, gets sidetracked and loses itself in its own unfolding, as it is wont to do, there is always someone to cut it off and then to get it started again on the right track: "Comment? (dist alors Pasquier) après vous avoir bien escouté, Compere, à qui parlez-vous? . . . Auquel respondit maistre Huguet qu'il luy pardonnast, et qu'il s'estoit forvoyé . . . et que, puisqu'il avoit tant poursuivi le conte, qu'il l'acheveroit. — Achevez donc (dist Lubin)" (87). The "propos" clearly generate their own energy and momentum; here they need to be completed primarily because they have begun. Elsewhere there are times when they move forth on their own, for example, even without the need for a "call"

---

appartenant soit à l'actualité immédiate, soit à un passé tout proche, 'de fraîche mémoire'; (3) non encore racontés, 'inouïs,' ou en tout cas non encore transcrits; (4) digne d'être rapportés, qu'ils soient 'exemplaires,' ou assez étonnants pour susciter l'intérêt des narrataires" (27).

[14] In *"Propos rustiques.* Caractérisation des devisants et statut du texte," in *Noël du Fail, Écrivain,* ed. Magnien-Simonin, 49–61, A. Leclercq-Magnien states that "presque d'elle-même la parole passe d'un personnage à un autre, d'un épisode à un autre" (54), but my reading suggests that the word does not circulate entirely "by itself."

(122). But in the interstices of discourse, where I have been looking, in the moments of exchange or "badinage" between the interlocutors that interrupt or follow the "propos," we can read the self-reflective activity of discourse itself and heed the signals by which it is re-motivated.[15]

Huguet's presentation of the rustic banquet ends with the return home of one of the peasants after the day's festivities, but the close of the day and of the festival is not the end of the story. In terms so vivid that his listeners imagine themselves present at the scene, the storyteller realizes the goal of *enargeia* and this gives impetus to further tales: "Par mon ame! (feit alors Lubin) le conte nous est si bien mis devant les yeux (ô compere!) que proprement me semble y estre et voir le bon homme Robin Chevet s'esbatant ainsi à jazer" (71). The act of seeing is, of course, one of seeming, as Lubin's own language reveals, and we remain properly in the duplicitous realm of rhetoric, but one whose copiousness cannot be contained. What Lubin has "seen" must be said; with the interlocutors' help the discourse moves on: "Puisque le compere Lubin ha mis en termes ce bon lourdaut Robin Chevet (dit Pasquier), il me semble qu'il ne sera que bon qu'il die ce qu'il luy ha veu faire." The call is issued and answered, and not by coincidence Robin Chevet is himself a "jaseur" like Lubin and his cronies, and *his* talk helps to propel Lubin's own. Robin invents new words, sings songs, and, in a further elaboration of this discursive *mise en abyme*, recounts fables about animals who speak: "le bon homme Robin (après avoir imposé silence) commençoit un beau conte du temps que les bestes parloient" (72). In the conventional setting for storytelling, Robin holds forth before the hearth as his family does its chores, whiling away the hours in the leisure of the evening, like the proverbial women who entertain each other with their tales while spinning. And if he fails as a storyteller and loses his audience's attention, he recuperates their interest by practical jokes and laughter; he makes himself the center and the butt. In a parodic narrative gesture, after words have failed him, he farts; instead of the wine-inspired breath of the narrator that enraptures his audience, there is the degraded, but equally inspired, polyphonic *flatus* that also delights his listeners and ensures his future success: "Que s'ilz rioient de ce, le preudhoms faisoit un pet à trois parties qui esbaudissoit tous, et rioient desmeshuy à toutes restes" (74).

---

[15] An important critical perspective has been gained in the study of the novella in recent years by the shift in focus from the subject matter of the stories—which has tended to produce mostly thematic readings—to the discussions among the storytellers that frame them, to what I am calling the interstices. This has allowed important new readings of the *Heptaméron*, for example, by critics like John Lyons, Gisèle Mathieu-Castellani, and others.

Thus the mock figure of the storyteller emerges anonymously out of the banquet to be given the name Robin Chevet, and in numerous other incarnations and under a variety of names he dominates the rest of the *Propos rustiques* as a parody of all purveyors of "propos," confounding the real and the imaginary, inventing fictions and revealing truths, creating illusions, enchanting, deceiving, entertaining his audiences, making a mockery of everything and a monkey of himself. Thenot du Coin is another of these originals, the subject of Pasquier's "propos" ("Or bien, dites donc quelque cas de vostre village, Pasquier!") and the source of his own, telling stories about his relations with the birds, "jazant avec son compere Triballory," teaching the young Pasquier how to speak "à propos," spending the evening "à caquetter," engendering further "propos" from others in the form of a poem written on his door by a passing bard (91–96). And engendering Tailleboudin, his son, who reveals himself as the parodic counterpart of his saintly father, the "jazeur" as scoundrel and confidence man, as perpetrator of "propos" that deceive and exploit the listener. But that also amuse and delight the listener, Anselme's listener, as the old crony makes Tailleboudin the matter of his own "propos" (96–106). Whose *own* "propos"? we might ask, because in this proliferation and confusion of "jazeurs" and of "propos," Anselme narrates Tailleboudin's story and ventriloquizes the first-person discourse in which Tailleboudin himself is his own narrator. In another of those mirroring, mimicking moments so prevalent in the *Propos*, Tailleboudin tells the tale of his life through Anselme, and he also tells the tales he tells others that constitute that life, all tales in which he is both raconteur and actor, imitator and dissimulator, entertainer and persuader (is this just another "tale" that he is telling Anselme?). In this parody of imitation, Tailleboudin is the mummer, the master of illusion, the mouthpiece of a fictional rhetoric and a rhetoric of fiction. Or is it Anselme?

The eponymous Pierre Claquedent is Anselme's excuse to hold forth near the end of the day, but Claquedent himself needs no excuse. He never misses a banquet or the occasion to "jaw"; his mouth seems simultaneously and inexhaustibly to inhale food and to exhale speech: "nul estoit mieux adroit que luy et qui mieux tinst son ordre, tousjours en contant quelque fable, quelque cas de nouveau, quelques nouvelles fresches qu'il inventoit sur le champ, ou bien de quelque procès qu'il promptement intentoit, et tellement par divers incidents le continuoit qu'il venoit à son honneur" (144–45). In Anselme's "propos" Claquedent becomes a first-person speaker, unleashes a discursive flow without logic or evident coherence, an extended *coq-à-l'âne* that parodies Rabelais's already comic "Propos des bien yvres" as the expression of verbal folly. Here, too, wine intoxicates and facilitates *garrulitas*, to the point that Anselme himself, as if contaminated, has to be cut off: "Compere

Anselme (dist maistre Huguet), je vous prie, soyez brief, et le faire court: car je veux (avant que la nuict soit plus avancée) vous dire quelque cas d'assez bon gout, le tout pour entretenir le propos de celle antique preudhommie" (147). Discourse expands as if on its own and knows no bounds, as I indicated earlier; and if Huguet is in his turn to prolong the "propos" of the day, then Anselme must cede the floor so that the word can circulate. This he does graciously so that the figure of Gobemouche's son Guillaume can appear as the final "jazeur," so that the popular, conventional wisdom of his mother, the old wives' tales and superstitions that form his early education, can be satirized along with the bookish learning and written culture that later make him the parodic embodiment of an "habile homme et bon clerc" (151). The "propos" formally end with the endless wagging of tongues, Guillaume chattering incessantly about his new-found knowledge ("tint les conclusions à tous venans" [153]) and provoking others to chatter about him ("on parloit de luy jusques à Becherel, à son bien grand avantage" [154]).

Sandwiched between this gallery of "jazeurs," the "grande bataille des habitants de Flameaux et ceux de Vindelles" performs a mock epic battle that reveals its discursive status. As a lesser Picrocholine war, we might call it a parody of a mock epic, to suggest both that the attempt to imitate genius results inevitably in unintended self-parody (to Du Fail's disadvantage) and that the text displays, nevertheless, a genuine parodic dimension (to Du Fail's advantage). Heroic terms announce a titanic physical struggle ("grand debat," "enorme et perilleuse bataille," "chappliz" ["bataille où l'on porte de grands coups"]), but a verbal war ensues, an exchange of ludicrous insults which ragtag bands from neighboring peasant villages hurl at each other. Stones, sticks, and planks accompany words as the material of this burlesque encounter. But if peasants armed with farm tools are the degraded image of chivalric warriors, the arrival of their women to carry on the battle, screaming, scratching, and pulling hair, provides a second level of parodic degradation, a comic *mise en abyme* that culminates in an accumulation of insults worthy of Rabelais. Unlike Rabelais's war, however, there is no obvious moral dimension to the presentation, no social or political lesson either, and one could argue that the episode takes place for no other reason than to provide the occasion to tell a story, to invent "propos." This "fait de donner coups et de babiller" (121) has no victor, no other outcome than to generate the name of the road where it took place, and no rationale other than to become the stuff of further stories, to proliferate "babil" ("ainsi que depuis ils en plaisantoient" [115]).

> A peine les *Propos rustiques* étaient-ils sortis des presses qu'ils furent remaniés, interpolés, augmentés de deux chapitres

nouveaux, par les soins d'un personnage resté jusqu'ici inconnu, qui publia à Paris . . . le résultat de son bizarre travail. Malgré l'édition de 1549, revue par l'auteur "luy mesme" et qui rétablissait, sauf certains changements, le texte authentique, les interpolations et additions reparurent dans toutes les éditions ultérieures, et cela jusqu'en 1878, date à laquelle La Borderie sépara enfin le bon grain de l'ivraie.[16]

In my discussion of the *Propos rustiques* I have been focusing on the generation of discourse within the fictional world of the text and on the operation of those mechanisms by which it is prolonged, enlarged, proliferated. But it appears that the work itself was not immune to its own preoccupations, that it opened itself up from within to one final *mise en abyme*, to more monkey business, to augmentation, to imitation, to parody. For what else are these interpolations and additions than surplus discourse "in the style of" Du Fail, a form of discursive mimicry that supplements the writing, an excess like the chaff but also a signal of a central void or absence, an imperfect whole that always invites completion? And what else, I might add, is parody that imposes itself on a work, not entering explicitly as interpolation does, but mimicking from alongside, intruding, interfering, interjecting something that was always already there, already subversively contained within, implicit? As in the case of the four old cronies, the "propos" circulate from Du Fail to the interpolator and back, and when Du Fail takes up the reworked text he does not expunge the "chaff" but recuperates one hundred and twenty-eight revisions and additions and makes them his own, as if they were (because they are already?) the wheat. We cannot ultimately tell the wheat from the chaff, Du Fail from the interpolator or from Ladulfi, the man from the monkey. There is thus nothing "bizarre" about the supplementary text, as Philipot puts it; there is not even (and never was) an "authentic," that is, single-voiced text. Multiple voices and multiple discourses always engender textuality, and inhabit it. When Du Fail imitates, copies, parodies the works of the ancients, and that of Rabelais and other contemporaries, when he invents his fictional frame and cedes his voice to his narrative *alter ego*, and finally, when he himself endorses the augmentation of his writing by the interpolator, he confirms what his characters seem already to know, that discourse always circulates, and is always shared. It is always a question of monkey business.

---

[16] Philipot, *La Vie*, 222–23. Philipot did solve the mystery of the unknown interpolator by identifying him as the Angevin Jean Maugin. See also pp. 224–33 which indicate the degree to which Maugin writes "in the style of" Du Fail and the way in which that writing affects (engenders) Du Fail's later texts.

Jeanne Flore and Erotic Desire: Feminism or Male Fantasy?

Floyd Gray

If the complete meaning of a story is not inherent in its structure or words, then it may depend also on narrative strategy and reader perception. Thus a story proclaiming and extolling feminine sexual freedom would be read differently according as it was written by a male or female author and directed towards a male or female audience. If written by a male posing as a female, knowing that the intended audience would be primarily masculine, then it would acquire a radically new configuration, shaped by culturally programmed expectations and reactions.

While Jeanne Flore's *Comptes amoureux* have been attributed to a woman and read both as an apology for women's sexual liberation and as a condemnation of arranged marriages, there would seem to be an element of play at work in the author's emphatic and systematic reversal of previously gender-coded texts and situations, adding a measure of parodic undecidability to their meaning.[1] Read as self-conscious exercises in male fantasy in favor of men's sexuality and to their inevitable advantage, these stories become a kind of in-joke (orchestrated perhaps, as was probably Rabelais's *Pantagruel*, by an editor's commercial instincts) which a sixteenth-century public, essentially masculine, would have had no difficulty in recognizing and appreciating as such. Rather than serious feminist statements from a female author to a female audience, the *Comptes amoureux* appear, from this particular vantage point, to be ludic rewritings by a male author (or authors)

---

[1] Especially if, as Jean-François Marmontel proposes in his *Eléments de littérature*, "une excellente *parodie* serait celle qui porterait avec elle une saine critique." See idem, *Œuvres complètes*, 7 vols. (Geneva: Slatkine Reprints, 1968), 4:828. Moreover, these stories include large excerpts, even translations, recast in a different mode of, among others, Francesco Bello's *Menbriano*, Francisco Colonna's *Hypnerotomachia Poliphili*, Ovid's *Metamorphoses*, Boccaccio's *Decameron*, Boiardo's *Orlando Innamorato*, and Petrarch's *Trionfi*.

of prevailing Platonic and Petrarchan literary conventions appertaining to codes of feminine discourse, dress, and conduct, addressed primarily to a male audience. This, obviously, is a hypothetical reading, which an analysis of (1) the fiction of the female narrator, (2) the rhetoric of the portrait and of dress, (3) the dialectic of love, and finally (4) the displaced ideology of the story of Echo and Narcissus may help to substantiate.

What is unclear either from available documentary evidence or from reading Jeanne Flore's work is whether the person behind the author's name is a man or a woman, and consequently whether the text affords an example of a woman's looking at women or of a man's looking at women.[2] Both perspectives seem possible, depending on whether or not the text is perceived as feminist, calling for sexual and spousal freedom, or ironic, reversing and depreciating contemporary discourses tending to idealize women and their relationship with men. Not to be excluded, moreover, is the possibility that the author is a man looking at women in the way he would want women to look at men, making the work reflective of the kind of disabused or realistic sexuality voiced later by Hircan or Saffredent in Marguerite de Navarre's *Heptaméron*.

Less elaborate as a frame-story than the *cornice* of Boccaccio's *Decameron* or the prologue that Marguerite de Navarre, taking Boccaccio as a model, imagined for the *Heptaméron*, Jeanne Flore's dedicatory epistle, addressed to a cousin, brings together, somewhat arbitrarily, a select group of ladies who had agreed to tell stories "à ces vendanges dernieres." In it, she recounts that she suddenly realized, as she was preparing to transcribe them for her cousin as promised, that it would be agreeable and pleasing to all young ladies in love, and who delight in reading such stories, if she were to have them printed, making them thereby more widely available.[3] Whereas the

---

[2] Since we know nothing about Jeanne Flore's identity, we can only speculate on the background of her life and her probable association with Lyons. It is most likely, however, that the author's name is a pseudonym. Significantly, François de Billon includes Marguerite du Bourg, Claudine and Jeanne Scève, Jeanne Gaillarde, Pernette du Guillet, and Hélisenne de Crenne in his list of women authors in *Le Fort inexpugnable*, but the name of Jeanne Flore is conspicuously and inexplicably absent. Claude Longeon advances a series of circumstantial arguments to bolster his contention that the final version of the *Comptes* should be attributed to Etienne Dolet. See his "Du nouveau sur les *Comptes Amoureux de Madame Jeanne Flore*," in idem, *Hommes et livres de la Renaissance* (Saint-Etienne: Institut Claude Longeon, 1990), 259–67.

[3] "Puis tout soubdain je me suis advisée que je feroys chose tres agreable et plaisante aux jeunes Dames amoureuses, lesquelles loyaulment continuent au vray service d'Amour, et lesquelles se delectent de lire telz joyeulx comptes, si je les fai-

pretext advanced by Boccaccio's and Marguerite's group of noble ladies and gentlemen is more diversionary than exemplary, in that they resort to storytelling in order to pass the time of day, Jeanne Flore's is purposeful, since her group means to convince one of their own, Madame Cebille, of the dangers of disobeying Venus and manifesting hostility towards men.

Another significant departure from Boccaccio's or Marguerite's later model is that all of Jeanne Flore's storytellers are women. There is some fluctuation, however, in their number and names. Eight are mentioned in the opening *Epistre*: Madame Melibée, Madame Cebille, Madame Hortence, Madame Lucienne, Madame Salphionne, Madame Sapho, Madame Andromeda, Madame Meduse; but the actual *devisantes* turn out to be called Melibée (1), Andromeda (2), Meduse (3), Minerve (4), Solphionne (5), Cassandre (6), and Briolayne Fusque (7), while Madame Cebille remains a silent listener throughout.

Supposedly, they voice the conventional feminine point of view on love, marriage, and sexuality; but their declarations are somewhat perfunctory, even simplistic, reiterated rather than logically reinforced or developed, leading one to wonder if they are meant to represent a woman's viewpoint or to overstate it with parodic intentions, as is suggested by the emphatically erudite language and convoluted examples of the following typical passage:

> Sçachés, cheres et amoureuse [*sic*] dames, que l'ire et corroux inevitable d'Amour ou tost, ou tard a de coustume faire telles punitions: telles que souffrit par son peché la nimphe Castalia du Dieu Apollo. Et par celle mesme offense, la belle fille de Phorcus, laquelle de tout son povoir aspre et incivile envers ceulx qui la vouloient aymer, luy furent par sa ferme rigueur des celestes Dieux ses cheveux blondz et dorez muez en horribles et tortués serpens: dont elle après desirant en l'amoureuse et contemnée compagnie se retrouver, eulx espoventez du chef serpentin s'en fuyoient, et elle autant embrasée de desirs libidineux que le mont de Vesuvio de ses flammes sulphurines, de plus fort les desiroit et poursuyvoit. (163)

sois tout d'ung train gecter en impression": Jeanne Flore, *Contes amoureux*, ed. Le Centre Lyonnais d'Etude de l'Humanisme, sous la direction de Gabriel-A. Pérouse (Lyon: Presses Universitaires de Lyon, 1980), 97. The quotation in the previous sentence is found on the same page. Further references, incorporated into the text, are to this edition. Note that *Comptes*, rather than *Contes*, was the original spelling of the title.

Some of the uncertainty as to the authorship and focus of the collection arises quite obviously from the seemingly truncated state in which sixteenth-century editions have transmitted it. There is internal evidence which suggests that we have neither a complete text nor the original order of the stories. Moreover, those we have are strikingly unequal in length, erudition, and presentation. Some are more fully developed, more carefully written and structured than others, displaying a sure sense of narrative economy and development as well as a wide knowledge and appropriate use of classical antecedents. On the other hand, the order in which they appear seems arbitrary, even confused. Thus the work opens with a reference to two stories which have already been recounted, one by Madame Salphionne, the hostess of the group, and one by Madame Lucienne, but which are not included in the published collection, making the transition to the extant first story both awkward and abrupt.[4] Moreover, at the end of the fifth story, once the gentlemen from Lyons have been invited to join the women for the evening's celebration, Madame Salphionne expresses both her disappointment that they have not been present these past ten days to hear the stories, and her pleasure that they have arrived in time to hear the last one, implying that there were originally ten stories in all, and that what is now the sixth was once probably the tenth.

Furthermore, not all of the *devisantes* named initially actually participate in the storytelling, whereas others, not previously mentioned, unaccountably do, thereby confirming the suspicion that the work as we know it is not only defective but also, as variations in style and standpoint would seem to indicate, the product of several different authors, male or female.[5] If female, the work is radical, even revolutionary, in its call for the recognition and legitimization of female sexuality. If male, its ideology is expressed tongue-in-cheek, putting into the mouths of women what was already in

---

[4] "Madame Melibée après que la jeune Salphionne eust mist fin à son compte, où receut assez plaisir toute la compaignie, print la parolle, et dit . . ." (101). In addition, the reader is not made privy to Madame Cebille's "acerbe accusation à l'encontre de la sacrosaincte divinité d'Amour" (101) which Madame Melibée mentions as the reason for her own story. Madame Cebille is punished at the end of the sixth story. She is caught by her husband with "ung vilain et sale palefrenier" (215); he ties the two of them together and exposes them naked in public for all to see their shame.

[5] Régine Reynolds-Cornell argues for the collective nature of the work, with Clément Marot as one of the participants. See her "Madame Jeanne Flore and the *Contes amoureux*: A Pseudondym [*sic*] and a Paradox," *Bibliothèque d'Humanisme et Renaissance* 51 (1989): 123–33.

the minds of men, reversing in a sense the roles Floride and Amadour will play in the tenth story of the *Heptaméron*.

Already in her lifetime, little more was known about Jeanne Flore than that a collection of seven *Comptes amoureux* appeared under her name in an undated edition, published around 1537, and that the volume continued to be printed until 1574, when the last edition was published at Lyons. Several unsuccessful attempts have been made to discover who Jeanne Flore really was, but her identity is less crucial finally to the meaning of the work than the function of the female narrator, whether the real author be male or female, for it is this primary fiction which establishes the context in which the stories are told as well as the way in which they are to be read, shaping both our perception of the intended relationship between writer and reader and our reception of the stories themselves.

In the introductory "Epistre" to "Madame Minerve sa chiere Cousine," Jeanne Flore acknowledges that her style is less polished than that of a male author,[6] a disclaimer which, judging from a similar profession of humility Marguerite de Navarre addressed to the readers of her *Miroir de l'âme pécheresse*, was already a topos in female writing of the day;[7] but her learned allusions, and her Latinized language and syntax, belie the statement, showing her to be highly skilled in the art and artifice of rhetoric—which is quite unusual, generally speaking, for women of the day.

What is even more unexpected, especially given the restrictions which contemporary social and religious codes placed on women's sexuality, is that each story defends the rights and prerogatives of *fol'amor* and calls for the punishment of all who refuse to submit to its authority, as the programmatic title clearly indicates: *Comptes amoureux par Madame Jeanne Flore, touchant la punition que faict Venus de ceulx qui contemnent et mesprisent le vray Amour*. Initially, the author plays with the ambivalence inherent in the

---

[6] "Ce que j'ay faict presentement: neantmoins soubs espoir que vous, et les humains lecteurs excuserez le rude et mal agencé langaige. C'est œuvre de femme, d'où ne peult sortir ouvraige si limé, que bien seroit d'ung homme discretz en ses escriptz" (97).

[7] "Si vous liséz ceste œuure toute entiere, / Arrestéz vous, sans plus, à la matiere: / En excusant la Rhyme, et le langaige, / Voyant que c'est d'une femme l'ouuraige: / Qui n'a en soy science ne sçauoir...": "Au Lecteur," *Le Miroir de l'âme pécheresse*, ed. Renja Salminen (Helsinki: Suomalainen Tiedeakatemia, 1979), 165. Similarly, Christine de Pisan speaks of herself with pretended modesty and humility, disclaiming learning and ability in her reply to the treatise of Jean de Montreuil. For a discussion of the "affected modesty" topos, see Ernst Robert Curtius, *European Literature and the Latin Middle Ages*, trans. W. Trask (New York: Harper and Row, 1953), 83–85.

proposition that men and women, being sexually equal, have an equal right to sexual satisfaction, adopting a strategy which makes it possible, even necessary, for men and women to read and receive these stories differently, each according to his or her own prejudices and fantasies.

Much of Jeanne Flore's apology for sexual freedom would seem to be ironic, intended to ridicule coded discourses of female behavior, whether marital or courtly. What one needs to ask is to what purpose and to whose advantage. Is she taking an extreme position for the purpose of creating irony, or is she representing uncritically and straightforwardly an extreme position which appears ironic only when viewed from a masculine, or maybe a Renaissance standpoint? In any event, there is frequently a rhetorical playfulness in her arguments as well as in her examples, which needs to be addressed.

Marguerite de Navarre writes *nouvelles*, stories which, as the word itself indicates, are *new*, founded on contemporary events rather than inspired by literary models, events either experienced by her *devisants* or related to them by someone who had. Jeanne Flore, on the other hand, is an author of *comptes*, stories which, if not mythical or legendary, are old and immemorial, as if the past were a source and guarantee of truth.[8] Thus writing for her is first of all reading, or rather rereading and therefore rewriting, classical or canonical authors, most prominently, perhaps, Virgil, Ovid, and Jean Lemaire de Belges. Not only does she appropriate allusions and situations from the *Aeneid*, the *Metamorphoses*, and the *Illustrations de Gaule et Singularitez de Troie*, but she regenders them frequently as well, interpreting classical mythology and literature with a feminine bias, transforming men into women and women into men. Thus in the second of the seven stories, related by Andromeda, Pyrance's final, fatal monologue, and the expression of public consternation upon learning of his death, recall Dido's last words and the subsequent panic Rumor spread in Carthage (*Aeneid* 4. 651–666). Meridienne's "laniation," in the same story, is reminiscent of the demise of Orpheus who, disdaining the love of the women of Thrace, is torn asunder by the Maenads. Juno takes pity on Dido in the *Aeneid* (4. 688–695), but Venus takes pity on Pyrance in the *Comptes*, and Meridienne replaces Aeneas in the comparison with an oak tree (*Aeneid* 4. 445–446).

---

[8] There are numerous allusions to the fact that her stories take place in the distant past: "Icy fine mon compte tel qu'il est veritablement jadiz advenu" (154); "vous toutes icy, moult eslongnées du temps que cela advint" (158); "jà a longtemps y eust en ceste ville . . ." (158); "Et celle merveille veoit on encores en la forestz Garboniere jusques à aujourd'huy, et si a plus de cinq cens ans que cela premierement advint" (184).

Moreover, the story of Meridienne, as told by Andromeda, is a rewriting of the story of the mythological Andromeda. According to legend, Cassiopeia, Andromeda's mother, angered Poseidon by saying that her daughter (or possibly herself) was more beautiful than the Nereids. To avenge himself of this insult, Poseidon sent a sea monster to lay waste to the country and was appeased only by the sacrifice of Andromeda. Chained to a rock by the shore, she was rescued by Perseus, who killed the monster, fell in love with her and, later, married her. Meridienne's story, contrary to Andromeda's, is not a love story but a revenge story, the tale of a woman punished by Venus, not for her beauty, but because she misuses her beauty and rejects the love of another for love of self.

Significantly, the order of physical description in the *Comptes* is structured as well as gendered by the model and rhetoric of the *blasons du corps féminin*. Thus all of the heroines are young and beautiful. Their dress and physical attributes are amply, even sensually, described, with details eroticized in keeping with a masculine rather than a feminine perspective. In the first story, Rosemonde, rescued by her lover, is presented

> simplement vestue d'une robbe faicte d'ung blanc taffetas armoisi, dont les bords estoient de passemans d'or: par dessoubs, la deliée chemise joignoit à sa chair blanche et ferme: si que quant le doulx vent Zephirus venoit à entresoufler parmy ses habillemens, ores il demonstroit à qui le voulait veoir, la composition de la cuisse, ores du ventre, et ores de sa jambe longuette et bien faicte. (122)[9]

And in the bedchamber scene, her lover contemplates her sensuously, lingering on "la blancheur delicieuse de sa gorge," "la rondeur des petitz tetons," "le ventre uny et dur," "ses cuysses bien tournées" (126). Such erotic insistence upon a woman's physical charms seems incongruous and unlikely from a Renaissance woman's viewpoint or pen.

Their male counterparts, equally young and handsome, are presented much more succinctly, as would undoubtedly be the case if the narrator were a man, with emphasis placed on their strength and stamina. Pyrance, the man who loves Meridienne, is summarily described as "jeune, beau,

---

[9] Quite obviously, such descriptions are literary, as a Renaissance reader would have immediately realized. This one conflates Virgil's evocation in the *Aeneid* of the divine grace of Venus's measured step (1. 405) and Jean Lemaire de Belges's display of her charms in the judgment of Paris episode (*Les Illustrations de Gaule et Singularitez de Troie*, in *Œuvres*, ed. J. Stecher, 4 vols. [Geneva: Slatkine Reprints, 1969], 1:255–56).

riche et gracieux" (140). Jeanne Flore does not look at him, however, only at her and at her cruel pleasure in his surrender to the seductive power of her eyes: "Subtilement s'en apperceut la cruelle Meridienne, et estoit fort joyeuse et contente de veoir ainsi l'imprudent jeune homme se perdre en la lueur de ses beaulx yeux, resemblante au serpent appellé Basilique, qui occit quiconque il aura attainct de son regard venimeux" (140). Finally, women are depicted as sexually deprived, but the young lover is praised for his ardor, which is how a male author might imagine him:

> La belle Dame, qui auparavant se mouroit entre les impotens et sans chaleur accollemens de Pyralius, maintenant s'esjouyt de manier les membres refaictz et en bon poinct de son nouvel amy, et de veoir sa belle et bien colourée face: ses vers yeulx: sa blonde barbe: sa poictrine forte, et plaine de chaleur: ses bracs non rudes au delicieux exercisse d'amours. (125)[10]

Husbands, on the other hand, most of whom are old, ugly, and impotent, are the true villains, and not men in general, especially not young men. Their portraits are compilations of grotesque details. Thus Pyralius, Rosemonde's husband, in the first story, is characteristically repulsive:

> il eust la teste grosse et lourde, herissée de rude et aspre cheveleure, jà envieillie et grise, le front ridé, les sourcilz gros et espaix, les yeulx tous chassieux et enfoncez en la teste. . . . De l'estomach luy issoit une espaisse et fetide haleyne à travers une puante, noyre et baveuse bouche . . . (102–3)[11]

Everything in this portrait seems to point to the rhetoric of *enargeia*, the art of presenting a vivid picture, reinforced here by an accumulation of increasingly negative details. These are not, of course, real persons, but rather

---

[10] Although onomastics suggests ardor for both, only Pyrance lives up to his name.

[11] The portrait of the *senex amans* is a classical set-piece. See, for example, Erasmus's bridegroom, "with his snub nose, dragging one leg after him, but not as easily as the Swiss were wont [the allusion to the "Suiseri" in the Latin original is not clear], with itchy hands, a stinking breath, heavy eyes, a bound-up head, with pus running from his nose and ears": *Colloquia*, ed. L.-E. Halkin et al, in *Opera omnia Desiderii Erasmi Roterodami* (Amsterdam: North Holland Publishing Company, 1972), 1. 3:593, my translation.

characters, even caricatures, composed of a series of qualities belonging to the conventions of the topos in question, piled up with comic emphasis by a hand intent upon portraying sexual incompatibility.

This kind of descriptive accumulation, as Apollo's portrait of those who remain loveless in Louise Labé's *Débat de Folie et d'Amour* clearly shows, could easily express feminine disgust with loathsome husbands. It could also translate into a feature of masculine rhetoric designed not only to denigrate troublesome and impotent husbands, but also, and more pertinently, to praise the vigor of young love and lovers. Thus the following passage could easily be dictated from the standpoint of masculine self-interest:

> Par laquelle cause, cheres compaignes, povez considerer en quelle melancolie estoit la dolente espousée: laquelle estant totallement frustrée de son intention, ne luy peult oncques, tant sceut elle bien user des actes que font les amoureuses couchées avec leurs jeunes amys, exciter les membres prosternez et endormis de sa vieillesse enorme et sans vigueur. (162)

It seems obvious, despite what Pérouse and others have claimed, that the *Comptes amoureux* are not the work of a young author; or if they are, then of a young author who has read well and widely, and whose prose is replete with references to classical authors and, more directly perhaps, reminiscences of Rhétoriqueur prose. In any event, one of the most significant characteristics of the *Comptes amoureux* is the pronounced disproportion between personal and derivative discourse. Jeanne Flore has little to say on her own; both her stories and language are borrowed, and what is properly hers is limited to exercises in imitation and rhetorical amplification.[12]

In imitation there is always an element of parody, if by parody one understands, as etymology dictates, a *second singing*. Because of the double meaning of the preposition *para*, "against" and "beside" or "along with," this second singing can be opposed to the first or complete it. In a sense, parody is akin to irony, which, according to rhetorical treatises, is a trope by which one says one thing while meaning another.[13] The interest of parody

---

[12] For the classical theorist, *amplificatio* was a device used in judicial and demonstrative rhetoric to give weight and substance to an argument or to praise a person or an act. In the Renaissance, *amplificatio* is conflated with *copia*, the search for linguistic and semantic abundance.

[13] Dilwyn Knox's *Ironia: Medieval and Renaissance Ideas on Irony* (Leiden: Brill, 1989) provides a detailed review of the meaning and applications of the term. For an equally useful study, from a more literary standpoint, see C. Jan Swearingen,

as, moreover, of irony, lies therefore in the difference, the hiatus between two texts, rather than in their similarity, and it is in this critical space between the two that the author has room to manipulate writing, displace reading, and display originality.

Through parody, Jeanne Flore's stories acquire a double dimension, and coexist in the past as well as in the present. There is a constant play of text and intertext, the distinct action of two discourses, side by side on the same page. Thus in the second story, Lemaire de Belges's authoritative depiction of Venus's seductive costume is grafted onto Jeanne Flore's depiction of Meridienne's dress, setting up reverberations between the two, awakening literary memory on the one hand and stimulating the reader's imagination on the other.[14] In this particular context, intertextuality is a form of parody: neither repetition or imitation, nor the absorption and transformation of other texts, but the ironic rewriting of a prior and commonly recognizable text.

The most striking feature of irony is the peculiar relation it creates between author and reader. In incorporating another text within the text, the author invites the reader to correlate them, less perhaps in an attempt to provide a criterion of relevance than to encourage recognition of critical difference. Distanced from the reader, as the reconstruction of a world in which the masculine past and the feminine present are juxtaposed and coexist, the text seems to aspire towards a rereading of literature itself, or, perhaps more accurately, towards a playful readjustment of its themes and conventions.

Generally speaking, Jeanne Flore's prose is disconcerting in its accumulation of erudition. At every step, there is a name, an allusion, or a detail which diverts the narrative present to the literary or mythological past. Thus Meridienne's arrival in public is conflated with Venus's departure for Mount Pelion:

> Donc après les aultres plusieurs ceremonies feminines, et qu'elle eust prins conseil de son mirouer trois et quattre fois, la voicy apparoistre en la presence de ceulx qui l'attendoient: et à l'yssue de son palais resembla la grande Venus, laquelle partoit de l'isle de Chippre pour tirer droit au mont Pellion à l'assemblée des nopces du Roy Pelleus et de Thetis: puis de là en Phrigie à la contention des

---

Rhetoric and Irony: Western Literacy and Western Lies (New York: Oxford University Press, 1991).

[14] Lemaire de Belges, *Œuvres*, 1:255.

beaultez, montée sur son doré chariot trainé par douze colombes blanches comme laict. (138)

And the description of the effect of her beauty calls up reference in quick succession to Juno, Phoebe, Cleopatra, Cupid, Aeneas, Carthage, Mars, Adonis, Ganymede, and Psyche, creating a significant textual disproportion between the arts of telling and remembering.

What is more significant perhaps is the fact that Jeanne Flore's references to figures or events are frequently allusive or periphrastic, indicating that she expected her public to have read the same books she has. Her language requires cross-reading, which alone would seem to limit the intended public considerably. In fact, it is not everyone who would have read widely enough in Roman history or literature to understand this reference to Cleopatra: "Et pas n'eust sceu à mon advis, la femme de Marc Anthoine lorsqu'elle desploya les forces de son parler pour à soy rendre captif qui venoit pour la subjuguer soubz l'empire Romain, la surpasser d'eloquence et bien dire" (137). Familiarity with classical mythology is taken for granted, as in this indirect reference to the peacock: "Aultres jectans l'œil sur la chevelure blonde et desliée à l'entour du large front moderement undoiante, et de beaucoup meilleure grace que n'espand pas sa queuë l'oiseau de la Déesse Juno" (138). Either Jeanne Flore was writing for a humanist audience, which means an essentially masculine one, or there was at Lyons at the time a group of women sufficiently educated to be able to understand and appreciate the subtleties of her language, as well as numerous enough to make the publication of successive editions of the *Comptes* commercially worthwhile.

What the author of these stories has assembled is a collection of the conventional situations and clichés of earlier romances concerning rejected suitors. In this sense the work is also metafictional, commenting or reflecting upon other texts in a way which allows the reader to recognize the irony inherent in their rewriting and regendering. In any event, appropriation in the *Comptes* has a twofold dimension in that it introduces a semantic intention that is different from the original text. Sexual comportment for Jeanne Flore, contrary to Platonic or Petrarchan conventions, is dictated by nature rather than by social or cultural codes. Thus she recognizes and promotes the imperatives of female sexuality, without always recognizing the necessity of taking masculine reciprocity into consideration. Rather than degendering sexuality, she regenders it from a different perspective. Although her language reflects the influence of the courtly love tradition, the game aspect it supposes, with intricate steps and rules to follow, is largely absent.[15] Sexual union is quite clearly the immediate goal of the lovers in the first story (Rosemonde and Jean Andro) and the sixth (Theodore and Daurine), but also of the anonymous lady of the third.

The *Comptes amoureux* privilege female eroticism over male eroticism, but is this because their author is a woman or a man? To be sure, Jeanne Flore's men are generally loathsome, especially husbands too old to be capable of sexual arousal, whereas her women are always young and beautiful: either filled with love and unsatisfied by their husbands, or filled with hate and causing the despair and death of their lovers. In either case, it is the woman's sexuality or lack of it which determines the happiness or misery of the men in her life. Moreover, female sexuality is depicted as natural and not to be repressed. Those who refuse to honor love are cruelly punished. Sexual pleasure is not to be denied or postponed, nor is procreation its aim. Jeanne Flore celebrates sexuality for and of itself; here woman is ruled by desire, which is not presented as tragic or reprehensible, except when denied or suppressed.

Admittedly, because of the bars of semi-seclusion and parental arrangements of marriages, a maiden's love could not easily run a romantic course in sixteenth-century French society. Consequently, it is not only women who might imagine a relaxation of sexual mores, but also men, and more especially young men. Mockery of marriage was not new in the Renaissance; it was already traditional in Greek and Roman comedy, not to mention its prevalence in medieval farce. Not surprisingly, therefore, the *devisantes* are prepared to practice what they preach, inviting young men for a visit and entreating them to remain for the night, taking the initiative in what is an obvious reversal of traditional gender roles, and just the kind of reversal which a male author and audience would appreciate and applaud.

In the fourth story, which celebrates female sexuality and the inability of old husbands to satisfy women's young desires, Madame Minerve calls for wives to deceive their husbands:

> Veu ce, nous n'avons doncques tort, amoureuses compaignes, si pour mitiguer noz martyres venons à choisir qui puisse supplier aux faultes que font noz maris impotens, lesquelz possible, quoy qu'ilz meslent le ciel et la terre ensemble quand ilz nous surpreignent en noz larcins

---

[15] See Roberta Kay Binford, "The *Comptes amoureux* of Jeanne Flore: A Critical Study" (Ph.D. diss., University of Iowa, 1972), 179.

amoureux, sont bien joyeulx de trouver œuvre faicte. (168)

While not exactly reversing roles here, she gives the situation a new twist when she portrays the wife as a martyr and justifies adultery as a necessary means to self-satisfaction.

On the other hand, it is precisely because Jeanne Flore's heroines live out their sexuality that they conform to the misogynistic stereotype of the wanton woman propounded by the antifeminist literature of the *Querelle des femmes*. Renaissance medicine and medical authors, uniformly male, informed primarily by the Galenic or Hippocratic model, taught that women had a voracious sexual appetite and that this was a purely physiological phenomenon. Satisfaction for them is not associated with any pleasure other than simple relief of the unbearable pressures emanating from the uterus. And whereas a man was expected to be able to control his desires, it was believed to be impossible for a woman and injurious to her health that she should try. Thus in the third story a young girl, more enamored of learning than of men, is afflicted by Venus with a fatal malady. The doctor who examines her diagnoses her illness as sexual and prescribes marriage as a remedy. Hoping to save her life, her parents marry her off as quickly as possible to an old man who, unfortunately, is sexually dysfunctional. In despair, she finally stabs herself to death, symbolically enough, on her marriage bed. Here we find the counterpart of the hysterical woman who, in Hippocratic gynecology, is unable to control her sexual appetite, and who, in the antifeminist literature of the day, is an object of scorn and laughter.

There is something willfully paradoxical in Jeanne Flore's praise of unrestricted sexual desire. Since the codes of conventional love mandated chastity to the unmarried woman and fidelity to the married, her appeal for absolute obedience to the dictates of Venus is both provocative and polemical. Whereas a woman, traditionally, is the pursued, here she becomes the pursuer, either bestowing or withholding her love as she pleases; the man, at least in the second story, dies helplessly of unrequited love, which is more in conformity with the destiny of a woman in fiction as in life. Marriage, when it appears, is a source of discord, and the heroine in the first story, who is bound to an old, repulsive husband, is finally rescued by a young and dynamic lover. Christian morality does not come into play; the only rule of order is one of unhesitating allegiance to Venus, with punishment reserved for those who fail to honor her properly. In this sense, Jeanne Flore's representation of the nature of woman's love is liberating. Unfortunately, the argument works both ways, for in confirming the voraciousness of female sexuality, she confirms as well what popular and scientific tradition had said about it all along.

What finally are intended readers, presumably masculine as well as feminine, supposed to learn from the experience of the author's characters? If female, that they are justified in fulfilling their erotic expectations, legitimately, through marriage, or otherwise. If male, that women have equally strong sexual fantasies and desires. Hence there is a lesson for both, grounded simultaneously in past and present history. In cross-writing and displacing themes and stories from the past, Jeanne Flore imagines a strange new fictional reality. There is something utopian, even dream-like, in her world, and it is precisely this quality which awakens and stimulates the reader of her rewriting of the myth of Echo and Narcissus.

In Ovid's story there are several potential morals, and this is undoubtedly one of the reasons for its lasting appeal.[16] In the first place, it argues against the desire and pursuit of the unattainable. More specifically, it illustrates the destructive effect of self-love on others as well as on oneself. But the complexity and elaboration of his treatment are not directed solely to privileging any lesson which the story may imply, nor does the poet call attention to any of its moral implications. His interest is in combining the story of the punishment of Echo with the story of the punishment of Narcissus in a way which brings out the paradox, indeed the absurdity, of their interrelationship. Thus in its sequential development, Ovid's narrative alternates between the story of Echo and the story of Narcissus.[17]

Ovid first introduces a beautiful and proud Narcissus, then tells how the nymph Echo, condemned by Juno to repeating in abbreviated form other people's words, falls in love with him, only to be cruelly spurned. As a consequence of his rejection, her body wastes away, leaving only her synonymous voice. Narcissus is punished for his disdain when, chancing upon a forest pool, he falls in love with his reflected image. If for Echo, the other was another, for Narcissus, the other is himself, a reflected image which touch or desire are unable to reach. Realizing this in a monologue marked by rhetorical amplification and temporization, Narcissus dies at last from

---

[16] Ovid, *Metamorphoses*, ed. and trans. Frank Justus Miller, 2 vols. (Cambridge, MA: Harvard University Press; London: William Heinemann, 1984), 1:148–61 (Book 3. 339–510).

[17] For a deconstructive reading of Ovid's text, see John Brenkman, "Narcissus in the Text," *Georgia Review* 30 (1976): 293–327. For a detailed discussion of Brenkman's analysis of the disruption of narrative schemes in Ovid's story, see Jonathan Culler, *On Deconstruction: Theory and Criticism after Structuralism* (Ithaca: Cornell University Press, 1982), 251–57.

love of himself. In place of his body, his mourners find only an emblematic flower, white petals clustered round a cup of gold.

Ovid makes no moralizing generalizations on his characters or their fate. He simply tells a story which is at once intense and dramatic. Jeanne Flore, in her rewriting, underscores from the outset the lesson she reads into it. Thus she begins by admonishing women who are loved to love their lovers in return, reminding them of "Dido, Philis, Oenone, Phedra, Adrianne, et Medée," who came to love reluctantly and who were abandoned subsequently by their lovers: "Et chascune de cestes cy . . . au premier eurent Amour et ses flambeaux à despris, jusques à ce que le printemps de leur aage se veit estre converty en pluyes ameres, et en esté tempestueux" (169–70). The example of their misfortune reminds her of Echo and Narcissus.

In retelling the story, the narrator begins with a brief reference to Narcissus's great beauty, followed by three pages of complaint on the part of the Nymphs who blame themselves for their inability to express adequately the consuming passion he inspires in them. Echo is introduced obliquely as one who, had she not been deprived of her "doulce loquence" (173), might have found the words to do so. In keeping with her penchant for explanatory amplification, Jeanne Flore then recounts with copious detail the story of Echo's punishment by Juno for complicity in Jupiter's philandering, establishing thereby narrative causality between her loveless solitude and her subsequent rejection by Narcissus. When she finally encounters him in her lonely wanderings through the forest, she is unable to speak for herself, and can only express herself by repeating the final words he speaks, distorting their meaning to suit her own purposes.

Jeanne Flore's rendition of the scene of their meeting expands on the incidental comedy that Echo's linguistic disability entails. When Ovid's Narcissus says "Here let us meet," Echo, to follow up on her own words, comes forth from the woods and throws her arms around the neck she longs to clasp. Jeanne Flore's Echo reacts with considerably less dignity and restraint, as though she were being viewed though masculine eyes:

> Prenant de là Echo esperance de jouir de ses amours, lascha la bride à ses ardens desirs, et donna telle hardiesse à son hatif vouloir comme de venir vers Narcissus, luy plorant et larmoiant par force d'amour dans le sein: et s'efforce luy monstrer à plain en profondement souspirer sa douleur surpassante toute aultre douleur. Et à l'heure quoy qu'elle doubta et trembla de paour, si est ce qu'elle baisa la bouche de l'amy fugitif. (175)

And whereas Ovid's Narcissus says only "manus conplexibus aufer!" (v. 390) ("Remove your hands from me!"), Jeanne Flore's apostrophizes her with a misogynistically coded epithet: "Je puisse, dist il, *lascive* Damoiselle, estre resolu en pouldre premier que je consente à tes vouloirs!" (176, my italics). Moreover, while Ovid devotes more than twice as many lines to Narcissus than to Echo, Jean Flore gives more attention to Echo, evoking at length the almost hysterical intensity of her passion, implying that her loss of love is fully justified by past behavior. This may be a woman's interpretation of the fate of Ovid's Echo, but it is definitely not a feminist one.[18]

Finally, it is important to note that in Ovid, Narcissus's demise is induced by a young man who, upon being scorned, raised his hands and prayed that Narcissus himself might love and never win his love, whereas in Jeanne Flore it is Echo who asks that "cestuy, à qui nature a donné si excellente beaulté qu'il en a deschassé de soy toute doulceur humaine, soyt amoureux de soy mesmes et ne vive plus en paix, puisqu'il a en ce poinct desprisé tant de gentilles Damoiselles" (176), making it perfectly clear that while their fates intersect, his is appropriate punishment for indifference towards the opposite sex. Additionally, and not insignificantly, while Ovid's Narcissus sees his own image reflected in the fatal pool, Flore's Narcissus wonders if he is not seeing a "Deesse" come down to earth, a logical Renaissance male rereading of the classical myth.[19]

Although Jeanne Flore retains the essential drama and general outline of Ovid's story, she omits the incident of the flower that bears Narcissus's name, presumably because, given the ideology which underlies all seven of the *Comptes amoureux*, anyone displaying contempt for love would not deserve the slightest hint of redemption. Her *translation* of Ovid's text is already *interpretation* in that she reads it differently, but not necessarily from a feminist standpoint. Her digressions, additions, and omissions tend to remotivate Ovid's myth, recontextualizing it into a story in which Narcissus becomes the brunt and the instrument of Echo's punishment for post-

---

[18] Ovid gives 45 lines to Echo and 108 to Narcissus. Flore reverses the ratio, devoting 7 pages to Echo and only 5 to Narcissus. Does more interest in Echo imply that the author is a man? Contemporary cultural and literary conventions relegate the female author to the role of Echo in relation to her male counterpart, and this is a situation which our author seems to accept without anxiety.

[19] Cf. Ronsard's mythological regendering in "Je vouldroy bien . . . / Estre un Narcisse, & elle une fontaine / Pour m'y plonger une nuict à sejour": *Les Amours* 1552–1553, XX, in *Œuvres complètes*, ed. Paul Laumonier with I. Silver and R. Lebègue, 20 vols. (Paris: Société des Textes Français Modernes, 1914–1975), 4:24.

poned love. Her version rereads an existing myth, and at one and the same time demands to be read as a myth itself.

It should be emphasized that Echo's death is portrayed as a function of feelings which she created within herself, making it appear as an inevitable consequence of the excesses of unsatisfied female desire. This reading is confirmed, moreover, by the closing moral instructing the *devisantes* not to neglect their lovers or delight in their martyrdom if they love heaven and themselves, for they will only regret their cruelty—a moral which has little to do with Narcissus. And while both Flore's and Ovid's Echo continue to echo even after death, her Narcissus simply dies, while Ovid's, received into the Underworld, continues, with final irony, to gaze upon himself in Stygian waters.

Ovid blames neither Echo nor Narcissus, but Flore clearly links his fate to her fault. Significantly, she omits Ovid's reference to the blind seer Tiresias whose prophecy that Narcissus will live to old age "if he himself shall not know" opens the story and is fulfilled by it. In both accounts, Narcissus is self-possessed and content before Echo intervenes. However, Flore frames her story differently, with a reference to Phoebus, "recteur du divin œil eterne," who "par preuve sçait quel dommage reçoit celuy qui contre l'amour se veult rebeller" (170), displacing Ovid's theme of self-love with that of women's unfulfilled love.[20] Far from being a submissive rewriting of a classical text, Jeanne Flore's story asserts its own meaning. Whereas a humanist would be intent upon finding and restoring the text's original meaning, she seems more inclined to reappropriate it, underscoring those features which translate most effectively her reading—which is, after all, what classical and Renaissance rhetoric understood by *invention*.

In this particular case, the narrator renews the story of Echo and Narcissus by representing it through feminine eyes. As described by her, both protagonists represent the torment and death resulting from unsatisfied desire. Her concluding address is an attempt to steer the readers and their fictional expectations in one direction, while the myth seems to go off in another. She instructs her *devisantes* to learn from Echo's example not to neglect their lovers nor rejoice in their martyrdom, but to love them with

---

[20] The motif of Love's revenge and victory is strongly emphasized in the metamorphosis of Narcissus in the medieval *Ovide moralisé*. Narcissus's fate is mainly looked upon as a warning against pride in physical beauty, or even pride in general. Cf. Louise Vinge, *The Narcissus Theme in Western European Literature up to the Early 19th Century* (Lund: Skånska Centraltryckeriet, 1967), 92–93. Vinge, unfortunately, was not aware of Flore's treatment of the theme.

mutual affection.[21] Thus her lesson has the effect of turning Ovid's essentially undetermined myth of Echo and Narcissus into a problematic *exemplum* whose solution is unequally experienced by the two protagonists.

Although we have no proof that Jeanne Flore was or was not a woman, there is some indication that authorship of the *Comptes amoureux* was actually collective and partially, if not totally, masculine.[22] While her program for woman's sexual equality anticipates Marguerite de Navarre's in the *Heptaméron* or Louise Labé's in the *Débat de Folie et d'Amour*, it is focused, even distorted, by a shift from the contrived reality of the frame-setting to the fictive atmosphere, fanciful setting, and elaborate writing of the stories.

Moreover, since there is a marked discrepancy between the urgency of the feminist theme and the fantasy of its narrative setting in a dream world of dwarfs and giants, fabulous lions and snakes, magical clubs and ointments, enchanted castles and dragons, sorcerers and monsters, valorous knights and beautiful princesses, the reader, confronted with an admixture of seriousness and play, can only react with corresponding familiarity and detachment towards the author's display of discursive irony.

Finally, if this work is indeed an apology for women, it is strange that it has them willingly assuming many of the defects and weaknesses attributed to them by the misogynistic literature of the *Querelle des femmes*: lust, lasciviousness, infidelity, duplicity, aggressiveness. Moreover, when Jeanne Flore states in the concluding address to the reader that all she has written is "fiction / De poësie" (225), she acknowledges the fantasy of her feminism and the distance with which she has treated it. Irony of this sort is a polemical device, suggesting that the author holds other views, alerting us therefore to the possibility of other readings and other meanings.

What provokes and supports the assumption that Jeanne Flore's *Comptes* are to be read otherwise, with an eye to possible critical attitudes towards them, is, first of all, everything we know about the reading public in Renaissance France. A collection of stories dealing with the proposed liberalization and legitimization of female sexuality, especially one recover-

---

[21] "ne vueillez, dis je, despriser vos serviteurs: ne vous esjouyssez de leurs martyres, sur tant que vous aymez le ciel, et vous mesmes. Que vous les debvez aymer de mutuelle amour, l'exemple que j'ay recité vous le montre assez: vous souvienne, je vous pry, que de peu sert le repentir" (181). Curiously, her injunction echoes the *sententia* with which Guillaume de Lorris ends his version of the Narcissus myth: "Dames, cest essample aprenez, / Qui vers voz amis mesprenez; / Car, se vos les laissiez morir, / Deus le vos savra bien merir": *Roman de la rose*, ed. Ernest Langlois, 5 vols. (Paris: Firmin-Didot, 1914–1924), 2:78 (vv. 1507–1509).

[22] See Gabriel-A. Pérouse, *Nouvelles françaises du XVIe siècle: Images de la vie du temps* (Geneva: Droz, 1977), 84–85.

ing and reversing easily recognized classical or Italian models, would have provided an essentially masculine public with the kind of referentiality needed to detect the distortions arising from ironic rewriting. Early modern readers would not have failed to appreciate the subtle humor inherent in the depiction of a group of women realizing their erotic fantasies through the medium of fiction. It is not certain, however, to what extent they would have realized that, in locating their thematic ideology outside the laudatory or depreciative parameters of the *Querelle des femmes*, the *Comptes amoureux* effectively place the whole question of women's sexuality in a new and problematic context, one shared, moreover, by other women writers of the day.

History or Her Story? (Homo)sociality/sexuality in Marguerite de Navarre's *Heptaméron* 12

Gary Ferguson

The twelfth *nouvelle* of Marguerite de Navarre's *Heptaméron* recounts the story of Lorenzo de' Medici, who, on the night of 6 January 1537, murdered his cousin Alessandro, the first Duke of Florence. Of all the *Heptaméron*'s protagonists, Lorenzo has had one of the most successful literary careers, being taken up most famously in the nineteenth century by Musset. Yet the story, in its various versions, proliferated from the beginning, and Lorenzo himself seems to have encouraged and even exploited its ambiguous character, giving varying accounts at different times and in different contexts. One of these versions Marguerite may well have heard from Lorenzo in person, for, a little less than a year after committing the murder, he sought refuge at the French court. Although the dauphine, Catherine de' Medici, was in all likelihood Alessandro's half-sister, Lorenzo was able to exploit the hostility that existed between François I and the Emperor, the latter having been Duke Alessandro's father-in-law and protector.[1] Lorenzo was to remain in France until October 1544, at which point, in the wake of the Peace of Crépy, the improved relations between the two monarchs rendered his situation increasingly precarious.

If we take literally its opening words ("Depuis dix ans en ça . . ."),[2] the twelfth *nouvelle* was most likely written in 1547—a supposition corroborated by the fact that no mention is made of Lorenzo's own murder, which occurred in 1548.[3] Since several versions of Lorenzo's story remained in

---

[1] Alessandro was the bastard son of either Lorenzo de' Medici, Duke of Urbino (the father of Catherine de' Medici), or of Giulio de' Medici, who, in 1523, became Pope Clement VII.

[2] Marguerite de Navarre, *L'Heptaméron*, ed. Michel François (Paris: Garnier, 1967), 90. All subsequent references will be to this edition.

[3] This date also fits with Renja Salminen's account of the genesis of Marguerite's collection, cf. *Heptaméron*, ed. Renja Salminen (Geneva: Droz, 1999), xliii–xliv.

manuscript for many years, to be published only long after their initial composition, it is impossible to establish a complete and accurate "genealogy" for them, indicating which versions may have influenced others.[4] Despite the possibility that it postdates the event by as many as ten years, Marguerite's *nouvelle* remains one of the earliest accounts of the murder. Even though the story was circulating already in letters, only the account given by Girolamo Cardano in his *De Sapientia* (1543) was published before the time at which Marguerite was probably writing.[5] Guillaume Paradin included a short version of the story in Latin in his *Memoriae nostrae* (1548), but his long account in French was published only in 1550, a year after Marguerite's death.[6] Although it was not published until 1723, Lorenzo composed his own *Apologia* before 1548 and probably as early as 1538. The *Storia fiorentina* of Benedetto Varchi (1503–1565) has an equally late publication date (1721), but its account of Alessandro's murder also claims to be based on Lorenzo's own testimony.

Heptaméron 12 differs from all other contemporary versions of the story in a number of respects, but most strikingly perhaps in its portrayal of Lorenzo's motivation. This is generally presented in the chronicles as political—to rid the city of Florence of a tyrant and to restore its republican freedoms—and writers adopt positions pro- or anti-Lorenzo, depending upon their own political convictions. *Heptaméron* 12, by contrast, seems to minimize political considerations: the political context is only barely sketched; political motivations for the murder are merely alluded to. Rather, Marguerite presents the events almost entirely as a story of personal and familial honor played out among a triangle of related protagonists: Lorenzo determines to murder the duke—his master, cousin, and friend—rather than become an accomplice in his own sister's sexual exploitation.[7] None of

---

For a dissenting view, see Marie-Madeleine Fontaine, "Les Enjeux de pouvoir dans l'*Heptaméron*," in L'*Heptaméron de Marguerite de Navarre: Actes de la journée d'étude Marguerite de Navarre, 19 octobre 1991*, ed. Simone Perrier, Cahiers textuel 10 (Paris: L'U. F. R. «Sciences des textes et documents» avec le concours du Conseil Scientifique de l'Université de Paris VII, 1992), 133–49 and 155–60, here 138 and 149 n. 15.

[4] For the most complete list, arranged chronologically to the extent possible, see Fontaine, "Les Enjeux," Appendice II, "Principaux documents contemporains sur Lorenzino de Médicis," 155–60.

[5] For Fontaine, there is no doubt that Marguerite had read Cardano ("Les Enjeux," 137).

[6] Guillaume Paradin, *Memoriae nostrae libri quatuor* (Lyons: Jean de Tournes, 1548), 120–21; *Histoire de notre tems* (Lyons: Jean de Tournes and Guillaume Gazeau, 1558), 329–33 (first edition, 1550).

[7] In *nouvelle* 12, the duke's wife is initially too young to play any part in the story,

the other versions of the story presents the motivation for the murder in terms of Lorenzo's desire to protect his sister from the duke's sexual advances; at most, the assignation he arranges between his sister and the duke offers him the opportunity for carrying it out. Accounts even disagree as to whether Lorenzo was defending one sister, his two sisters, or his aunt. In some versions, the woman involved is not named at all.[8]

Despite its peculiarities, critics have generally emphasized *Heptaméron* 12's historical veracity,[9] or at least argued that Marguerite invents little, repeating the version of events that Lorenzo presented to the French court.[10] It is pointed out not only that Marguerite heard the story at first

---

except to the extent that her unavailability as a sexual object forces the duke to pursue other women: "et, pour ce qu'elle estoit encores si jeune, qu'il ne luy estoit licite de coucher avecq elle, actendant son aage plus meur, la traicta fort doulcement; car, pour l'espargner, fut amoureux de quelques autres dames de la ville" (90). Only at the end of the *nouvelle* does the duchess begin to emerge as a character. When the duke fails to appear, we are told that "la pauvre duchesse, qui commençoit fort à l'aymer, sçachant qu'on ne le trouvoit poinct, fut en grande peyne" (94).

[8] According to Varchi, Alessandro "voulut encore que Lorenzo lui procurât une sœur de sa mère du côté paternel. . . . Lorenzo, qui attendait une occasion de ce genre, fit entendre au duc que l'entreprise offrirait des difficultés, mais qu'il ferait son possible pour réussir, disant qu'en somme toutes les femmes étaient femmes": Extract from *Storia fiorentina*, trans. Paul de Musset, published in Alfred de Musset, *Lorenzaccio* (Paris: Larousse, 1991), 227. Paradin's account runs as follows: "Alexandre de Medicis, premier Duc de Florence, estant fort amoureux d'une Dame, chercha tous les moyens qu'il put pour jouir secrettement d'elle, tellement qu'il fut contreint de mettre en œuvre ses parens propres, desquelz il n'estoit pas fort aymé, entre lesquelz estoit Laurent de Medicis, un sien cousin, qui de tout tems avoit conceu mortelle haine alencontre dudit Alexandre, tant pour estre amateur de l'ancienne liberté de leur Republique, que pour les facheuses et tyranniques complexions dudit Duc. Icelui, voyant l'ocasion s'estre offerte de delivrer la vile de tyrannie, s'adressa audit Duc son parent, et lui promit de lui amener la Dame dont estoit question" (Paradin, *Histoire*, 329). Cf. also Fontaine, "Les Enjeux," 141–42, 158; Joyce G. Bromfield, *De Lorenzino de Médicis à Lorenzaccio: Etude d'un thème historique* (Paris: Marcel Didier, 1972), 21, 39, 41, 46, 51–52; and Salminen, ed., *Heptaméron*, 698.

[9] See, notably, Pierre Jourda, *Marguerite d'Angoulême, duchesse d'Alençon, reine de Navarre (1492–1549): Etude biographique et littéraire*, 2 vols., Bibliothèque littéraire de la Renaissance, nouv. sér. 19 and 20 (Paris: H. Champion, 1930; repr. Geneva: Slatkine, 1978), 2:774–75.

[10] Alexandre Rally, "Commentaire de la XIIe nouvelle de l'«Heptaméron»," *Revue du seizième siècle* 11 (1924): 208–21. The idea that Lorenzo gave an account of the murder in France alleging as his motive the defense of his sister or sisters is advanced by Luigi Alberto Ferrai, *Lorenzino de' Medici e la società cortigiana del cinquecento* (Milan: Ulrico Hoepli, 1891), 290–91, and Pierre Gauthiez, *Lorenzaccio (Lorenzino de Médicis) 1514–*

hand, but also that she would have been acquainted with Laudomia, Lorenzo's sister, who accompanied her brother into exile.¹¹ There were good reasons, moreover, why Lorenzo might have chosen not to stress his political ambitions when he told his tale at the French court in 1537;¹² there were equally good reasons why Marguerite herself, writing perhaps a decade later, may have wished to avoid sensitive political issues.¹³ More recently, however, Marie-Madeleine Fontaine has demonstrated with acuity the problems of reading Marguerite's story as an historical account. Having shown how Marguerite shapes, even falsifies the raw historical material, Fontaine concludes: "Il est clair que Marguerite infléchit les données, ... la nouvelle XII n'est donc pas une version officielle, mais celle qui lui convient. . . . La réussite narrative est totale: Marguerite a fait observer à son récit toutes les règles nécessaires à son enchaînement, à son intensité et à sa résolution. Elle a aussi imposé une vraisemblance, qui a été prise pour une véracité."¹⁴ The narrative details that *Heptaméron* 12 shares with the

---

1548 (Paris: Albert Fontemoing, 1904), 245, 274, 296, 440. Referring to a Florentine manuscript that mentions the different versions of the story (cf. also Gauthiez, *Lorenzaccio*, 454, n. to 296 and Fontaine, "Les Enjeux," 158, n° 15), Ferrai goes on to affirm that Lorenzo told his story in front of Marguerite and the court. As Rally notes, the manuscript quoted stops short of saying this ("Commentaire," 213, n.). Gauthiez also refers to a letter of Jean de Vauzelles to Aretino, dated 20 February 1539 (*Lorenzaccio*, 449, n. to 274), that, according to Fontaine, affirms that Lorenzo presented himself to Marguerite as the avenger of his sister, and the content of which Marguerite may well have influenced ("Les Enjeux," 158, n° 14 and 142).

¹¹ Cf. Rally, "Commentaire," 208; 210, n. 6; 212 (and ff.), n. 1; 219 (and ff.), n. 1; also Bromfield, *De Lorenzino*, 31, 34.

¹² Rally suggests that Lorenzo may well have wanted to occult the political nature of the murder given, first, that he was seeking refuge at the court of an absolute monarch, and secondly, in view of negotiations aimed at securing the release of Filipo Strozzi, whom the Emperor had agreed to ransom only on condition that he was in no way implicated in the murder of Alessandro ("Commentaire," 213–14, n.). Cf. also Fontaine, "Les Enjeux," 158, n° 15.

¹³ Mention has been made already of her brother's improved relations with the Emperor in the wake of the Peace of Crépy. Marguerite's attachment to the dauphine, Catherine de' Medici, who was probably the murdered duke's half-sister, may also have been a consideration (cf. Bromfield, *De Lorenzino*, 34). Fontaine outlines some of the multiple and complex relations among the Medici, the Strozzi, and the court of France that would have encouraged Marguerite to minimize the political import of her story at whatever date she may have been writing ("Les Enjeux," 139–40). Renja Salminen comments: "Par prudence, la Reine glisse sur les raisons politiques; sous sa plume, l'assassinat devient un exploit romantique" (*Heptaméron*, ed. Salminen, 698).

¹⁴ Fontaine, "Les Enjeux," 142–43.

accounts of the chroniclers, Fontaine insists, are inflected in particular ways and take on specific functions within the fictive economy of the *nouvelle*. Even so, Fontaine shares the view that Marguerite tells Lorenzo's story in the way she does in order to avoid sensitive political issues.[15] While *Heptaméron* 12 largely avoids such issues, and while it may broadly reflect the version told by Lorenzo at the French court, these considerations alone do not adequately explain Marguerite's conscious choice to recount the story as she does. In this essay, I shall examine the terms in which Marguerite casts her version of the story of Lorenzo; I shall argue that her transformation of her material into a piece of short narrative fiction, a *nouvelle*, not only allows her to avoid politically sensitive topics, but also enables her to explore issues of particular interest to her, issues that preoccupy the *Heptaméron* as a whole.

In his study of literary erotic triangles, René Girard demonstrates how the choice of the beloved is often determined by the choice of the rival with whom the beloved must be disputed.[16] Triangular desire, as analyzed by Girard, generally involves two men who desire the same woman sexually. In the *Heptaméron*, however, we find alternative triangular structurings of desire and narrative. Carla Freccero, for example, has pointed out the importance of triangles of characters comprised of two women and one man, one of the former normally being in a position of authority as mother or queen.[17] We also find a number of stories like *nouvelle* 12—and like *nouvelle* 4, to which I shall compare it below—that present a triangle of characters which involves a sister and a brother. This

---

[15] "L'enjeu de Marguerite, qui n'a pas voulu s'interdire un récit aussi impressionnant que fameux, a été de protéger de toute accusation la politique de son frère, en minimisant incroyablement les intentions «républicaines» de Lorenzino et en éliminant le soutien qu'il aurait pu recevoir en France. Elle sauvegarde toutes les relations avec Charles Quint et avec la cour de Florence, elle éloigne de toute complicité la famille Strozzi et n'engage à aucun degré, ni en Italie, ni en France, les exilés florentins": Fontaine, "Les Enjeux," 144.

[16] René Girard, *Mensonge romantique et vérité romanesque* (Paris: Bernard Grasset, 1961), trans. Yvonne Freccero, *Deceit, Desire, and the Novel: Self and Other in Literary Structure* (Baltimore and London: Johns Hopkins University Press, 1966).

[17] Freccero suggests that this "challenges both Freud's and Girard's oedipal models for the structuring of desire and the novel and announces the entry of feminine desire and feminine subjectivity as a thematic preoccupation and structuring agent of prose narrative": "Patriarchy and the Maternal Text: The Case of Marguerite de Navarre," in *Renaissance Women Writers: French Texts/American Contexts*, ed. Anne R. Larsen and Colette H. Winn (Detroit: Wayne State University Press, 1994), 130–40, here 130.

model is similar to Girard's but substitutes a sibling for an erotic relationship between two of the parties.[18] The need further to refine Girard's model has also been demonstrated by Eve Sedgwick, who has argued for the necessity of taking into account "historically variable power asymmetries, such as those of class and race, as well as gender."[19] For Sedgwick, the male-male-female erotic triangle is implicated in the very structures of patriarchy, which makes power relations between men and women dependent on power relations between men.[20] It is precisely to issues of gender and social status that this analysis of triangular desire in *Heptaméron* 12 will seek to attend.

Despite their secondary importance, the possible political motivations for Lorenzo's killing his cousin are not entirely absent from *nouvelle* 12; yet they surface only briefly and are presented as being inextricably linked with questions of family honor. Immediately following the murder, for example, the narrator states that Lorenzo "se veid victorieux de son grand ennemy, par la mort duquel il pensoit mettre en liberté la chose publicque"; a little earlier, the protagonist had determined his course of action by coming to the following conclusion: "que plustost debvoit delivrer sa patrye d'un tel tyran, qui par force vouloit mettre une telle tache en sa maison" (92–93). Thus, the Republic benefits from the death of Lorenzo's enemy; the tyrant is the one who would sully Lorenzo's family name.

The impossibility of demarcating personal and political motivations is also highlighted in the discussion following the *nouvelle*. The terms in which the story is presented cause a hermeneutic split among the *devisants* which is different from that found among the chroniclers. The divergent interpretations no longer reflect only a republican or an autocratic ideology, but also a female or a male point of view. Initially the narrator tells us that the story "engendra diverses oppinions": "les ungs" contend that Lorenzo

---

[18] Susan Snyder has suggested a link between Marguerite's personal situation and her use, in the *Miroir de l'âme pécheresse*, of the sister-brother relationship as an analogy for that of the soul and God. Unlike the other paradigms invoked (those of wife, mother, and daughter), the figure of the sinful sister is not a commonplace of devotional writing. It is equally tempting to relate the prominence of the brother-sister couple in the *Heptaméron* to the well-attested centrality in Marguerite's own life of her relationship with her brother François I. See Susan Snyder, "Guilty Sisters: Marguerite de Navarre, Elizabeth of England, and the *Miroir de l'âme pécheresse*," *Renaissance Quarterly* 50 (1997): 443–58.

[19] Eve Kosofsky Sedgwick, *Between Men: English Literature and Male Homosocial Desire* (New York: Columbia University Press, 1985), 7.

[20] Sedgwick, *Between Men*, 25.

has acted dutifully, defending the honor of his sister and freeing his city from tyranny; "les autres" tax him with ingratitude towards his benefactor. While the emergence of a diversity of opinions is wholly in keeping with the *Heptaméron*'s much discussed plurivocality, it is less common for this diversity to be signaled explicitly by the frame narrator. It is quickly revealed, moreover, that the opinions are not so much diverse, as clearly and deeply divided, split along the lines of gender: "les ungs" are in fact "les dames," for whom Lorenzo is both a "bon frere et vertueux citoyen"; "les autres" are "les hommes," for whom he is a "traistre et meschant serviteur" (95).

Yet the ideological and hermeneutic split, which here fractures explicitly along the fault line of gender, is discernible implicitly within the narrative of the *nouvelle* itself. Fontaine notes the change in tone and point of view that occurs after the murder of the duke.[21] Before that moment, as Francis Bright has argued, the *focalisateur* in the *nouvelle* is Lorenzo; subsequently, the narrative perspective shifts, being identified less and less with the point of view of the murderer.[22] The first sign of this shift comes through the voice of Lorenzo's servant, who, having helped his master to carry out the assassination, subsequently chides him for his desire to kill five or six more of the duke's associates. The narrator next tells us that Lorenzo follows his servant's advice to flee as a result of his bad conscience, which renders him cowardly: "le gentil homme, la mauvaise conscience duquel le rendoit crainctif, creut son serviteur . . ." (93). The culmination of this shift in focalization is marked by the discovery of the duke's body, for once slain, it is the duke, not Lorenzo, who elicits the sympathy of the narrator. When the duke fails to appear as usual in the morning, "la pauvre duchesse" and "les pauvres serviteurs" become increasingly anxious, until, discovering the murder, they come upon "le pauvre corps, endormy, en son lict, du dormir sans fin" (94). Bright has argued that the female listener identifies initially with both Lorenzo and his sister. After the murder, this identification shifts more firmly to the sister, without, however, being wholly withdrawn from Lorenzo. In this way, the *devisantes* of the frame, like the sister in the *nouvelle*, can identify in part with the murderer, voice approval for his actions, yet avoid sharing his guilt. Lorenzo's aristocratic male body thus provides a cover to a pre-emptive

---

[21] Fontaine, "Les Enjeux," 143.

[22] I am grateful to Francis T. Bright for providing me with a copy of his unpublished paper, "Phantasm and (Women's) Storytelling in *Heptaméron* 12," a preliminary version of which was read at the conference *Les Femmes Ecrivains sous l'Ancien Régime: Tentatives d'émancipation*, St. Louis, April 1995. Professor Bright's ideas, which coincided with my own on a number of points, have helped the development of my thought considerably.

response to rape that could not have been praised openly, had it been performed by a woman.[23]

As the split in the narrative perspective within the *nouvelle* anticipates the hermeneutic split between the male and female *devisants* in the ensuing discussion, it necessarily has the effect of incorporating into the narrative the viewpoint expressed later in the discussion by the men. While the women *devisants* express no reservations in their support for Lorenzo, the frame narrator (the *je* of the opening lines of the *Heptaméron*?), in a rare expression of judgment, does offer some support for the men's point of view, glossing the women's approval of the duke's murder as follows: "Mais les dames, selon leur coustume, parloient autant par passion que par raison" (95). It is at least possible to suggest, then, that this hesitation between "female" and "male" viewpoints may well reflect something of the attitude of the author, revealing her own ambivalent implication in patriarchal power structures, not to mention her deeply held religious beliefs.[24]

Such reservations notwithstanding, *Heptaméron* 12 constitutes a powerful example of the consequences of (men) privileging family ties over the homosocial bonds of patriarchy. It is, in effect, to these bonds that the duke appeals when he assures Lorenzo, "si j'avois femme, mere ou fille qui peust servir à saulver vostre vie, je les y emploirois . . . et j'estime que l'amour que vous me portez est reciprocque à la mienne; et que si moy, qui suys vostre maistre, vous portois telle affection, que pour le moins ne la sçauriez porter moindre" (90). As feminist scholars have shown, "traffic in women" is one of the principal mechanisms of patriarchy, enabling both the domination of women by men and the forming of hierarchical bonds of interdependence between men.[25] *Nouvelle* 12 does not so much eschew

---

[23] Bright, "Phantasm." On the question of rape in the *Heptaméron* in general, see Patricia Francis Cholakian, *Rape and Writing in the* Heptaméron *of Marguerite de Navarre* (Carbondale and Edwardsville: Southern Illinois University Press, 1991).

[24] The contradictory position of the aristocratic mother within patriarchy, evinced particularly in the contracting of marriages, has been explored in relation to Marguerite de Navarre by Carla Freccero. See "Marguerite de Navarre and the Politics of Maternal Sovereignty," *Cosmos* 7 (*Women and Sovereignty*, ed. Louise Olga Fradenburg) (1992): 132–49; eadem, "Margaret of Navarre," in *A New History of French Literature*, ed. Denis Hollier (Cambridge, MA and London: Harvard University Press, 1989), 145–48; and eadem, "Patriarchy and the Maternal Text."

[25] Gayle Rubin, "The Traffic in Women: Notes on the 'Political Economy' of Sex," in *Toward an Anthropology of Women*, ed. Rayna R. Reiter (New York: Monthly Review Press, 1975), 157–210. Also see, notably, Heidi Hartmann, "The Unhappy Marriage of Marxism and Feminism: Towards a More Progressive Union," in *Women*

political considerations then; rather it redefines them, recasting them essentially in terms of power and gender. These are issues that other versions of the story ignore.

As is often the case in the *Heptaméron*, questions of gender and power are explored here initially through the inversion of gender roles. A particularly revealing comparison can be made between *nouvelle* 12 and *nouvelle* 4. The latter tale relates the attempted rape of the sister of a powerful prince by a "gentil homme." Successfully parrying the attack, the woman sends her assailant bleeding back to his own room to reflect on his folly in front of a mirror. In the triangle of characters in tale 4, the powerful brother remains a shadow in the background of the drama, with the "gentil homme" directing his violence against the woman. In *nouvelle* 12, it is the desired sister who remains in the background as the story is played out between the two men: the murder of one man by another thus replaces the attempted rape of the woman. As Bright has again argued, the duke in *nouvelle* 12 initially plays the role of seducer; he addresses his words of seduction to Lorenzo, however, not to Lorenzo's sister. To Lorenzo are directed the discourse on friendship, the declaration of the secret, the blandishments, the threats, the tears. Finding himself in a situation similar to that of many female characters, Lorenzo is thus compelled to respond to male desire while seeking to preserve personal and familial honor. Like much of the traditional courtly rhetoric of seduction, the duke's discourse involves a play of dependence and submission, a pretense that the other exercises the power to give life or inflict death: "Parquoy, je vous declaireray un secret, dont le taire me met en l'estat que vous voyez, duquel je n'espere amandement que par la mort ou par le service que vous me pouvez faire" (90). Lest Lorenzo forget the real distribution of power, however, the duke reminds him that if anyone must lose his life in the affair, it is Lorenzo: "Si vous aymez ma vie, aussi feray-je la vostre" (91).[26]

The *devisants*' discussion also highlights the degree to which Lorenzo's dilemma resembles that so often encountered by women. When Dagoucin

---

and Revolution: A Discussion of the Unhappy Marriage of Marxism and Feminism, ed. Lydia Sargent (Boston: South End Press, 1981), 1–41 (esp. 14–15); Luce Irigaray, *Ce sexe qui n'en est pas un* (Paris: Editions de Minuit, 1977), 167–69, and eadem, "When the Goods Get Together," in *New French Feminisms*, ed. Elaine Marks and Isabelle de Courtivron (Amherst: University of Massachusetts Press, 1980), 107–10.

[26] The fiction of the lover's subjection to the beloved is discussed openly at several points in the *Heptaméron*. At the end of the first day, for example, Saffredent quotes the proverb: "De bien servir et loyal estre, / De serviteur l'on devient maistre" (84).

sees what a heated disagreement his story has provoked, he attempts to shift the terms of the debate: "Pour Dieu, mes dames, ne prenez poinct querelle d'une chose desja passée; mais gardez que voz beaultez ne facent poinct faire de plus cruels meurdres que celluy que j'ay compté" (95). If Dagoucin is trying to smooth over the division between the men and the women, he fails singularly however, since he only serves to underscore the gender differences on which it rests. As is so often the case in the *Heptaméron*, the binary that appears opposes a feminine code of "honneur" and "vertu" to a masculine code of "plaisir": "Vous vouldriez doncques, dist Parlamente, pour saulver la vie d'un qui dict nous aymer, que nous meissions nostre honneur et nostre conscience en dangier?" (95). Parlamente's words recall strikingly the description of Lorenzo in the *nouvelle*, torn between "sa seur et l'honneur de sa maison" and "le plaisir du duc" (91). The women sympathize with the murderer then, not only because he defends his sister, but because he substitutes for her, taking her place. Acting not as a woman but as a man, however, Lorenzo successfully turns the tables on the duke, who in his turn is compelled to play the part of the woman.

The extent to which the duke's murder mirrors and inverts the rape plot of *nouvelle* 4 is underscored by a series of parallels between the two tales. Like the would-be seducer in tale 4, the duke spends considerable time dressing for the encounter, and both men don their best perfumed shirts and bonnets (29, 92). Instead of entering the woman's chamber, however, the duke is led by Lorenzo into a bedroom; he is then undressed and put to bed, where, with the curtains coyly drawn, he waits. The process of feminization, which we see beginning here, is complete when Lorenzo returns, brandishing "une espée *toute* nue . . . de laquelle il frappa le duc qui estoit *tout* en chemise" (92–93, my italics). The sexual tension spills over here in the first redundant, over-excited "*toute*," describing the naked sword as if it were a woman. The adverb has the paradoxical effect of re-concretizing the metaphor ("nue") by introducing an idea of degree which might have meaning only in a literal sense referring to a person. This is the case with the later expression "*tout* en chemise," which, describing what the duke is wearing, has the effect of underlining the degree of his un-dress. The redundant "toute" thus draws attention to the substitution of the phallic sword for the expected woman, again underscoring the inversion that makes the murder look like a rape.[27] Now, like the princess in *nouvelle* 4

---

[27] The substitution of the sword for the woman is prepared by Lorenzo's earlier highly ambiguous statement to the duke: "Mon seigneur, je vous vois querir celle qui n'entrera pas en ceste chambre sans rougir; mais j'espere que, avant le

(but without her success), the duke defends himself by biting and scratching his assailant (30, 93).

A second peculiarity of *Heptaméron* 12, however, concerns its description of the relationship between the two men, Lorenzo and the duke, and particularly its emphasis on the closeness of their initial friendship.[28] The reader is introduced to Lorenzo as "un gentil homme que le duc aymoit comme luy-mesme, et auquel il donnoit tant d'autorité en sa maison, que sa parolle estoit obeye et craincte comme celle du duc. Et n'y avoit secret en son cueur qu'il ne luy declarast, en sorte que l'on le pouvoit nommer le second luy-mesmes" (90). While the vocabulary of perfect friendship may be viewed as an expression of the idiolect of the narrator Dagoucin,[29] its effect is to establish a particular dynamic between the two men. Their relationship represents an intense and reciprocal emotional engagement, a communion which minimizes differences between them. The question of friendships between rulers and subjects was a thorny one, however, precisely because of the distinctions the former must maintain between themselves and the latter in order to preserve their authority.[30] Although Aristotle had maintained that such friendships were not in theory impossible, provided the ruler were not a tyrant (that is, that he looked to the interests of his subjects before his own), many Renaissance writers,

---

matin, elle sera asseurée de vous" (92). On the motif of the sword in the *Heptaméron*, with particular reference to *nouvelle* 12, see Michel Bideaux, "Figures, thèmes, motifs et configurations: Propositions pour une sémantique narrative de l'*Heptaméron*," in *La Nouvelle: Définitions, transformations*, ed. Bernard Alluin and François Suard, Collection UL3 (Lille: Presses Universitaires de Lille, 1991), 73–88. Bideaux's survey leads him to conclude: "Le rôle thématique de l'épée est le plus souvent frappé d'une valorisation négative.... Ce qui se trouve par là mis en question, c'est (sous bénéfice d'inventaire) un réseau de valeurs viriles et guerrières" (80).

[28] For example, Varchi notes merely that Lorenzo was favored by the duke over his second cousin Cosimo (*Storia fiorentina*, 227); Paradin states that the two were enemies (*Histoire*, 329); cf. n. 8 above.

[29] *Nouvelle* 47, recounted by Dagoucin, also concerns a close friendship between two men, which is disturbed by the introduction of a woman. More generally, a number of Dagoucin's stories deal with neo-Platonic or sublimated relationships, reflecting the narrator's views on love. See most notably *nouvelle* 9 and the preceding discussion (47–54).

[30] For the most recent and comprehensive study of the subject of early modern friendship, see Ullrich Langer, *Perfect Friendship: Studies in Literature and Moral Philosophy from Boccaccio to Corneille* (Geneva: Droz, 1994).

most notably perhaps Machiavelli, warned of their pitfalls.³¹ The French political theorist Jean Bodin also advised rulers to avoid close friendships, by which their authority was necessarily compromised. In *Les Six Livres de la republique*, Bodin writes:

> les droits royaux sont incessibles, inalienables, et qui ne peuvent par aucun traict de temps estre prescrits; et s'il advient au Prince souverain de les communiquer au subject, il fera de son serviteur son compagnon: en quoy faisant, il ne sera plus souverain, car souverain (c'est à dire, celuy qui est par dessus tous les subjects) ne pourra convenir à celuy qui a faict de son subject son compagnon. . . . Aussi pouvons nous dire que le Prince . . . ne peut faire un subject egal à luy, que sa puissance ne soit aneantie.³²

The lack of distinction between the duke and Lorenzo in *Heptaméron* 12 is clearly detrimental to the former's authority. Were the duke's officers not in the habit of obeying Lorenzo's orders as if they were those of their prince, Lorenzo would have been unable to flee the city after committing the murder (cf. 93–94).

Demonstrations of reciprocity in friendship were often expressed through the metaphor of a combat, with each man seeking to prove his love "stronger" than that of the other.³³ Asking Lorenzo for his help, the duke seems to invoke this idea of friendship rivalry: "et j'estime que . . . si moy, qui suys vostre maistre, vous portois telle affection, que pour le moins ne la sçauriez porter moindre" (90). The problem is that the duke justifies his expectation that Lorenzo will rival him in affection by alluding to the real power inequality that exists between them. His invitation thus turns into a threat, initiating an inimical rivalry, of which the only possible resolution is that one man will come to dominate the other.

In relation to the duke's "seduction" of Lorenzo, we noted that the duke's play of submission resembles that often adopted by men and addressed to women. In the context of the "friendship" relationship also, the duke now initiates a fiction of submission, as he comes to his courtier seeking his "favor."³⁴ As with men's seduction of women, however, the

---

[31] Cf., for example, chapter 17 of *Il Principe*, on whether it is better for the prince to be loved or feared.

[32] Jean Bodin, *Les Six Livres de la republique* (Paris: Jacques du Puys, 1580), 215.

[33] See Langer, *Perfect Friendship*, 214.

[34] Within the context of friendship theory, it is possible to consider the "favor"

invocation of this fictional dependence cannot operate outside the social power structures in place; it necessarily serves, therefore, to underscore the real inequality between the two men. Apart from the duke's veiled threat against Lorenzo's life, quoted already, the vocabulary of domination and subjection plays in tense counterpoint to the expressions of perfect friendship. The whole exchange is fraught, as the two men vie with each other, the one affirming "suys vostre maistre," the other acknowledging "je suis vostre creature" (90–91).

While they differ concerning the motivation of the murder, the versions of Lorenzo's story display a high degree of conformity with regard to the details of the killing itself. A number of these recur frequently, making the scene read almost like a set piece. Repeatedly we are told of the long struggle in which the two men were locked in such physical intimacy that Lorenzo's servant had difficulty intervening, and of Duke Alessandro biting his assailant's thumb. As Fontaine has suggested, however, these details serve different functions in Marguerite's *nouvelle* from those they have in the chronicles; more precisely, they take on particular significance by pointing to earlier moments in the *nouvelle*, or, more generally, to common literary motifs. In other accounts they are sometimes given a logical explanation, or else they simply take their place in a narrative sequence, having little reference to anything beyond their immediate context.

It is the description of the closeness of the men's initial friendship, for example, that gives particular resonance to the later description of the murder, for, at the moment when they lock in physical combat, they are again so united as to become indistinguishable. As the duke defends himself against Lorenzo's attack, the latter calls his own servant-accomplice to help him, "lequel, trouvant le duc et son maistre si liez ensemble qu'il ne sçavoit lequel choisir, les tira tous deux par les piedz, au millieu de la place" (93). The image of the wrestling men thus recalls and inverts the image of perfect friendship at the precise moment when the two men must be differentiated: the one must rise to the top, the other must succumb. We discussed above the shift in narrative perspective following the duke's murder that is signaled initially by the words of Lorenzo's servant, named in other accounts as Scoronconcolo. It is also the introduction of Scoronconcolo before the murder that marks Lorenzo's passage from bottom to top, since in the eyes of the former, Lorenzo, not the duke, is "maistre." Lorenzo's subjection of the duke requires as guarantee the

---

the duke requests a kind of perverse *beneficium* ("the service or favor one performs for a friend": Langer, *Perfect Friendship*, 102).

presence of Lorenzo's own subordinate. Only a little perversity is needed to read a grammatical ambiguity into the account of Scoronconcolo's entry into the fray (just whose master is it that he sees?): "lequel, trouvant le duc et *son* maistre si liez ensemble . . ." (my italics).

Of all the details of the murder, however, without doubt the most striking (the most singular, as well as the most often repeated and commented upon) is Alessandro's biting of Lorenzo's thumb. The historical veracity of the episode is well attested;[35] however, whereas in several historical accounts (e.g. Varchi and Cardano) it is given a logical, pragmatic motivation (Lorenzo puts his hand over the duke's mouth in order to prevent him from crying out), *nouvelle* 12 omits any such explanation, presenting the duke's action instead as a sign of his complete defenselessness: "Et, voiant qu'il n'avoit autres armes que les dentz et les ongles, mordit le gentil homme au poulce" (93). Such a presentation—particularly given the introduction of "les ongles," found only in the *nouvelle*—clearly invites the reader to draw the analogy, as we did earlier, between the duke's situation and that of a female victim of sexual aggression (as in tale 4). The gesture also takes on particular significance in *Heptaméron* 12, however, since it recalls an earlier moment when the duke bit his own finger. As Fontaine remarks: "La littérature de fiction est là, dans cette conscience de la répétition formelle des détails, choisis expressément ici pour fausser le sens de l'histoire."[36] The duke's earlier biting of his own finger had occurred at the end of his "seduction" of Lorenzo, when the latter revealed his hesitation in acquiescing to the duke's demand that he procure his sister for him: "le duc, tout enflambé d'un courroux importable, mint le doigt à ses dentz, se mordant l'ungle, et luy respondit par une grande fureur: «Or bien, puisque je ne treuve en vous nulle amityé, je sçay que j'ay à faire»" (91). At this point the duke bit his finger precisely to remind Lorenzo of his subordinate status, and that he would lose his life if he refused to bend to his master's pleasure.[37] This

---

[35] See Rally, "Commentaire," 217, n. 2.

[36] Fontaine, "Les Enjeux," 139.

[37] According to Giuseppe di Stefano, to bite one's fingers was normally a sign of grief: *Dictionnaire des locutions en moyen français* (Montréal: Editions CERES, 1991), 266. A more usual sign of anger was to bite one's thumb, hence Randle Cotgrave gives "Mordre les poulces. To bite his thumbes for anger": *A Dictionarie of the French and English Tongues* (Amsterdam: Theatrum Orbis Terrarum; New York: Da Capo Press, 1971), s.v. "Poulce." It is most likely that the gesture described here is that associated with swearing an oath. Again according to Di Stefano, "Toucher, hurter son doit au dent" signifies "affirmer avec geste de serment" (*Dictionnaire*, 266). In any case, the duke's fury is evident, as is his solemn intention to exact retribution.

narrative repetition, linking as it does the two moments when the duke first threatens Lorenzo and when the latter responds with force, invites us to examine further the duke's biting of Lorenzo's thumb, not only as a sign of the duke's feminization, but also in the context of male rivalry and its literary depiction.

Rivalries between men of different social status and age directed through women are central to the plots of many courtly romances. While more commonly the desire of a younger, less powerful knight or *juvenis* is directed toward the wife of his lord or *senior*, there are also examples of the reverse, as in "Equitan," one of the *lais* of Marie de France. In any case, homosocial desire is reciprocal in the courtly triangle: the lord's need of the knight, equal to the knight's need of his lord, ensures their rivalrous bonding. In a number of the best-known French romances, the sexual consummation of the relationship between the knight and his lord's wife is accompanied by a flow of the knight's blood: in Chrétien de Troyes's *Chevalier de la charrete*, Lancelot cuts his finger in prizing open the bars of Guenièvre's window; in Béroul's *Roman de Tristan*, the hero opens a wound in his thigh as he jumps into Yseut's bed.[38] I have argued elsewhere that it is possible to understand this inversion of sexual roles as symbolic of the knight's initiation. At the moment he sleeps with his lord's wife, the knight undergoes a symbolic wounding, a gesture, like adolescent circumcision, ambivalent in gender associations, which marks his desired passage from *juvenis* to *senior*, from boy to man.[39] The specific associations of the thumb, moreover, lend themselves particularly well to such symbolism, for as Montaigne tells us in his essay *Des pouces*, the ancients associated the thumb with virility: etymologically, *pollex* (thumb) was said to derive from *pollere* (to be powerful). The thumb guaranteed the hand's ability to manipulate the instruments of manly power: arms, the oar, the male member; its amputation, inflicted on one's enemy or on oneself, functioning as a kind of castration, rendered the victim incapable of military exercise. In this light, it is possible to understand the practice of Spartan schoolmasters,

---

[38] Chrétien de Troyes, *Le Chevalier de la charrete*, ed. Mario Roques (Paris: Champion, 1983), 141–45; Béroul, *Le Roman de Tristan*, ed. Ernest Muret, 4th ed. rev. L. M. Defourques (Paris: Champion, 1982), 23–24.

[39] Gary Ferguson, "Symbolic Sexual Inversion and the Construction of Courtly Manhood in Two French Romances," *The Arthurian Yearbook* 3 (1993): 203–13. I have also argued that other stories in the *Heptaméron* rewrite motifs from the medieval romance, undermining as they do so the courtly tradition: idem, "Pedestrian Chivalry: Novella 50 and the Unsaddling of Courtly Tradition in the *Heptaméron*," in *Heroic Virtue, Comic Infidelity: Reassessing Marguerite de Navarre's* Heptaméron, ed. Dora E. Polachek (Amherst: Hestia Press, 1993), 118–31.

who, in order to chastise their charges, would bite their thumbs.[40] As Lorenzo strives to pierce his master's body with his sword, his thumb penetrates the latter's mouth, simultaneously risking and affirming his manhood. The scene of the duke's biting of his servant's thumb thus functions iconically as a sign of the intimate rivalry between the two males and signals the moment at which the younger and less powerful challenges and symbolically accedes to the status of the older and more powerful.[41]

A striking difference, however, between the triangle of protagonists in the courtly romance and that in *Heptaméron* 12 is the virtual absence, in the latter, of the woman. Despite her role as object of the duke's desire and motivator of her brother's actions, Lorenzo's sister plays no active part in the *nouvelle*. She is never more than a shadowy character, remaining wholly ignorant of events until they are past. In conclusion, we learn that she approves of the murder, and that she subsequently marries, thus avoiding the poverty to which the confiscation of the family's wealth would have exposed her. But she survives the story precisely because she has played no active part in it. The *nouvelle*'s final sentence splits her in two; thus she lives a doubly virtuous life, remaining essentially a thing of repute: "Et continua de plus en plus sa vie honneste en ses vertuz, tellement que . . . trouverent sa seur et elle des mariz autant honnestes hommes et riches qu'il y en eust poinct en Itallie; et ont toujours depuis vescu en grande et bonne reputation" (94).[42] Since, then, the sexually charged rivalry is played out almost exclusively between the two men, their conflict may be illuminated by reference not only to the structures of homosociality but also to those of contemporary homosexuality.

As with their heterosexual counterparts, homosexual sexual relations appear, in the Renaissance, to have been determined by patriarchal power

---

[40] Michel de Montaigne, *Essais*, 2. 26, in idem, *Œuvres complètes*, ed. Albert Thibaudet and Maurice Rat, Bibliothèque de la Pléiade (Paris: Gallimard, 1962), 670–71. I am grateful to Marian Rothstein for drawing my attention to this essay.

[41] In reality Lorenzo was younger than his cousin by only four years, Alessandro having being born in 1510, Lorenzo in 1514 (cf. Rally, "Commentaire," 210–11). He was, however, the eldest member of the "junior" branch of the family, excluded from power until the death of Alessandro (cf. Bromfield, *De Lorenzino*, 15–17). Age, in any case, is only one consideration in the power dynamic we are describing. Many of Henri III's *mignons* were barely younger than the king himself.

[42] Lorenzo's younger sister Maddalena also fled to France with her brother. The double marriage between the two sisters, Maddalena and Laudomia, and the two Strozzi brothers, Robert and Pierre, took place in 1539. Cf. Rally, "Commentaire," 220, nn. 2, 3, and 4.

structures. As Alan Bray expresses it: "What determined the shared and recurring features of homosexual relationships was the prevailing distribution of power, economic power and social power, not the fact of homosexuality itself."[43] Renaissance Europeans seem to have largely represented sexual roles in terms of activity and passivity, of domination and submission: to penetrate the other and "to take" one's pleasure, was to be on top; to allow oneself to be penetrated, "to give" pleasure, was to be on the bottom. From medical treatises to scurrilous anecdotes, the need to observe proper coital positions was a commonplace of Renaissance discourse on heterosexual sex; indeed, failure to do so might have a variety of potentially serious consequences. Some maintained, for example, that a woman mounting a man might result in the conception of a hermaphrodite—the unmanning of the man being made manifest in the offspring.[44] The larger social and hierarchical structures, to which these sexual positions stood in synecdochical relationship, are made particularly clear by the seigneur de Brantôme: the person on the bottom in sex is "abattue," "subjuguée," "foulée," "sousmise," "suppedit(ée)."[45] Having told of one woman who refused systematically to submit to convention in this respect, Brantôme comments with a mixture of admiration and horror:

> Voilà une terrible et plaisante humeur de femme, et bizarre scrupule de conscience genereuse. Si avoit-elle raison pourtant; car c'est une fascheuse souffrance que d'estre subjugée, ployée, foulée, et mesmes quand l'on pense quelquefois à part soy, et qu'on dit: «Un tel m'a mis sous luy et foulé», par maniere de dire, sinon aux pieds, mais autrement: cela vaut autant à dire.[46]

In homosexual relations, the person on top was also a man, the one on the bottom, a boy. Commenting on the fact that the myth most frequently used to figure homosexual desire was that of Ganymede, Bruce Smith writes: "The scenario of 'one above' taking his pleasure of a 'boy' reflects the mores of medieval Europe and early modern England no less than the

---

[43] Alan Bray, *Homosexuality in Renaissance England* (London: Gay Men's Press, 1982), 56; see also 45–56 in general.

[44] Cf. Jean Liébault, *Thresor des remedes secrets pour les maladies des femmes* (Paris: Jacques du Puys, 1585), quoted in Guy Poirier, *L'Homosexualité dans l'imaginaire de la Renaissance*, Confluences-Champion 7 (Paris: Champion, 1996), 63.

[45] Pierre de Bourdeilles, seigneur de Brantôme, *Les Dames galantes*, ed. P. Pia (Paris: Gallimard, 1981), 72–75.

[46] Brantôme, *Les Dames galantes*, ed. Pia, 73.

mores of ancient Greece and Rome. . . . That is to say, Renaissance Englishmen, like the ancient Greeks and Romans, eroticized the power distinctions that set one male above another in their society. Sexual desire took shape in the persons of master and minion; sexual energy found release in the power play between them."[47]

As for other Western European countries in the Renaissance, evidence relating to France suggests something of an ambivalence in attitudes towards sodomy. Strict legal sanctions, for example, seem in practice to have been relatively rarely imposed.[48] Again, on the one hand, sodomy was associated with the overturning of the natural and social orders, with treason and the overthrow of the state.[49] On the other hand, a certain tacit tolerance of sodomitical relationships seems also to have existed, within certain circumstances. It appears, for example, that servants may often have been expected to help satisfy their masters' sexual desires, either by submitting themselves or by procuring others to do so.[50] In support of his argument that the "passive" partner often acts under compulsion and therefore deserves more lenient treatment than the "active" sodomite, the jurist Jean de Coras (1515?–1572) invokes Seneca: "Et l'impudicité, dit Seneque defendant le libertin, deferé et accusé pource qu'il avoit esté le mignon du patron, est crime au noble et de franche condition, nécessité au

---

[47] Bruce R. Smith, *Homosexual Desire in Shakespeare's England: A Cultural Poetics* (Chicago and London: University of Chicago Press, 1991), 193–94; cf. also 189–223 in general. On the myth of Ganymede, see also James M. Saslow, *Ganymede in the Renaissance: Homosexuality in Art and Society* (New Haven and London: Yale University Press, 1986), 155–60.

[48] On France, see David F. Greenberg, *The Construction of Homosexuality* (Chicago and London: University of Chicago Press, 1988), 314–23, and Poirier, *L'Homosexualité*, 45–59; on England, see Bray, *Homosexuality*, 50–53, 70–76; on Florence, see Michael Rocke, *Forbidden Friendships: Homosexuality and Male Culture in Renaissance Florence* (New York and Oxford: Oxford University Press, 1996), 22–25, 32, 68, 76, and elsewhere.

[49] Cf. Poirier, *L'Homosexualité*, 153–61. In England, sodomy was frequently associated with popery. Cf. Alan Bray, "Homosexuality and the Signs of Male Friendship in Elizabethan England," in *Queering the Renaissance*, ed. Jonathan Goldberg (Durham and London: Duke University Press, 1994), 40–61, here 41–42, and idem, *Homosexuality*, 19–26. In France, both parties in the religious conflict branded their opponents sodomites.

[50] See Robert Oresko, "Homosexuality and the Court Elites of Early Modern France: Some Problems, Some Suggestions, and an Example," in *The Pursuit of Sodomy: Male Homosexuality in Renaissance and Enlightenment Europe*, ed. Kent Gerard and Gert Hekma (New York and London: Harrington Park/Haworth Press, 1988) (published simultaneously as a special issue of the *Journal of Homosexuality* 16, nos. 1 and 2), 105–28, esp. 117 and 127, n. 41.

cerf, et office au libertin et affranchy."[51] Ruler and courtier, nobleman and page, teacher and pupil, artist/craftsman and apprentice, ship's mate and cabin boy were so many power relationships within which the sexual might find expression.

It is in this light, perhaps, that we best understand the Renaissance taste for women cross-dressing as boys. A female transvestite must not look like a man, however, or she would excite derision rather than desire. Brantôme describes as follows a style of dress adopted by Marguerite de Valois:

> il n'est bien seant qu'une femme se garçonne pour se faire monstrer plus belle, si ce n'est pour se gentiment adoniser d'un beau bonnet avec la plume à la guelfe ou gibeline attachée . . . ; mais pourtant à toutes il ne sied pas bien; il faut en avoir le visage poupin et fait exprés, ainsi que l'on a veu à nostre reine de Navarre, qui s'en accommodoit si bien qu'à voir le visage seulement adonisé, on n'eust sceu juger de quel sexe elle tranchoit, ou d'un beau jeune enfant, ou d'une tres-belle dame qu'elle estoit.[52]

---

[51] *Resolutions de droict etc.* (Paris: Jean Houzé, 1610), 303 (Jacques Baron's translation of Coras's *Memorabilium Senatus Consultorum Summae etc.*). Citing the above passage, Guy Poirier comments: "nous ne pouvons que nous poser la question à savoir s'il [l'auteur] croyait vraiment qu'un tel raisonnement cynique quant à l'impudicité pouvait véritablement être le reflet des structures sociales de son époque. La nécessité attribuée au serf de faire acte d'impudicité, par exemple, pourrait laisser entendre bien des choses à propos des relations entre nobles et serviteurs, ou du moins de ce qu'on pouvait en penser": *L'Homosexualité*, 50–51. The source is Seneca, *De Beneficiis*, 3. 18–28.

[52] Brantôme, *Les Dames galantes*, ed. Pia, 295. Cf. Ronsard's famous sonnet for Cassandre, "Soit que son or se crespe lentement":

> Quel plaisir est-ce, ainçois quelle merveille,
> Quand ses cheveux troussez dessus l'oreille,
> D'une Venus imitent la façon?
>
> Quand d'un bonnet sa teste elle Adonise,
> Et qu'on ne sçait s'elle est fille ou garçon,
> Tant sa beauté en tous deux se desguise?

(Pierre de Ronsard, *Œuvres complètes*, ed. Jean Céard, Daniel Ménager, and Michel Simonin, 2 vols., Bibliothèque de la Pléiade [Paris: Gallimard, 1993–1994], 1:72.)

This description may be compared with that given by Pierre de L'Estoile of Henri III's *mignons*:

> Ces beaux Mignons portoient leurs cheveux longuets, frisés et refrisés par artifice, remontans par dessus leurs petits bonnets de velours, comme font les putains du bordeau.[53]

While male transvestism seems to have been tolerated to some extent within certain festive contexts,[54] the infraction of Henri's *mignons* is to render masculine dress "effeminate." This, for L'Estoile and many of his contemporaries, can only be construed in terms of moral degeneracy. The comparison with prostitutes is doubly revealing, since it suggests a willingness to provide sexual services to men, and to do so in return for financial or social gain. The effect of the *mignons*' dress is not simply to equate them with women, however; rather, as the comparison with Marguerite's "Adonized" dress reveals, in rendering them less clearly virile, it makes them more boyishly ambiguous.[55] In Renaissance England, it was customary for female characters to be played on stage by boys. Examining this practice, Stephen Orgel makes a number of observations regarding the respective social positions of boys and women, and the areas of overlap and differentiation between them. Orgel notes that "boys were, like women—but unlike men—acknowledged objects of sexual attraction for men," concluding that "the homosexual, and particularly the pederastic, component of the Elizabethan erotic imagination is both explicit and for the most part surprisingly unproblematic." At the same time, he cautions: "That the analogy between boys and women was naturalized does not imply that boys are substitutes for women; it implies just the opposite: both

---

[53] Pierre de L'Estoile, *Registre-Journal du règne de Henri III*, ed. Madeleine Lazard and Gilbert Schrenck, vol. 2 (1576–1578) (Geneva: Droz, 1996), 42. Unless indicated otherwise, subsequent references will be to this edition.

[54] Henri III's cross-dressing is discussed extensively by Gilbert Robin, *L'Enigme sexuelle d'Henri III (Etude psycho-sexuelle du trans-sexualisme)* (Paris: Wesmael-Charlier, 1964), esp. 116 ff. As Robin points out, however, the king was not alone in engaging in transvestitism. Cf. also Pierre Chevallier, *Henri III, roi shakespearien* (Paris: Fayard, 1985), 357–58.

[55] Such an impression can only have been reinforced by the momentary fashion, launched by the king, of carrying a "bilboquet," a child's toy. Cf. L'Estoile, August 1585 *(Journal de L'Estoile pour le règne de Henri III (1574–1589)*, ed. Louis-Raymond Lefèvre [Paris: Gallimard, 1943], 388).

are treated as a medium of exchange within the patriarchal structure, and both are (perhaps in consequence) constructed as objects of erotic attraction for adult men."[56] Moreover, in the hierarchically organized society of the Renaissance, most men were "boys," were feminized, in relation to someone.[57]

In his study of the policing of sodomy in Renaissance Florence, Michael Rocke also demonstrates convincingly the extent to which the practice of sodomy in this city was profoundly implicated in wider homosocial structures: "sodomy was inextricably enmeshed in broader forms of male association and sociability in this community, from youth-group camaraderie to neighborhood ties, from occupational solidarities to patron-client relations, from kinship bonds to networks of friends. In the intensely homosocial world of Florence, *l'amore masculino* . . . was one of the threads that helped to create and reinforce bonds between males and to fashion the texture of their collective life."[58] The city in which *Heptaméron* 12 is set was, in fact, widely reputed in the Renaissance to be a city particularly tolerant of sodomy—a policy seemingly associated at times with the Medici family's courting of political support.[59] While detailing a number of important exceptions to dominant codes of sexual behavior, Rocke again emphasizes the prevalence of the pederastic model of sodomitical relations.[60] Particularly suggestive for our reading of *nouvelle* 12 is Rocke's contention that "the highly structured form of these relations helped to distinguish boyhood from manhood and to mark out the transition from the one to the other."[61] Refusal of a "passive" sexual role and adoption of

---

[56] Stephen Orgel, *Impersonations: The Performance of Gender in Shakespeare's England* (Cambridge: Cambridge University Press, 1996), 70, 103; cf. also, in general, the end of chap. 3 and chaps. 4 and 5.

[57] Orgel, *Impersonations*, 124.

[58] Rocke, *Forbidden Friendships*, 149; see also in general chap. 5 (148–91).

[59] Rocke, *Forbidden Friendships*, 42–43, 65, 195–204, 223, 228–35.

[60] Rocke describes a variety of cases which involve, for example, older men taking the passive role or sexual partners (normally adolescents) playing both. While ultimately these exceptions can be seen as serving to reinforce dominant codes in one way or another, they also deserve to be taken seriously in their own right. Deviances from sexual patterns inherited from antiquity should also not be understated. In Renaissance Florence, there is evidence of fellatio being performed on a younger partner by older men, many of whom remained unmarried (cf. *Forbidden Friendships*, 91–94). While still maintaining a distinction between "active" and "passive" roles, such a practice nevertheless inaugurates other sexual configurations.

[61] Rocke, *Forbidden Friendships*, 88.

an "active" one (whether homo- or heterosexual) marked entry for a male into the world of adult sexuality.

Although Renaissance discourses of sodomy and friendship customarily occupied opposite ends of a spectrum running from execrable to admirable, their relation to each other and to social practice was slippery and complex. The word "mignon," for example, originally designated a "passive" homosexual, a meaning that, by the early sixteenth century, had disappeared, giving way to hetero- or non-sexual meanings.[62] Nevertheless, the revival of the word's earlier sense later in the century, and particularly in relation to Henri III and his *mignons*, might suggest that it had always remained latent, never quite having been forgotten.[63] The *mignon*-favorite and the *mignon*-catamite might thus be less disparate figures than might at first appear.

Similarly, "friendship" was a term often used to describe patronage relationships, that, despite the idealized nature of friendship discourse, were contracted neither between equals nor in a spirit of disinterest. "Friendships" representing a pragmatic compromise, and based on a courtier's hope for gain in the form of his master's favors, seem to have been widespread in Renaissance courts.[64] In this important respect, at least, relations between a client and his patron were not dissimilar from those between a boy and a sodomite. Rocke notes that Florentine pederastic relationships, including those maintained over long periods, almost invariably involved the older "active" partner rewarding the younger "passive" one with money or gifts in kind, or exerting influence on the latter's behalf and perhaps even that of his family.[65] Similar conditions prevailed in Elizabethan England, where, as Alan Bray has shown, the outward signs of mutually beneficial friendships—physical and emotional intimacy and the giving and receiving of favors—could also be read, under certain circumstances, as evidence of a sodomitical relationship. This was the case particularly if the subordinate partner was of low birth and his

---

[62] Cf. Poirier, *L'Homosexualité*, 132–33; and *Dictionnaire historique de la langue française* (Paris: Dictionnaires Le Robert, 1992), s.v.

[63] In 1610, Baron renders Coras's "in Cynaedis" as "ès bougerons et mignons" and "patroni Cynaedus" as "le mignon du patron": *Resolutions de droict*, 302–3; cf. *Memorabilium Senatus Consultorum Summae* (Lyons: B. Vincentius, 1599), 251–52.

[64] Cf. Langer, *Perfect Friendship*, 199–221. In "De l'amitié," Montaigne also distinguishes common social (mutually beneficial) friendships from perfect friendship (*Essais*, 1. 28).

[65] Rocke, *Forbidden Friendships*, 165–68.

"friendship" was perceived to have a *primarily* mercenary motivation.[66] These were the very objections raised against Henri III's *mignons*. More than by their dress, accusations of sodomitical behavior appear to have been fed by the *mignons'* relatively low birth (lesser provincial nobility) and the seemingly endless stream of gifts lavished upon them by the king. What triggers the accusations is the meteoric rise of these "boys" to positions of power, from where they lord it over members of the traditionally influential noble families.[67]

The fiction of the disinterested nature of mutually beneficial friendships and the play of some kind of equality and reciprocity between two parties of noble but unequal birth were so important, then, because they served to distinguish a patron-client relationship from a sodomitical one. In *Heptaméron* 12, Lorenzo is known as the duke's friend, but the duke is also his master and benefactor. While Lorenzo is not of low birth, he clearly occupies the slippery terrain of "amy"-"serviteur"-"creature." In undermining the appearance of their equality and of the free and disinterested nature of their relationship, in

---

[66] "If someone had acquired a place in society to which he was not entitled by nature and could then perhaps even lord it over those who were naturally his betters, the specter likely to be conjured up in the mind of an Elizabethan was not the orderly relationship of friendship between men but rather the profoundly disturbing image of the sodomite, that enemy not only of nature but of the order of society and the proper kinds and divisions within it." Bray relates this development to "the sixteenth-century decline in the hordes of retainers in the great houses of an earlier and different England and the conventions of personal service associated with them. . . . As a social form the personal service of early Tudor England was in decay by the end of the sixteenth century, but as a cultural form it was not": "Homosexuality," 51–53.

[67] The prodigality of the king and his *mignons* is one of the major themes of the satirical verse recorded by L'Estoile (*Registre-Journal*, 43–49, 182–87). The spectacular career of the *archimignon* Epernon provoked satirical comparisons with that of Gaveston, the favorite of the English king, Edward II. As Poirier remarks: "c'est effectivement la préférence accordée à des favoris au détriment de la noblesse en place qui demeure la clef du rapprochement" (*L'Homosexualité*, 154). Cf. also Smith's analysis of Marlowe's treatment of this relationship in his *Edward II* (*Homosexual Desire*, 209–23). Modern historians tend to emphasize the political function of the "système des mignons," which helped the king to hold in check the competing ambitions and interests of the great noble families. See Arlette Jouanna, "Faveur et favoris: L'Exemple des mignons de Henri III," in *Henri III et son temps: Actes du colloque international du Centre de la Renaissance de Tours, octobre 1989*, ed. Robert Sauzet (Paris: Vrin, 1992), 155–65; see also Chevallier, *Henri III*, 16–17, 365, and, most recently, the vast study of Nicolas Le Roux, *La Faveur du roi: Mignons et courtisans au temps des derniers Valois (vers 1547–vers 1589)* (Seyssel: Champ Vallon, 2001).

demanding that Lorenzo become a provider of sexual pleasure or an object of violence, the duke would insist that his cousin become his boy, his friend become his minion.[68]

The story of Lorenzo's murder of Duke Alessandro was told by the chroniclers largely or exclusively in terms of political ideology, that is, the desire to overthrow a tyrant and to restore to the city of Florence its former republican privileges. As we have seen, *Heptaméron* 12 alludes to this political framework through the binary of traitor/citizen. But by linking this to and privileging the concomitant binary of servant/brother, Marguerite's *nouvelle* focuses on the relationships of personal engagement which, in any patriarchal society, whether more or less hierarchically or equitably organized, men make between themselves through their use of women. Contemporary political theorists like Bodin, and even the proverbially pragmatic Machiavelli, warned rulers of the importance of respecting their subjects' material goods and their women.[69] The reason is clear: these are the currency of patriarchy. If Lorenzo's decision to defend his sister overturns homosocial patriarchal bonds, these bonds had already been stretched to their limits when the duke spoke openly to Lorenzo of his desire to sleep with the latter's sister, and demanded his servant's explicit compliance. This demand ruptures not only the working fictions of "friendship," but also those of the courtly triangle whose functioning was dependent upon tacit complicity, not explicit compliance. The convention of secrecy, the fiction of silence, protected not only the lady and her lover, but also the two rival men, allowing their mutual needs and desires to remain in the shadows. Only a text parodying the courtly tradition would

---

[68] Whatever the historical reality of the relationship between Lorenzo and Alessandro, it was represented variously by contemporaries. Varchi portrays Lorenzo as the duke's procurer; he also stresses Lorenzo's own debauchery with both women and men (*Storia fiorentina*, 225–27). Basing his history in part on Varchi, Gauthiez claims that, after a youthful passion for Francesco de' Medici, Lorenzo became the minion of Pope Clement VII at age 16 (the Pope was 52). Of Alessandro and his relationship with Lorenzo, Gauthiez writes: "S'il voulut de Lorenzino pour mignon, il l'eut sans doute; mais on ne trouve pas les traces d'une influence pareille" (*Lorenzaccio*, 99; cf. also 59, 63–71). Despite his other failings, modern historians do not generally impute sexual impropriety to Clement VII. Cf. Eamon Duffy, *Saints and Sinners: A History of the Popes* (New Haven: Yale University Press, 1997), 157; *The Oxford Dictionary of the Christian Church*, 2nd edition, ed. F. L. Cross and E. A. Livingstone (Oxford: Oxford University Press, 1974), 301; Herbert M. Vaughan, *The Medici Popes (Leo X and Clement VII)* (London: Methuen, 1908).

[69] Bodin, *Six Livres*, 15; Machiavelli, *Il Principe*, chaps. 17 and 19.

flout this convention utterly, as do a number of the branches of the *Roman de Renart*, in which the rivalry between Ysengrin, the "wronged husband," and Renart, the "lover"/"rapist," is pursued openly. It is not insignificant for my argument that this conflict comes to a head in a scene of single combat, in the course of which the cuckolded Ysengrin bites Renart's finger:

> ses doit en la boche dedanz
> li chiet, et cil le prant as denz,
> la char li tranche jusqu'a l'ous.[70]

In *Heptaméron* 12, rivalrous homosocial desire is foregrounded as a direct result of the strategy, unique to Marguerite's telling, whereby Lorenzo's sister is a principal motivator of the action, but a minor actor— necessary to the economy of desire, but marginal to the acting out of desire. As Bright has argued, the fact that Lorenzo stands in for his sister enables women to identify with him in part, and, from a safe distance, to approve a pre-emptive vengeance for rape. That distance is afforded principally by an aristocratic male body that supplies a cover to the act of revenge. This same strategy, however, also has the effect of turning the spotlight on the relationship between the two male protagonists. Rendering the sister inaccessible to the duke and distancing her from the action means that, this time, the men must play out by themselves the old patriarchal plot of mediated desires and rivalries. Indeed, when the duke sets about "seducing" his servant at the beginning of the *nouvelle*, it is not so much, perhaps, that Lorenzo is standing in for his sister, but that, *this time*, a woman is *not* standing in for a man. The duke's subsequent murder looks like a rape, not only because it substitutes for the intended rape of the murderer's sister, but also because a minion refuses to succumb, and a master finds himself "foulé," "suppedité," "subjugué," "abattu." In *nouvelle* 12, Marguerite de Navarre thus takes a doubtful and contested history and casts it in terms of the *Heptaméron*'s own narrative interests and structuring preoccupations. The result is her own "true story"—a "veritable histoire"[71]—which exposes

---

[70] *Le Roman de Renart*, ed. Mario Roques, 6 vols. (Paris: Champion, 1955–1966), 3:92; Cangé, branch 8, vv. 8549–8551. While Renart and Ysengrin are both married and established each in his own domain, they are named, respectively, after human prototypes who are said to be (like Tristan and King Marc) nephew and uncle (2:19; Cangé, branch 3, vv. 3829–3856).

[71] *L'Heptaméron*, 9. André Tournon has also examined the different kinds of "truth" at work in Marguerite's text: "Conte véritable, véritable conte," in *Conteurs et romanciers de la Renaissance: Mélanges offerts à Gabriel-André Pérouse*, ed. James Dauphiné and Béatrice Périgot, Colloques, congrès et conférences sur la Renaissance 7 (Paris:

the latent violence of male homosocial relations, and lets those relations play out without the cover of a female aristocratic body.

Champion, 1997), 379–93. Tournon notes that when they take up the aborted project of the French court to imitate Boccaccio's *Decameron* while telling only true stories, the *devisants* establish a process of testimony as mediation between the real and their own *nouvelles*: "Leur engagement . . . interpose entre le réel et les récits qu'il cautionne l'équivalent d'une procédure quasi-testimoniale, en vertu de laquelle la véracité du témoin oculaire (qui a «vu») ou le crédit reconnu à un garant («homme digne de foi») seraient les voies prescrites pour l'accès à la vérité" (380). Tournon subsequently analyzes how the complex play of factual truth, truthful testimony, and literary truthfulness is foregrounded and explored in the opening *nouvelle*.

Fictions of the Eyewitness

John O'Brien

The circumstances of Marguerite de Navarre's first *nouvelle* will be familiar to all readers of the *Heptaméron*, not least because of the attention it has received from Natalie Zemon Davis.[1] At the climax of the tale, Saint-Aignan employs Gallery the sorcerer to make five wooden images of his allies and enemies. Gallery says that wax images must next be made of Saint-Aignan's enemies, foremost among whom is his wife, "cause de tout son mal."[2] Unfortunately for his plans, Saint-Aignan's wife is a witness to his conversation with Gallery: "ung matin elle l'espia et veid que le dict Gallery luy monstroit cinq ymaiges de boys" (16). A subsequent reference is more explicit still: "sa femme . . . voyoit tout par le pertuis de la porte" (17). The end of the affair comes speedily with the husband and his accomplice consigned to the galleys while "la mauvaise femme, en l'absence de son mary, continua son peché plus que jamais et mourut miserablement" (17).

The keyhole is commonly associated in the Renaissance with illicit knowledge, the domain of the voyeur or the spy (cf. "espia" here).[3] In the present context, it not only serves as one more marker to designate the "méchanceté" of the woman, but also does so in particularly gendered terms, for the errant wife is the subject of a male narrative from which she is by definition excluded: any knowledge that she has is marked *ipso facto* as

---

[1] Natalie Zemon Davis, *Fiction in the Archives: Pardon Tales and their Tellers in Sixteenth-Century France* (Stanford: Stanford University Press, 1987), 58–59; and eadem, "1526, July: Life-Saving Stories," in *A New History of French Literature*, ed. Denis Hollier (Cambridge, MA: Harvard University Press, 1994), 139–45.

[2] Marguerite de Navarre, *L'Heptaméron*, ed. Michel François (Paris: Garnier, 1960), 17. Subsequent references, incorporated into the text, are likewise to this edition.

[3] The major example is Jean de Léry, *Histoire d'un voyage faict en la terre du Bresil*, ed. Frank Lestringant (Paris: Livre de poche, 1994), 399–401 for the episode of the "pertuis" among the Tupi; and cf. Michel de Certeau, *L'Écriture de l'histoire* (Paris: Gallimard, 1975), 215–48, esp. 239–40 for the incident concerned.

illegal, so making epistemology a sphere to which she has no automatic right and gains access only by happenstance. The woman thus appears as an epiphenomenon in male plots (variously understood), an accessory to male power. What she overhears is a scheme to destroy her, which she successfully prevents by adopting a male mode of power display; she does not try to rewrite the plot entirely on her own terms but to wrest power control from male hands and turn the tables on her male opponents. And in this she is very nearly successful.

While this episode in *L'Heptaméron* is in some senses an emblematic moment, the deterministic model it presents of gender relations—an enduring problem of power-based interpretations—gives an insufficiently nuanced account of the pressures and resistances composing the pattern of relationships in early modern France. One particular field that may serve as a test case is widowhood. Studies of widows and their status in early modern society point out the unease that their presence inspired.[4] Ruth Kelso emphasizes that "widowhood . . . in the general opinion constituted practically a kind of rebirth."[5] She adds: "The woman, standing out free from the governance of a husband, from anybody's governance, and therefore freer than before marriage when she was under the control of her father or guardian, has a choice to make for herself. Shall she, or shall she not remarry? Her whole future way of life depends on her answer."[6] The absence of the paternal signifier occasioned by the death of a husband thus left a cavernous void which early modern authorities were at pains to fill by actively encouraging the remarriage of young widows and limiting the legal rights of elderly widows; the latter nevertheless came to be a presence of increasing importance in a community ravaged by the civil wars of the latter part of the sixteenth century. Widows thus occupied by default a distinct social position. They might also exercise economic power, or contribute to the economic output, as when women printers carried on their dead hus-

---

[4] Merry E. Wiesner, *Women and Gender in Early Modern Europe*, 2nd ed. (Cambridge: Cambridge University Press, 2000), 89–93, esp. 90–91: "[Widows] were still very disturbing to notions of male authority, however, both because they were economically independent and because they were sexually experienced women not under the tutelage of a man"; cf. Barbara Diefendorf, "Widowhood and Remarriage in Sixteenth-Century Paris," *Journal of Family History* 7 (1982): 379–95.

[5] Ruth Kelso, *Doctrine for the Lady of the Renaissance* (Urbana and Chicago: University of Illinois Press, 1958), 121. The same point is made by Constance Jordan, *Renaissance Feminism: Literary Texts and Political Models* (Ithaca and London: Cornell University Press, 1990), 71, quoting St Jerome's *Ad Eustochium* in a discussion of Trissino's *Epistola . . . de la vita che dee tenere una donna vedova* (1524).

[6] Kelso, *Doctrine*, 121.

bands' activities, so ensuring the survival of a business and supplying deficiencies in the workforce.⁷ It may be argued all the same that while such early modern women had power (the ability to shape events, often behind the scenes), they did not exercise authority (the ability to hold hierarchically dominant positions).

A pervasive fear nevertheless subsisted about the widow's sexual availability, uncontrolled by the "legitimate" authority and appetites of the husband. Brantôme puts the matter with his usual candor:

> L'amour des vefves est bon, aisé et profitable, d'autant qu'elles sont en leur plaine liberté, et nullement esclaves des peres, meres, freres, parens et marys, et ny d'aucune justice, qui plus est; et a-on beau faire l'amour à une vefve et coucher avec elle, on n'en est point puny, comme l'on est des filles et des femmes.⁸

In this light, it is unsurprising to find conduct books for widows dealing with the issue of chastity as their primary concern. The whole problem attracted the attention of writers from Savonarola and Erasmus to Cabei and Trotto.⁹ Their general trend is to align chastity with other virtues, of a distinctively religious nature, as the pattern for widows' behavior. Thus in effect, although the husband is absent, the paternal signifier has itself not disappeared, but has been reasserted in dominantly religious mode as a renewed source of containment and regulation. The widow occupies an uneasy position in Renaissance society, as an excuse for male sexual license, and as the object of moralizing claustration. Few writers in the conduct-book tradition suggest that widowhood may be an opportunity for the

---

⁷ See Roméo Arbour, *Les Femmes et les métiers du livre (1600–1650)* (Chicago: Garamond Press, 1997), especially 29–50; Wiesner, *Women*, 126, 130–31; Jordan, *Renaissance Feminism*, 71.

⁸ Pierre de Bourdeilles, seigneur de Brantôme, *Recueil des dames*, ed. E. Vaucheret (Paris: Gallimard, 1991), 493. For further equivocations about widows, see, for example, Guillaume Bouchet, *Les Serees* (Lyons: Rigaud, 1614), Livre premier, "Cinquiesme seree," 193–200.

⁹ Kelso, *Doctrine*, 122–23, summarizing Savonarola, *Della vita viduale* (c. 1495); Erasmus, *Vidua Christiana* (1529); Cabei, *Ornamenti della gentil donna vedova* (1574); Trotto, *Dialoghi del matrimonio e vita vedovile* (1578). On the last of these, see Jordan, *Renaissance Feminism*, 154–57. For Book 3 of Juan Luis Vives's *Education of a Christian Woman*, entitled *On Widows*, see *De Institutione Feminae Christianae*, ed. C. Fantazzi and C. Matheeussen, trans. C. Fantazzi, vol. 2 (Leiden: Brill, 1998), 199–241; and *The Education of a Christian Woman*, trans. C. Fantazzi (Chicago: University of Chicago Press, 2000), 297–326.

widow to develop her own talents; Kelso in fact cites only one, Horatio Fusco.[10] Against this background of cultural stereotyping, it is important to examine other data that allow alternative, less settled perspectives to emerge. As our initial example from Marguerite de Navarre indicates, the *nouvelle* holds a potential for focusing on and examining this stereotype, a potential largely absent from "official" narratives; such at least will be one of the hypotheses of this essay.

Of the range of evidence afforded by the *Heptaméron*, *nouvelle* 4 offers an important reflection on the whole issue of widows and their social and sexual status. The widow who in this case has outlived two husbands now lives with her brother, "fort grand seigneur, et mary d'une fille de Roy" (28). The widow is "la plus joyeuse et meilleure compaigne qu'il estoit possible, toutesfois saige et femme de bien," characteristics that will be activated in the course of the tale. As for the gentleman who shows an interest in her, his "grandeur, beaulté et bonne grace passoit celle de tous ses compaignons" (28), an iconic indication of his social standing and appropriateness. As often in the *Heptaméron*, the narrative complication is precipitated by a promise, a pact between the characters, inasmuch as the gentleman is allowed intimate friendship with the widow provided he does not proceed further. At this point he breaks his promise:

> non qu'il entreprint de se hazarder par parolles, car il avoit trop, contre son gré, experimenté les saiges responces qu'elle [la veuve] sçavoit faire. Mais il se pensa que, s'il la povoit trouver en lieu à son advantaige, elle qui estoit vefve, jeune, et en bon poinct, et de fort bonne complexion, prandroit peult-estre pitié de luy et d'elle ensemble. (29)

The gentleman does not wish to hazard himself in words, but to embark on a more dangerous course by which he takes advantage of his privileged access to the lady's person in order to force his attentions on her. As in *nouvelle* 10, the attempted rape has the effect of polarizing the gender positions and, narrativally, of precipitating the action to its next crucial stage. The turning point is symbolized in concrete form. Before he approaches the lady's bedroom, he dresses to seduce:

> Et, quant il eut prins la plus gorgiase et mieulx parfumée de toutes ses chemises, et ung bonnet de nuict tant bien

---

[10] Kelso, *Doctrine*, 127; Fusco, *La vedova di Fusco* (1570).

accoustré qu'il n'y failloit rien, luy sembla bien, en soy mirant, qu'il n'y avoit dame en ce monde qui sceut refuser sa beaulté et bonne grace. (29)

This moment of self-regarding narcissism, in which he attributes supreme beauty to himself rather than his hoped-for lover, has its parallel when the gentleman returns to his bedchamber after his failed rape:

> Il trouva son mirouer et sa chandelle sur sa table; et, regardant son visaige tout sanglant d'esgratineures et morsures qu'elle luy avoit faictes, dont le sang sailloit sur sa belle chemise, qui estoit plus sanglante que dorée, commença à dire: «Beaulté! tu as maintenant loyer de ton merite, car, par ta vaine promesse, j'ay entrepris une chose impossible, et qui peut-estre, en lieu d'augmenter mon contentement, est redoublement de mon malheur, estant asseuré que, si elle sçaict que, contre la promesse que je luy ay faicte, j'ay entreprins ceste follie, je perderay l'honneste et commune frequentation que j'ay plus que nul autre avecq elle; ce que ma gloire a bien deservy.» (30)

The scratches and bites that deform the gentleman's face recall the self-mutilation which Floride undergoes in *nouvelle* 10 or, from another perspective, the chalk marks that are left on Jambicque's clothes in *nouvelle* 43.

The reversal that takes place here is of great significance. Frequently, marks are left on the female body as a sign of male aggression, as a token of male sexual power. In the present *nouvelle*, the fierce resistance that the widow puts up leaves its traces on the male body, traces which will be "tesmoing(s) de (s)a chasteté" (31), at the same time that they are marks of recognition by which the gentleman's hidden passion is made known. The scratches are thus part of the narrative turning point between concealment and discovery that are in turn tied in with their physical counterparts, dark and light, night and day.[11] The gentleman's soliloquy, part of which has already been quoted, represents his coming to terms with the criteria of honor from which he has departed. There are two references in his speech to his broken promise—the symbol of his dishonor—along with his "visaige si deschiré" (31), both tokens of the way he has expelled himself

---

[11] On the prevalence of this imagery here and in other tales, see Marcel Tetel, *Marguerite de Navarre's* Heptaméron: *Themes, Language, and Structure* (Durham, NC: Duke University Press, 1973), 96, 101.

from his caste and denied his identity, which depends on a specific code of conduct appropriate to his place in the social hierarchy.

While the gentleman laments that he "debvoi(t), par long service et humble patience, actendre que amour en fut victorieux" (31), it is the widow who is aware that she has been in control of the physical situation ("la dame . . . estoit demorée victorieuse" [31]). The question that now preoccupies the lady is control of representation—control of how the physical situation is narrated. The lady herself invokes those abbreviated narratives, the hieroglyphs etched on the gentleman's face in the form of "marques." Against the lady's insistence that the gentleman must pay with his life as a "tesmoing" to her chastity—so relying on her brother to preserve decorum through the exercise of hierarchical power—the lady-in-waiting hatches a scheme by which storylines can be turned to female advantage, and representations made to convey a woman's point of view. Such a representation should not, the lady-in-waiting urges, reveal "la verité du faict" (31); concealment is a preferable device, inasmuch as it counterpoints the gentleman's own concealment, yet also deploys a strategy widely used by both sexes throughout the *Heptaméron*.[12] The course of action, the lady-in-waiting argues, should be inactivity: "Si vous desirez estre vengée de luy, laissez faire à l'amour et à la honte, qui le sçauront mieulx tormenter que vous" (31). In order to point up the contrast, the *dame d'honneur* sketches out the "normal" situation by which a lady might defend her honor, and she does so in ways that envisage the very differing narratives that might be made of her mistress's position. Thus the mistress might make complaint (*la plaincte*) about the gentleman, but "courra le bruict partout qu'il aura faict de vous à sa volunté; et la plus part diront qu'il a esté bien difficille que ung gentil homme ayt faict une telle entreprinse, si la dame ne luy en donne grande occasion" (32). The consequence then follows: "Et vostre honneur, qui jusques icy vous a faict aller la teste levée, sera mis en dispute en tous les lieux là où cette histoire sera racomptée" (32). The astuteness of the lady-in-waiting lies not just in suggesting—in a typical piece of *Heptaméron* strategy—the social necessity of concealment in order to preserve reputation, but also in foreseeing how far reputation depends on the narratives that can be made of it. She accordingly advocates a twofold feigning: a social deception, and a skilful manipulation of narrative and counter-narrative so as to maintain social rank and the appearance of public virtue. Reputation depends on (a) fiction.

---

[12] On which, see Gisèle Mathieu-Castellani, *La Conversation conteuse: Les Nouvelles de Marguerite de Navarre* (Paris: Presses Universitaires de France, 1992), 231–42 ("Des voiles et des masques").

Or else on God. In her second speech, the *dame d'honneur* advises the widow to thank God for her victory and for the "honnesteté" and "vertu" he has given her: "et, congnoissant que tout bien vient de luy, vous l'aymiez et serviez mieulx que vous n'avez accoustumé" (33). The piety that the speech embodies is entirely consistent with the morality of conduct books for widows, but sits uncomfortably with the duplicities of the lady-in-waiting's previous speech—duplicities that are present once more in the terms *faire semblant* and *faindre* which must, she urges, define her mistress's future attitude towards what has happened to her. The stark contrast between the divine and the profane throws into particularly sharp relief the tensions that underpin this *nouvelle*. They are reconfigured in the subsequent pages in forms that can be echoed elsewhere in the *Heptaméron*: disfigurement as in *nouvelle* 10, silence as in *nouvelle* 21, concealment as in *nouvelle* 70, all these being set alongside the widow's joy at the strategies she has marshaled. These ideas are brought together after the gentleman's withdrawal from and subsequent return to court:

> Quant il fut retourné devers luy, et qu'il se retrouva devant sa victorieuse ennemye, ce ne fut sans rougir; et luy, qui estoit le plus audacieux de toute la compaignye, fut si estonné, que souvent devant elle perdoit toute contenance. (33)

This passage epitomizes all the reversals that the *dénouement* enacts. The scars on the gentleman's countenance lead to his refusal to be seen and his subsequent loss of face when he is in the lady's presence. Similarly, the gentleman's physical concealment following the scratches he receives leads directly on to the concealment of his love. The play of literal and figurative wounds, as well as literal and figurative concealment, stands under the general sign of a conflict between the sexes in which the widow is victorious.

The special power of *nouvelle* 4 is not just that it draws together and focuses in one exemplary moment strands found elsewhere in Marguerite's work, but that it does so in a way that invites comparison with the gender and hierarchical situation of Jambicque in *nouvelle* 43.[13] The parallels between the two stories are striking. Both the widow and Jambicque occupy positions of influence in a hierarchically stratified household to which they are related by blood or friendship. Both entertain a lover in private. Both

---

[13] On this tale, see Hope Glidden, "Gender, Essence, and the Feminine (*Heptaméron* 43)," in *Critical Tales: New Studies of the* Heptameron *and Early Modern Culture*, ed. John D. Lyons and Mary B. McKinley (Philadelphia: University of Pennsylvania Press, 1993), 25–40.

vanquish the lover who has declared his passion. The similarities are not, however, followed through into the moral judgments passed by the *devisants* on the protagonists of the embedded narratives. Jambicque is condemned for preferring the glory of the world to her conscience, for covering "sa malice du double manteau d'honneur et de gloire, et se faire devant Dieu et les hommes aultre qu'elle n'estoit" (301). By contrast, the widow in *nouvelle* 4 is praised by the storyteller Ennasuite for her "vertu" and for the "bon sens" of her lady-in-waiting. One does not, of course, have to agree with the *devisants*, especially as the story of Jambicque is interpreted by Parlamente in contradistinction to that "autre fondement" that defines women in terms of "doulceur, patience et chasteté" (301). Indeed, one might contend that both narratives are about rank and the ways in which power is maintained, exercised, and extended by women who are the beneficiaries of hierarchy. *Nouvelle* 4 is, from that standpoint, less specifically about widows than about the ways in which narratives of authority and control are constructed. The destructive narrative of rumors that the lady-in-waiting foresees is successfully countered by the strategies that are put in place to preserve social position—strategies that build into a story of how to take charge of narrative. There is no real sense that this *nouvelle* is specially gender-inflected to serve the needs of widows or even women as a larger category. The important question here seems to be one of class and rank to which a particular conduct is deemed appropriate. The women in *nouvelle* 4, like Jambicque in *nouvelle* 43, are less subversive of power than in collusion with it; and collusion here means marshaling the resources of established authority so as to preserve status.

It is not just the moral position of the woman that varies, but also her role and function. Both the widow and Jambicque constantly cross and recross the divide between conformity and transgression. They are manipulators of power, not directly, but by the construction of plots implicating other characters (in these cases, the two gentlemen) in a scheme of things that reverse those characters' expectations of outcome. The *devisants'* comments suggest that the success of these female plots, although apparently similar, may in fact be regarded as opposites. The widow has been foolish but is anxious to retain her good name, whereas Jambicque has been hypocritical and is anxious to retain her social position. Neither the widow nor Jambicque loses her autonomy, yet it is how each handles the moral code of behavior that will determine how she will be regarded by the interpretive community of the *devisants*.

Nouvelle 16, told by Geburon at the behest of the young widow Longarine, shows a more decided gender orientation. The female protagonist is the widow of an Italian count who lives with her brother-in-law, never wishing to hear about remarriage. She is initially defined by those stereotypes of seemly conduct straight out of conduct books: ". . . se conduisoit si saigement et sainctement, qu'il n'y avoit en la duché Françoys ny Italien qui n'en feist grande estime" (129); "les François . . . feirent grande estime de sa beaulté et de sa bonne grace" (129). The tale itself follows the usual pattern of display and concealment, with the suitor "ostant son masque" while the lady remains in "crespe noir" (129); their meeting in church further masks illegitimate passion under acceptable social activity. Yet the elegant codes suddenly venture onto more dangerous territory. The church, space of the religion of love where gentleman meets lady, prefigures that other space of the lady's house which the gentleman resolves to penetrate, with encouragement from the lady as a reward in the face of "plusieurs refus, peynes, tormentz et desespoirs" (131). The vocabulary accordingly turns to the lexis of danger. Its implications are not just sexual, but also social. The gentleman must defend his life and the widow's honor; he must act not just "saigement" but like a gentleman, and display the valor associated with his class and his caste. In the event, his prowess is unnecessary. The scene turns to comic bathos, as the approaching enemies are revealed to be chambermaids rattling swords at their mistress's command in order to test the gentleman. The latter uncovers the subterfuge, strips off the mask of things, which then, after the satisfaction of *his* desire (132), leads to the lady's explanation. She reiterates the promptings of honor, which she links to widowhood, as at the beginning of the tale. The image of the wounded deer, also used at the outset, likewise recurs:

> Mais, ainsy comme la bische navrée à mort cuyde, en changeant de lieu, changer le mal qu'elle porte avecq soy, ainsi m'en allois-je d'eglise en eglise, cuydant fuyr celluy que je portois en mon cueur, duquel a esté la preuve de la parfaicte amityé qui a faict accorder l'honneur avecq l'amour. (132)

Placed at the conclusion of the tale, this passage epitomizes all the widow's attitudes and values. If the gentleman's own desire can be explicitly named earlier on the page, the widow's cannot, or at least it is not. She maintains, by contrast, the vocabulary of decorum, perceptible in phrases such as "parfaicte amityé" and by her description of her lover as "ung parfait homme de bien," defined by "plus de beaulté, de grace, de vertu et de hardiesse que l'on ne m'en avoit dict" (132). The widow, indeed, ends with the determination to commit her honor to the gentleman, since she finds in him "son pareil en toutes vertuz" (132). This reassertion of prudence is no doubt crucial in the depiction of the social status of the widow—of what is publicly permissible to a person of her rank and class.

Behind and beyond this description lies the image of the wounded hind. In combination with the churches that the widow attends, it underlines the twin "religions" to which she subscribes. Yet it is more than an elegantly reapplied topos from the love tradition.[14] By its overt foregrounding of woundedness, it hints at the widow's underlying pain and dilemma, her uncertainty of finding the love and the trust that would be the satisfaction of her desire. That is, the image of the hind suggests a "personal" reflection by the widow on her status. She is keenly aware that the terms appointed for her by her class are not necessarily those endorsed by human beings in the throes of passion. Hence the necessity of the test she imposes on her lover. Hence also the cynical reflections with which Geburon closes the embedded narrative he has just told:

> Et, comme si la volunté de l'homme estoit immuable, se jurerent et promirent ce qui n'estoit en leur puissance: c'est une amityé perpetuelle, qui ne peult naistre ne demorer au cueur de l'homme; et celles seulles le sçavent, qui ont experimenté combien durent telles oppinions! (132–33)

The summary of the tale informs us that the widow and the knight swear eternal love to each other (129). Geburon's comments actually say the opposite. And as if to underscore the importance of the hunting metaphor and the image of the hind, Geburon takes up the idea at the very beginning of the discussion:

> Et pour ce, mes dames, si vous estes saiges, vous garderez de nous, comme le cerf, s'il avoit entendement, feroit de son chasseur. Car nostre gloire, nostre felicité et nostre contentement, c'est de vous veoir prises et de vous oster ce qui vous est plus cher que la vie. (133)

The metaphor is sustained throughout the first part of the dialogue, which develops into larger points about male behavior. The status and nature of the widow's desire are forgotten, while the image of the wounded hind is reappropriated for the different purpose of bantering exchange between the

---

[14] On this tradition (the source of which is ultimately *Aeneid* 4. 68–73), and its extension into emblems, see Daniel Russell, "Some Ways of Structuring Character in the *Heptaméron*," in *Critical Tales*, ed. Lyons and McKinley, 203–17, here 212.

devisants. Even so, it remains, in its original context, a striking instance of the way a woman handles literary conventions in order to write, however briefly, her own history. Whatever its subsequent use in this *nouvelle*, the image provides an essential glimpse through the keyhole into a moment of a woman's story in all its uncertainty, contingency, and vulnerability.

Just how wavering and changeable this story can be is seen in *nouvelle* 20. It essentially reverses the situation of *nouvelle* 16.[15] In this revised version—as it might be, an inverted sequel to the previous tale—the sieur de Riant, in love with a widow, "croyoit fermement ce qu'elle luy juroit souvent: c'est qu'elle l'aymoit plus que tous les hommes du monde, et que, si elle estoit contraincte de faire quelque chose pour ung gentil homme, ce seroit pour luy seullement, comme le plus parfaict qu'elle avoit jamais congneu, et le prioit de se contanter de ceste honneste amityé" (153). The terms resonate with decorum and propriety, in what will prove to be a mocking echo of the words used by the widow in *nouvelle* 16. The detail is accurate even down to the religious overtones: the widow in *nouvelle* 20 returns from Vespers and goes into a bower in her garden "pour parachever son service" (154). As in the previous tale, the enclosed space is the *locus* of the gentleman's desire ("il commença à plus que jamais esperer quelque bonne fortune pour luy" [154]). What takes place within the bower is, however, the opposite of expectation: "Mais il trouva en son entrée, la damoiselle couchée dessus l'herbe entre les bras d'un palefronier de sa maison, aussy laid, ord et infame, que de Riant estoit beau, fort, honneste et aimable" (154). The gentleman's love is immediately extinguished, and after remonstrating with the widow he departs. It is the widow's reaction that claims our attention:

> La pauvre femme ne luy feit autre response, sinon de mectre la main devant son visaige; car, puisqu'elle ne povoit couvrir sa honte, couvrit-elle ses œilz, pour ne veoir celluy qui la voyoit trop clairement, nonobstant sa dissimullation. (154)

The expression of widows' stratagems, which elsewhere can have positive connotations as an expression of self-determination and resourcefulness, here holds negative—specifically morally negative—overtones, as fully

---

[15] On this *nouvelle* as a parodic variation also on the "roman de chevalerie," see Mathieu-Castellani, *La Conversation*, 95.

indicated by the word "dissimullation."[16] The addition of perceptual vocabulary opens up a new dimension of significance, especially as the visual had played such a crucial part in the very first *nouvelle* and provides one of the principal connections between the four tales examined so far. *Nouvelle* 20 is the closest in that respect to *nouvelle* 1, since in both the question of who sees what or whom is polarized into a gender issue, masculine being aligned with the positive (rightful knowledge, moral authority) and female with the negative (curiosity, specular transgression). Indeed, these tales, and their tellers, give the appearance of an essentialized gaze. The widow in *nouvelle* 20 remains trapped within the Other's gaze, as the gaze of sexual longing turns suddenly into the gaze of moral reproval. The male gaze, here, acts as a reminder of the codes of conduct that have been infringed—a reminder to the widow and to the reader that female action cannot take place unrestrictedly but relies on prudent negotiation of social as well as amorous space.

The message of *nouvelle* 20 is then recapitulated, at the start of the discussion, by Saffredent: "ne vous pensez poinct dissimuller à ung homme de bien, et luy faire desplaisir pour votre gloire" (154). The company is not altogether of Saffredent's view. Oisille finds it implausible that a woman of the widow's status would have abandoned a gentleman for a groom (although Hircan disagrees). Simontault discerns a pervasive hypocrisy in such behavior by which women "se font louer par les honnestes hommes" and fulfil their base desires by choosing lovers from those of "vile et orde condition" (155). Simontault's analysis is thus class-based as well as gender-based, and repeats some of the crucial terms from the tale itself. Significantly, it is left to the young widow Longarine to provide the retort:

> — Voylà, dist Longarine, une opinion que j'ay autresfois oy dire aux plus jaloux et soupsonneux hommes, mais c'est painct une chimere; car, combien qu'il soit advenu à quelque pauvre malheureuse, si est-ce chose qui ne se doibt soupsonner en aultre. (155)

Simontault had generalized the particular into the universal; Longarine reverses the paradigm: one notes that in the process Simontault and Saffredent's hypocrite has become simply a "pauvre malheureuse." As the company of *devisants* moves off to hear Vespers, Oisille reproaches Saffredent

---

[16] Cf. Glidden, "Gender," 36, on *nouvelle* 20: "Once again, masking is affirmative of feminine desire but is interpreted otherwise as a sign of shame—the patriarchal culture's way of foreclosing the idea of women's pleasure."

with recounting "une si grande villenye contre les dames" (155). Saffredent's reply is telling and, for our purposes, crucial:

> — Par ma foy, luy respondit Saffredent, combien que mon compte soit veritable, si est-ce que je l'ay oy dire. Mais, quant je vouldroye faire le rapport du cerf à veue d'œil, je vous ferois faire plus de signes de croix, de ce que je sçay des femmes, que l'on n'en faict à sacrer une eglise. (155–56)

"Faire le rapport du cerf à veue d'œil" is the expression of the (here, ironical) eyewitness. For the moment, the expression and the reality remain in the hypothetical conditional mood; Saffredent asserts that his story is true, but he has nevertheless only heard it at second hand. Yet the problem is endemic to a work such as the *Heptaméron*, with its narrative pact based on truth-telling: what happens if the eyewitness is disbelieved? What guarantees will ensure that the witness's testimony is accepted as the truth?

Nouvelle 20 leaves that question in abeyance, and indeed it receives no single unambiguous reply in the *Heptaméron*. One might argue, *a priori*, that truth claims in the *Heptaméron* should be treated with skepticism, subject as they are to distortion by gender hierarchy, ideology, or narrative standpoint. Nonetheless, one of the most salient features of this work is that it asserts repeatedly the imbrication of truth and fiction. On this view, fiction is not extraneous to truth, nor is it related to truth according to the well-worn image of *integumentum* and *medula*. In French Renaissance women's writing, it seems, a fictional dimension is integral to the presentation of truth. One should not assume that such "truth" comes across unmediated, transparent to the gaze. On the contrary, its intensest moments are those of equally intense symbolization. The widow in *nouvelle* 16 who appropriates for herself the image of the hind is a prime instance of such symbolization. It is an image deeply embedded in the male tradition of poetry. By applying it to herself, the widow highlights her own desirability as a love object, her own consciousness of that status, and yet simultaneously the vulnerability to which this condition exposes her. The fact that the image of the wounded hind acts as a leitmotif in the remainder of the tale and the subsequent discussion of it is confirmation of its importance. The wounded hind is but one instance of the way in which we can glimpse, in moments of intensity, compressed instances of female lives; the scene at the keyhole and the widow covering her eyes are no less significant examples of the same phenomenon, and a potent reminder that women's stories will not, unlike the tale of Jambicque, be consistently positive in outcome. In each case, however, the text contains some foregrounded moment of anomaly or unusualness, which may serve as a focus or a climax. That moment calls attention to itself by its sheer oddity in narratives in which widows attempt to imagine a space of being and action beyond (but sometimes within) the normal constraints of hierarchical power. Most importantly of all, it is the narrative itself which is that space; the way it is shaped by—in this case—widows' tales is crucial to its success.

If the intensity or anomalousness of symbolization is a central feature of female narrative, then we need to revise our notions of what an eyewitness account might be in those circumstances.[17] Pierre Matthieu, the historian of Henri IV, offers a critical perspective here, when discussing his own undertaking:

> Ceste Histoire est de choses que l'Historien n'a pas veu, & l'Histoire n'estant de la disposition d'vn tesmoin qui assure pour avoir veu, celui qui parle apres les autres n'est qu'vn faiseur de contes. . . . Quel Historien n'a escrit sur les memoires d'autrui? quel s'est obligé à n'escrire que ce qu'il avoit veu?[18]

The opening sentence implicitly summons up the familiar distinction between the historiographical eyewitness and the secondhand reporter, the "faiseur de contes" in Matthieu's arresting phrase. This distinction is immediately contested: no historian can have seen everything he writes about. The conclusion would seem to be that between the historian and the "faiseur de contes" the distance is not as great as one would imagine. As Matthieu emphasizes, "vn homme seul ne pourra escrire outre la portee de sa veuë."[19] The requirement that the historian should witness the events described and so guarantee and legitimate his own narrative is what Donald Kelley describes as the Thucydidean perspective,[20] according to which *historia* is linked to *opsis*; historical narrative, based on personal witness, unveils the truth through a progressive analysis of causation. It was a perspective

---

[17] On the specific difficulties of witnessing in the *Heptaméron*, see John D. Lyons, *Exemplum: The Rhetoric of Example in Early Modern France and Italy* (Princeton: Princeton University Press, 1989), 81–93, taking its cue from *nouvelle* 1.

[18] Pierre Matthieu, *Histoire de France, & des Choses Memorables aduenues aux Prouinces estrangeres durant sept annees de Paix, du regne du roy Henry IIII. Roy de France & de Nauarre* (Cologny: Porret, 1613), sig. eˇv.

[19] Matthieu, *Histoire de France*, eˇv.

[20] Donald Kelley, *Faces of History: Historical Inquiry from Herodotus to Herder* (New Haven: Yale University Press, 1998), 4.

reinforced by the Ciceronian dictum that truth was the first law of history.[21] The complementary pole is Herodotean, based as it is on storytelling, in both senses of the word: as Kelley points out, Herodotus's reputation is both as the father of history and the father of lies; he continues, "history has always been located in the realm of opinion, between poles of truth and falsehood, certainty and probability, and so it has indeed followed the fortunes of Herodotus."[22] Michel de Certeau makes the connection more uncompromising still: "L'histoire est sans doute notre mythe."[23] These contrasts are played out in Renaissance topoi about historiography, and it is hardly a surprise to find Matthieu reflecting on these notions. Yet his concessions and equivocations are significant. Matthieu is voicing something that is already implicit in women's literature, not by express theoretical pronouncements, but by a discernible practice of using narrative as a vehicle for the expression of women's lives. One might indeed claim that there is in the French Renaissance a women's historiography, written by women, but in "Herodotean" mode; in other words, in a way that exploits the resources of stories, myth, and writing. Hence the paradox—but no more than that— that the *Heptaméron* makes constant claims to truth-telling, while simultaneously highlighting literary forms that mediate that truth. This seeming contradiction highlights the specific gendered nature of the historiography involved. The use of narrative for the purpose of gendered historiography even became a standard medium in this respect, albeit in a variety of forms, as Natalie Zemon Davis has shown in the different narratives she studies in *Women on the Margins*.[24]

Derrida offers the following crisp formulation of our task and our opportunity in the field of witnessing and writing: "Le témoignage substitue le récit à la perception. Il ne peut voir, montrer et parler en même temps, et l'intérêt de l'attestation, comme du testament, tient à cette dissociation."[25] It is an ambitious statement and adumbrates an equally ambitious program. Importantly, in the complex interaction it posits between seeing and telling, French Renaissance women's writing illustrates at least one aspect of the dissociation of which Derrida speaks. For if witnessing and fiction are complementary, not opposite, activities, then the composition of women's history opens the way to invention. The medium of writing, of the story, is

---

[21] Kelley, *Faces of History*, 9.

[22] Kelley, *Faces of History*, 2.

[23] De Certeau, *L'Ecriture*, 29.

[24] Natalie Zemon Davis, *Women on the Margins: Three Seventeenth-Century Lives* (Cambridge, MA: Harvard University Press, 1995).

[25] Jacques Derrida, *Mémoires d'aveugle: L'Autoportrait et autres ruines* (Paris: Editions de la Réunion des musées nationaux, 1990), 106.

the site of possibility, and not just of record, of memory and memorialization. It acts not simply as an archive, but more dynamically as a storehouse replete with narrative choices and potential, ranging from fantasm to the subtle subversion of existing codes. The *nouvelle* looks not towards the past, but towards the future, or a series of futures, not all equally socially or existentially desirable, but all equally narratable.[26] The stakes are correspondingly high: against official records of the same, the female "faiseur de contes" tells stories of difference; against fixed positions in the gender hierarchy, she proposes speculation and *ouverture*; against the male language of sexual stereotyping, she singularizes her own situation. And in so doing, she becomes the (self) witness, witness to the eye and to the "I."

---

[26] Cf. Walter Mignolo speaking of Francesco Patrizi's *Della historia diece dialoghi* (1560): "Patrizi argued that history cannot only be conceived as a narrative of past events [= the Ciceronian model], but . . . of *present and future events*": *The Darker Side of the Renaissance: Literacy, Territoriality, and Colonization* (Ann Arbor: University of Michigan Press, 1995), 166 (author's italics).

Exemplarity as Misogyny: Variations on the Tale of the One-Eyed Cuckold

David LaGuardia

In the ninth *exemplum* of Petrus Alfonsi's *Disciplina clericalis*, a twelfth-century collection of *exempla* that was one of the major Latin sources for the *nouvelle* tradition, a philosopher tells the story of the one-eyed cuckold to his disciple. This anecdote was retold countless times in Europe in a number of different languages and cultural contexts.[1] A man goes to work, leaving his wife at home alone. Far from being idle, the wife invites her lover over in her husband's absence. Meanwhile, the husband is injured in one eye and rushes home. Somehow the wife manages to cover her husband's uninjured eye, and the lover escapes during this moment of blindness. The *Disciplina's exemplum* is framed by several preliminary statements:

> A philosopher said to his son: "Follow a scorpion, a lion, or a snake, but never follow an evil woman." Another philosopher has said: "Pray God that he keep you free from the tricks of good-for-nothing women, and take care never to be led astray." . . . A pupil said once to his teacher: "I have read in the books of the philosophers where the warning is given that a man must beware of the tricks of an evil woman. Solomon too warns against this in his book of Proverbs. If you therefore know of any story or proverb concerning the guile of such a woman, please tell it to me, so that I can learn from it." (119)[2]

---

[1] Petrus Alfonsi, *The Disciplina clericalis*, ed. and trans. Eberhard Hermes and P. R. Quarrie (Berkeley: University of California Press, 1977). All page references are to this edition. Hermes describes the successive variants of the anecdote as follows: "GR [*Gesta Romanorum*], 122; *Cent nouvelles nouvelles*, 16; *Heptaméron*, I, 6; Bandello, I, 23. Ex. IX–XIII were suggested by Vincent of Beauvais, *Speculum Morale*, liber III, pars 9, dist. 5" (184, n. 83).

[2] "Dixit quidam philosophus filio suo: Sequere scorpionem, leonem et draconem, sed malam feminam non sequaris!

Women are vilified in this transmission of "wisdom" from a man of one generation, the philosopher, to a man of another generation, his pupil. Perhaps the passage of wisdom, authority, and power from man to man in this context required that women be debased and devalorized in this story. Moreover, perhaps the transfer of power from male generation to male generation was virtually equivalent to the *telling* and *retelling* of this story of woman as the ultimate evil, which was firmly rooted in the exemplary narrative tradition derived from the Bible, as the pupil remarks.

As in the *Disciplina clericalis*, therefore, male power was disseminated for centuries through the telling of this story and others like it, which propagated and perpetuated misogynistic fantasy images of women and of female sexuality. If the purpose of *exempla* and of exemplary narrative in general is the moral instruction of those who listen to or read such stories, then the moral message of the one-eyed cuckold's tale in the original *exemplum* and its later variants, such as the two tales that I will examine from the *Cent nouvelles nouvelles*, is that men must learn to master a certain kind of knowledge about women and to pass that knowledge on to subsequent generations of men, for the purpose of controlling and dominating women. For hundreds of years, male narrators throughout the exemplary tradition told certain kinds of stories almost compulsively, unconsciously representing their own phobias and fantasies, and constructing a phantasmic identity for the figure of woman that undoubtedly was far removed from the reality of actual women living when these stories were told. In other words, the telling and retelling of exemplary stories about women within a narrative frame subtended the existence of unbalanced and gender-contingent relationships of power, in the most basic sense of the term. Male narrators throughout this tradition told stories in order to influence other men, to seduce them, at least metaphorically, to gain advantages over them, to extract something from them, to control them, or to bond with them, and all for the sake of subjugating women. Often, a male narrator's position in this type of narrative frame, or even his inclusion in a select group of men who served as

---

"Alius philosophus: Ora Deum et te liberet ab ingenio nequam feminarum, et tu ipse ne decipiaris provide tibi. . . .

"Dixit quidam discipulus magistro suo: Legi in libris philosophorum quibus praecipiunt ut ab ingenio feminae perversae custodiat se homo. Et Salomon in proverbiis hoc idem admonet. Sed tu si super ingenio illius sive de fabulis sive de proverbiis aliquid memoriter tenes, vellem renarrando me instrueres": Pedro Alfonso, *Disciplina clericalis*, ed. and trans. Angel Gonzalez Palencia (Madrid: Consejo Superior de Investigaciones Científicas Patronato Menéndez y Pelayo, 1948), 25. Latin quotations in the notes will be from this edition.

narrators, depended upon the types of stories that he was *compelled* to tell, which is the case for the pupil of the *Disciplina clericalis* as well as for the narrators of the *Cent nouvelles nouvelles*.

After centuries of this exemplary male bonding, Marguerite de Navarre produced a version of the one-eyed cuckold's tale, revealing the traps and pitfalls of the exemplary male tradition for both women and men, and proposing an alternate mode of interpreting stories that concerned the moral character of human beings as gendered subjects. Navarre's reframing of this tale was thus a revolutionary act of feminine or even feminist resistance against the male power that had previously dominated the narrative versions of the *exemplum*, as well as a crucial moment in the history of literary interpretation. Like all great writers, Navarre produces a work that is something of a paradox, which continues in the tradition of the *exemplum* at the same time that it performs a subtle yet powerful critique of the gender inequalities that were a constitutive element of the medieval genre. In order to appreciate the magnitude of her achievement, I will examine the original version of this story in the *Disciplina clericalis*, followed by its successive versions in French in the *Cent nouvelles nouvelles*, before addressing Marguerite de Navarre's revision of the tale in the *Heptaméron*.

The desire to communicate a specific kind of knowledge from narrator to narratee in the original *exemplum* from the *Disciplina clericalis* offers us an explicit interpretation of its significance in this context. According to the narrator's affirmations in the frame, the type of woman who cuckolds her husband is to be avoided, since she is closer to animals than to the male standard of the human being, and she is to be feared even more than the ferocious lion, the clever snake, or the scorpion with its quick sting. Far from being positive attributes, the strength, intelligence, and quickness of women are associated here with their desire to betray men. The passage of knowledge from man to man is thus coupled with the fear of women defined by these attributes, whose desires threaten to escape male control. This fear of (female) bodies and of (female) sexuality is also linked to the male dread of being drawn away from the realm of the spiritual and toward the realm of the physical, which is consistently identified with the supposedly uncontrollable physical needs of women. Further on in the frame that introduces the tale, the philosopher says to his pupil:

> I am afraid if naïve people read my story about the wiles and tricks of women, a story I have written to admonish them and instruct you and others, where you can read how *these women have without the knowledge of their husbands*

> *called their lovers to them and embraced them and kissed them and fulfilled all their lusts with them, I repeat, I am afraid, if all this be so, that they will naively believe that I too am as immoral as those women.* (119, my italics)³

Here the philosopher fears being excluded from the zone of morality, reserved for men, and characterized by corporeal control and restraint. Furthermore, he dreads being placed in the position of women, distinguished by immorality and unauthorized sexual activity. These comments equate the male with right and the female with wrong, and establish a hierarchy that demands the exercise of a certain kind of power on the part of the disciple, i.e., a refusal of the body for the sake of the spirit, which amounts to a repudiation of that which was identified by men with the female as such, women being body, men being mind and spirit. Finally, the relation of man to man develops as a call or request for precisely *this* kind of narrative discourse, which the philosopher who disseminates the story both dreads to tell, and is compelled to tell.

The philosopher's anguished perception of sex and of what he perceives as the feminine is accompanied by a symbolic threat to his manhood as well, which was described by Freud in his essay on "The Uncanny." Freud writes: "a study of dreams, phantasies and myths has taught us that anxiety about one's eyes, the fear of going blind, is often enough a substitute for the dread of being castrated."⁴ In the *exemplum* that the philosopher recounts, the husband is a vintner who is struck in the eye while he is out tending to his grapevines. He rushes home, where he interrupts his wife and her lover, who hides in the room. The husband demands that his wife prepare their bed so that he may lie down. The wife responds:

> "Why are you so eager to get to bed? Tell me first, beloved, what is grieving you?" So he then told her everything that had happened. She then said: "Allow me, my most dear Lord, to attend your good eye with medicaments and charms, so that the good eye too may not suf-

---

³ "Sed vereor ne si qui nostra simplici animo legentes carmina quae de mulierum artibus ad earum correctionem et tuam et aliorum instructionem scripsimus viderint, videlicet quomodo quaedam earum nescientibus viris suos advocent amasios et complectentes deosculentur advocatos et quae illarum expetat lascivia in ipsis expleant, earum nequitiam in nos redundare credant" (25–26).

⁴ Sigmund Freud, "The Uncanny," in *The Standard Edition of the Complete Psychological Works of Sigmund Freud*, ed. and trans. James Strachey (London: Hogarth Press, 1955), 17:231.

fer the same as the other eye which has already been damaged. For your pain is mine also." And with this she laid her mouth on his sound eye and kissed it until her lover removed himself from the place where he was hidden. (120)[5]

The husband in this scene is confronted by the greatest fear of the narrator who brings him to life: the image of the wife attending to her husband's good eye with her mouth evokes her dangerous sensuality, while the wounded eye incarnates the fear of castration. Moreover, the image of the wife placing her mouth over her husband's healthy eye represents perhaps the threat that she will engulf it or swallow it, another image of figurative castration. All of the male characters involved in this tale and in its frame are merely players in a drama that is directed entirely by the wiles and the desires of a female character. What is inscribed here is thus ultimately the male dread of losing power to women, which, in this religious and didactic context, manifests itself as the somewhat paradoxical dread of both sex and castration.

Ironically, then, power seems to be perpetuated among the men of this milieu precisely by the telling of stories about the fear and loathing inspired by "evil" women, i.e., by powerful and sensual women. As the pupil says after the story has been told:

> "You have given me good instruction, master, and what you have told me of women's tricks, I have taken to my heart that is thirsty and desirous for knowledge. All this that I know from your story, I would not change for all the riches of Arabia. But if you wish to continue please do so and *tell me of those things that I can utilise in my profession, when I too by virtue of my age will be asked for advice and guidance*." (120, my italics)[6]

---

[5] "Dixit ei: Quid tantum properas ad lectum? Dic mihi quid tibi sit prius! Narravitque ei totum ut acciderat. Permitte, inquit illa, karissime domine, ut oculum sanum medicinali arte confirmem et carmine, ne ita eveniat de sano ut mihi evenit de iam percusso, quia dampnum tuum commune est nobis. Apponensque os suum ad oculum sanum tantum fovit quousque amicus a loco ubi absconditus erat viro nesciente discessit" (26–27).

[6] "Tunc discipulos [*sic*] ait magistro: Bene me instruxisti, et quod de illarum artibus retulisti siticuloso et desideranti animo commendavi; nec quod inde scio pro divitiis Arabum commutare volo. Sed si placet progredere, et quod transferre in actum publicae administrationis futurorum valeamus edissere!" (27).

The master's instruction amounts to teaching his pupil how to tell this story about women's tricks, which means that narrative is a technique that the latter must master and pass on to other men once he has attained a certain level of authority within an implicitly described social structure. The Latin version of the text is even more emphatic on this point: the telling of this type of story must be fulfilled by the disciple *"in actum publicae administrationis."* The circulation of a tale about a woman to be feared is compared to economic wealth, and the narrative coin that circulates among these men is stamped with the face of a woman who bears the dreaded aspect of a sexual monster to be mastered. Her story, as it is told by the philosopher, is essentially about the strategies by which men who belong to a particular social group maintain their power via the transmission of a fantasy image of women *within* narrative, or even *as* narrative. The obsessive nature of its repetition over the course of centuries in diverse texts written by men leads one to believe that it embodied a collective male fantasy that was the unconscious foundation of a quite conscious male domination of women. And, as the Latin text reveals, the telling and retelling of this story was an important technical or even material basis of a masculinist "public administration" of the female body.

The first variant of this tale that I will examine appears as number 16 in the anonymous *Cent nouvelles nouvelles* of 1462. The frame of this first collection of French *nouvelles* is much more subtly developed than that of the *Disciplina clericalis*. At the beginning of each tale, the narrator is named, that of tale 16 being "Monseigneur," who is addressed in the anonymous author's introduction as "My most dear and formidable Lord the Duke of Burgundy, of Brabant, and so on" ("Mon treschier et tresredoubté seigneur Monseigneur le duc de Bourgoigne, de Brabant, etc.").[7] Philippe the Good of Burgundy was indeed one of the most formidable and important noblemen of the fifteenth century, and his court rivaled that of the French kings in artistic achievements and military power.[8] This context of the text's pro-

---

[7] *Les Cent nouvelles nouvelles*, in *Conteurs français du XVIe siècle*, ed. Pierre Jourda (Paris: Gallimard, 1965), 19. All page references are to this edition, as are my references to the *Heptaméron*, which appears in the same volume.

[8] "Louis XI, secondé par un concours heureux de circonstances et poussé par une ambition infatigable, avait contribué plus qu'aucun autre roi à l'agrandissement territorial et à l'unité politique de la France. Il avait profité de la mort de son redouté rival Charles le Téméraire, qui ne laissait qu'une fille, pour réunir à la couronne ... le duché de Bourgogne": M. Mignet, *La Rivalité de François Ier et de Charles-Quint*, 2 vols. (Paris: Librairie Académique Didier, 1886), 1:9. On the court of Philippe le

duction illuminates the parallel between the historical social structure of Philippe's court and the configuration of power that stratified the narrators and narratees assembled in the work. All of the narrators who are named at the beginning of each tale are men; furthermore, we know from several indices within the work that the listeners of these tales are men as well.[9] We can thus imagine the narrative frame of the *Cent nouvelles nouvelles* as a gathering of men, either friends or servants of the duke, who have been summoned to the court of their lord in order to contribute to his narrative stock. The narrator of tale 32, for example, asks that he not be "seclus du treseureux et hault merite deu a ceulx qui traveillent et labourent a l'augmentacion et accroissement des histoires de ce present livre" (139). Narrative is equated here to work that leads to the accumulation of wealth, and again the story that is told will be about the trade in women's bodies that is the basis of a male-dominated economy.

The protagonist of tale 16 of the *Cent nouvelles nouvelles* is a noble knight who goes to fight in the crusades. The semantic register of warfare is thus used metaphorically to describe the sexual infidelity that is at the heart of the tale. In fact, the tale derives much of its supposed humor from this type of semantic shifting between these two registers. The Christian metaphor of work in the garden of the *Disciplina clericalis* is substituted here by the image of the Good Christian sacrificing his body on the battlefield for the sake of his faith, as is made clear in the tale's opening description:

> [ce] chevalier, qui tresdevot et craignant Dieu estoit, delibera a Dieu faire sacrifice du corps qu'il luy avoit presté, bel et puissant, assovy de taille desirée autant et plus que nul de sa contrée, excepté que perdu avoit ung œil en ung assault ou avec son prince s'estoit tresvaillamment porté. Et pour faire son oblacion en lieu eleu et de luy desiré, après les congez a madame sa femme prins et de pluseurs ses parens et amys, se mect a voye devers les bons sei-

---

Bon, see Emmanuel Bourassin, *Philippe le Bon: Le Grand Lion des Flandres* (Paris: Editions Tallandier, 1983).

[9] See *Cent nouvelles nouvelles*, tale 81: "Puis que les comptes et histoires des asnes sont acevez, je vous feray en bref et a la verité ung bien gracieux compte d'un chevalier que la plus part de vous, *mes bons seigneurs*, congnoissez de pieça" (294, my italics). Cf. tale 89: "En ung petit hamelet ou village de ce monde, assez loing de la bonne ville, est advenue une petite histoire qui est digne de venir en l'audience de vous, *mes bons seigneurs*" (361, my italics).

> gneurs de Perusse, vraiz champions et defenseurs de la tressaincte foy chrestiane. (72–73)

The narrators of this collection often cast admiring glances at the anatomy of their noble male characters. In this tale, the conjoining and semantic "shuffling" of a limited number of elements attains an extreme level, with the implication being that this gentleman's hyperbolic body is both the most apt specimen to be sacrificed to his God, and most well-endowed for the sake of seducing women, which is borne out somewhat by the end of the story. To the reader initiated in the narrative tradition derived from the *Disciplina clericalis*, however, this passage also bears the signs of male paranoia and the fear of castration that lay at the foundations of the male subjectivity that I have been describing. From this serious point of view, the knight's partial blindness would certainly signify the dreaded possibility of female infidelity. In the comic context of the *Cent nouvelles nouvelles*, however, the certainty that feminine wiles would undermine male supremacy in the domain of marriage served merely as a pretext for a series of puns involving sex and warfare.

As we have already noted, an essential element of the male paranoia associated with the tale of the one-eyed cuckold is the parallel between the place of work and the place of sexual transgression, between the vintner who works in the field and the usurping lover who "plows the field" of the former's bed. In tale 16 of the *Cent nouvelles nouvelles*, this standard comparison assumes one of its most dramatic forms, with the working motif being replaced by descriptions of the knight as penitent Christian Crusader:

> Tandiz que monseigneur jeune et fait penitence, madame fait gogettes avecques l'escuier. Le plus des foiz monseigneur se disne et souppe de bescuit et de la belle fontaine, et madame a de tous les biens de Dieu si largement que trop; monseigneur au mieulx se couche en la paillace, et madame en ung tresbeau lit avec l'escuyer se repose. Pour abreger, tantdiz que monseigneur aux Sarrazins fait guerre, l'escuier a madame combat, et si tresbien s'i porte que, si monseigneur jamais ne retournoit, elle s'en passeroit tresbien. (73)

Within the context of late fifteenth-century narrative, this passage is a *tour de force* that combines the standard military metaphors for sexuality with the traditional symbols of abstinence and Christian suffering. This parallel comparison of the sacred and the profane merely prepares the way for the wife's trickery, which takes the familiar form of the uncanny combination of blindness on the part of the husband and insight on the part of the wife, which is shared by the gentlemen narratees gathered to listen to the story. The wife claims to have had a dream in which her husband could see out of his bad eye, and asks if she can demonstrate the truth of her premonition:

> Et monseigneur, qui est content de ceste epreuve, souffrit bien que madame luy bouchast son bon œil d'une main, et de l'autre elle tenoit la chandelle devant l'œil de monseigneur qui crevé estoit; et puis luy demanda: «Monseigneur, ne voiez vous pas bien, par vostre foy? — Par mon serment, nenny, m'amye, ce dit il.» Et entretant que ces devises se faisoient, le lieutenant de monseigneur sault de la chambre sans qu'il fust apperceu de luy. «Or actendez, monseigneur, ce dit elle. Et maintenant vous me voiez bien, faictes pas? — Par Dieu! m'amye, nenny, dit monseigneur, comment vous verroie je? vous avez bouchié mon dextre œil, et l'autre est crevé passé dix ans.» (75)

The figure of the one-eyed knight perfectly embodies the essentially ambivalent nature of the cuckold character. He is half avenging warrior, half pathetic dupe; one part devoted crusader, and one part victim of the game of blind man's bluff. Furthermore, the text makes it clear that the knight sees well out of his *right* eye and is blind in his *left* eye, reinforcing the Christian foundation of this anecdote, which is the battle between good and evil, light and dark, male and female, right and left. Here the candle evokes the entire realm of the visual, which is of vital importance in the *Cent nouvelles nouvelles*. The actions of many of its most important characters often have to be understood in relation to the concept of vision: they try to see what others try to hide from them, to hide what others want to see, to make others see what someone else is trying to hide from them, and so on. The scene from tale 16 in which an adulterous wife holds a burning candle before the blind eye of her cuckolded husband is thus a kind of emblem that represents the essential narrative structures of this type of *nouvelle*. The wife highlights her husband's blindness so that everyone who hears his story may see it.

The revision of this *exemplum* from the *Disciplina clericalis* is thus radically different from its model, at the same time that it serves to maintain and to disseminate male power. In the earlier work, the blindness of the husband within the anecdote served as an example intended to instruct the male reader in a moral code. The reader of the *exemplum* was meant to assume the moralizing position of the philosopher, from which the husband was excluded by his blindness. In the anecdote's revision in the *Cent nouvelles nouvelles*, however, the paranoia and anti-feminine dread of the philosopher and his pupil are transformed into a perverse pleasure on the part of the duke and his squires, carnivalesque characters who evidently take pleasure from seeing other people mocked and humiliated.[10] Instead of putting themselves in the position of the husband who is morally endangered by the tale's events, these listeners voyeuristically enjoy the description of sexual transgression as a spectacle, and indeed seem to delight in the fact that they can examine this situation from the wife's point of view. In this respect, the narrator particularly seems to enjoy the idea that the wife has had multiple sexual partners on the same day:

> Et a tant [mari et femme] s'entreacolerent et baiserent moult de foiz, et feirent grand feste. . . . Et a tant vindrent femmes et serviteurs qui bien be[g]neirent monseigneur et le deshouserent, et de tous poins le deshabillerent. Et ce fait se bouta ou lit avecques madame, qui le receut du demourant de l'escuier, qui s'en va son chemin, lyé et joieux d'estre ainsi eschappé. Comme vous avez oy fut le chevalier trompé. (75)

The formula of the husband who enjoys the "leftovers" or "remainders" of his "lieutenant" or "squire" in his own bed is repeated dozens of times in the *Cent nouvelles nouvelles*, to the evident satisfaction of the work's storytellers and listeners. The text substitutes a different economy of male domination for that of the *Disciplina*, while both are based on a male overestimation of the female body and its sexuality. The discourse of the *exemplum* was meant to serve as a means of moral instruction that would lead to male mastery and control of the female body within the realm of marriage; in contrast, the *Cent nouvelles nouvelles* celebrated an intensification of what the male narrators consistently perceived as the "over-sexed" female body, especially in so far as it served as a material foundation for the hyperbolic sexual activity of the text's male characters, such as the usurping lover and the knight himself in this case. The earlier text affirmed and reinforced the rule through serious narrative discourse; the later text undermined and cele-

---

[10] See Mikhail Bakhtin, "Forms of Time and of the Chronotope in the Novel," section 6, "The Functions of the Rogue, Clown and Fool in the Novel," in idem, *The Dialogic Imagination*, ed. and trans. Michael Holquist and Caryl Emerson (Austin: University of Texas Press, 1981), 158–67.

brated the transgression of the rule in comic narrative discourse. Both of these are, however, the complementary sides of an ambivalent male imaginary, constructed upon a fantasy vision of the relations between men and women, male and female. The pious philosophers of the *Disciplina clericalis* are replaced by the ribald warriors of the *Cent nouvelles nouvelles*, but the trade in fantasy images of female bodies remains the same.

Similarly, the variation of this tale that appears as *nouvelle* 87 of the *Cent nouvelles nouvelles* develops a subtext that tells the story of a male-dominated power structure. One of the major theses of feminist criticism asserts that the phallocentric social order is based upon the exchange of women among men. As Luce Irigaray has written:

> Ce qui assure donc le passage à l'ordre social, à l'ordre symbolique, à l'ordre tout court, c'est que les hommes, ou les groupes d'hommes, font circuler entre eux les femmes.... Femmes, signes, marchandises, sont toujours renvoyés pour leur production à l'homme ... et ils passent toujours d'un homme à un autre homme, d'un groupe d'hommes à un autre groupe d'hommes.[11]

Similarly, at the heart of the male organization of the *Cent nouvelles nouvelles* is the represented female body, which is passed from man to man in the form of a narrative representation. In tale 87, a knight who is staying in a royal house or *hôtel* falls in love with a young chambermaid who works there. The next sentence of the text unmasks the procedures through which narrative supports male homosocial domination, especially in this fantasy representation: "Et pour l'amour d'elle [ce chevalier] tant avoit fait au fourrier du duc de Bourgoigne, que cest hostel luy avoit delivré, affin de mieulx pourchasser et conduire sa queste, et venir aux fins et intencions ou il entendoit et ou amours le faisoient encliner" (310–11). Immediately, the network of influences that binds together the male characters involved in this story and its frame is apparent. The quartermaster whom the knight bribes is by definition in charge of supplying provisions to the duke's troops, and of preparing lodgings for the royal personage.[12] The protagonist of this tale curries favor with an officer of the ultimate male authority, who is responsible for

---

[11] Luce Irigaray, *Ce sexe qui n'en est pas un* (Paris: Editions de Minuit, 1977), 167–68.

[12] "Fourrier. Officier précédant en voyage les princes et les hauts personnages, et chargé d'assurer les logements": Edmond Huguet, *Dictionnaire de la langue française du seizième siècle*, 7 vols. (Paris: Didier, 1925–1967), 4:191.

providing the duke with merchandise of all kinds, even women, or *especially* women, as Irigaray remarked. By bonding with another male character economically, the knight secures the rights to the possession of a female body. In this way, the workings of narrative as a material support of male homosocial power are evident in the frame, as they are in the tale itself.

While the knight is pursuing the chambermaid, he falls victim to a serious eye infection. In the context of Freud's castration complex, to which I have already referred, the description of this infection is telling: "une maladie le print en l' œil si greve, qu'il ne le povoit tenir ouvert, tant en estoit aspre la doleur. Et pour ce que tresfort doubtoit de le perdre, mesmement que c'estoit le membre ou il devoit plus de guet et de soing, manda le cyrurgien de monseigneur le duc" (311). The duke's surgeon is of course the third character of the standard erotic triangle, who will attempt to usurp the "rights" that the knight has acquired to the chambermaid's body. From its beginning, the relationship of the knight to the surgeon is described in terms of exchange. "Si vous me voulez garir et delivrer de ce mal sans la perte de mon œil, je vous donneray bon vin," the knight says to the surgeon. "Le marché fut fait, et entreprint garir net cest œil" (311). A male character inscribed in the network of power relations thus calls out to another male character to save him from the fear of losing "his most cherished member"; the relationship between the two men is sealed by the promise of economic exchange, which of course will be transposed from the realm of material wealth to the realm of trade in the female body. The tale thus repeats the standard configuration of dread and desire that paradoxically unites and opposes male characters throughout the *Cent nouvelles nouvelles*.

When the surgeon is attending to the knight's eye, he is assisted by the chambermaid, whom he begins to desire. The chambermaid, who is no more than a stick figure in this process, reciprocates his desires, and the two of them formulate a plan. The knight agrees to have both of his eyes bandaged by the wily surgeon as a treatment for his infection, and his figurative cuckolding ensues:

> Quand . . . [le chevalier] eut les yeulx bandez, maistre cyrurgien fainct de partir comme il avoit de coustume, promectant de tantost revenir pour descouvrir cest œil. Il n'ala gueres loing, car assez près de son pacient, sur une couche jecta sa dame *et d'aultre palecte qu'il n'avoit remué son chevalier visita les cloistres secrez de la chambriere*. (312, my italics)

This mixed metaphorical description of the sexual act includes a fascinating transference of a phallic object from the body of the knight to the body of the chambermaid. This symbolic circulation of the phallus in the tale is a *mise en abyme* that mirrors the functioning of narrative in its frame. In other words, the transfer of narrative in the text and *as* the text is equivalent to the transfer and circulation of a symbolic marker of power and masculinity from man to man, via the material basis of the female body.

When the knight finally interprets the significance of the noises he hears coming from the other room, he tears the bandages from his eyes, and confronts the surgeon and chambermaid, vowing revenge. This potentially volatile situation is defused, however, in two brief sentences: "Le cyrurgien, qui estoit le plus gentil compaignon et des aultres le meilleur homme, commença a rire, et firent la paix. Et croy bien que tous deux, quand l'œil fut gary, s'accorderent a besoigner par terme" (313). The story ends when this male bonding via the exchange of a woman is institutionalized, with the two male characters agreeing to take turns with the body of the female character. The threat of castration and powerlessness is healed, in other words, when the exchange of the female body is made the basis of a social order that unites the two men. The real subject of the story is thus the system of exchanges based on gender difference that is the root of male power and domination, and which amounts to the "public administration" of a masculinist culture; furthermore, its subtext is the fear of castration, which is essentially a dread of being excluded from the network, or of being deprived of the essential attribute—the masculine marker—that allows one to have access to power within it. While the two tales that I have examined from this text are supposedly comic, in contrast to their all-too-serious model, it is clear that the net effect of both texts is the same. The telling of stories in both texts serves to establish and to maintain homosocial relationships among men, via the dissemination of fantasy images of women, and using the female body as a material base and literal conduit for exchange among men.

Marguerite de Navarre begins her response to this authoritative and misogynist narrative tradition by inscribing an emphatic inversion of exemplary stories as the media through which gender-contingent moral codes are communicated.[13] Since violence is implicitly associated with male sexuality

---

[13] "It has long been a commonplace that the series of *exempla* used by medieval preachers are the basis of the medieval and Renaissance genre of the novella collection. Marguerite de Navarre's novellas, published as the *Heptaméron* (1559), rise beyond this generic association of storytelling with example to mount a sustained, complex, and witty attack on the usefulness and even the possibility of creating

throughout the variants that I have examined, Navarre begins her version of the one-eyed cuckold's tale by placing a double frame around it, calling into question the justification of misogyny that is the explicit basis of the story. The first frame is, of course, that of the *devisants* or storytellers of the *Heptaméron*, who are equally divided on the basis of gender (five male and five female narrators), and who have equal access to the narrative discourse through which they attempt to communicate the truths of gender difference. The *Heptaméron* thus differs radically from its models in that it gives female characters an equal voice in the struggle for virtue that was the foundation of exemplary literature. While it may be true that seven women and three men are the narrators of Navarre's illustrious model, the *Decameron*, it is also clear that Boccaccio's intentions were not "feminist" in nature, since he proclaimed in the work's preface that his tales would be told for the delight of ladies in love who were trapped in what he undoubtedly perceived as their proper place, the home.[14] Marguerite de Navarre's inclusion of the female within the section of the literary artifice devoted to the moral interpretation of the tale substantially alters the configuration of power that underlies the male narrative tradition begun by the *Disciplina clericalis*, since female representatives actually interpret and comment upon the anecdotes in which their roles as gendered subjects are at issue. Such a

---

examples": John D. Lyons, *Exemplum: The Rhetoric of Example in Early Modern France and Italy* (Princeton: Princeton University Press, 1989), 72. It should be noted, however, that Navarre also attempted to describe counter-examples that would prove the validity of a particularly feminine virtue or "honnêteté," which is one of the key concepts of the work. Floride of tale 10 and Rolandine of tale 21 are clearly exemplary figures in the traditional sense of the term. Hence a simultaneous imitation and rejection of the *exemplum* is a consistent characteristic of the *Heptaméron*.

[14] In the *Heptaméron*, opinions that explicitly represent the points of view of women are given equal weight with those expressed by men, while Boccaccio's tales are written for women who are literally "put in their place" by the text's prologue: "E chi negherà questo, quantunque egli si sia, non molto più alle vaghe donne che agli uomini convenirsi donare? Esse dentro a' dilicati petti, temendo e vergognando, tengono l'amorose fiamme nascose, le quali quanto più di forza abbian che le palesi coloro il sanno che l'hanno provate: e oltre a ciò, ristrette da' voleri, da' piaceri, da' comandamenti de' padri, delle madri, de' fratelli e de' mariti, il più del tempo nel piccolo circuito delle loro camere racchiuse dimorano e quasi oziose sedendosi, volendo e non volendo in una medesima ora, seco rivolgendo diversi pensierir, li quali non è possibile che sempre sieno allegri": Giovanni Boccaccio, *Decameron* (Milan: Arnoldo Mondadori, 1985), 6. Boccaccio's purpose in writing is thus to delight and to instruct women who are in love, yet he speaks clearly as if women had a well-defined place and role in the social structure. In contrast, Marguerite de Navarre seeks to define new roles and a new sensibility for women.

feminine commentary is unthinkable in the context of the didactic literature from which the *nouvelle* originated, since the figure of woman was formerly spoken *about* in this tradition, while she seemingly was never allowed to speak for herself. The importance of the *Heptaméron* derives largely from its inscription of these feminine or even feminist voices in a misogynist tradition.

The second frame is more particularly suited to the tale of the one-eyed cuckold, in the sense that it makes an explicit reference to the function of exemplary stories in the moral education of women. Tale 5 of the *Heptaméron*, which tells the story of a clever woman who avoids being raped by two Franciscans, provides a critical context that Navarre uses to introduce her revision of the *exemplum*, which is tale 6. As numerous readers of the *Heptaméron* have shown in recent years, rape is a theme that traverses the entirety of the work, perhaps as a result of its author's own relationships with violent men.[15] Navarre thus counterposes what we might consider her experience of the "reality" of male violence to the fantasy figure of the insatiable female that was at the heart of the *nouvelle* literature and its antecedents. The revised female characters of the work, such as the clever "batelière" of tale 5, substitute the attributes of constancy, intelligence, and virtue for the ones that the *nouvellistes* conventionally assigned to women, that is, frivolity, a malicious intelligence devoted to betrayal, and vice. This transformation of the role of female characters is carried out methodically and explicitly in tales 5 and 6 of the *Heptaméron*.

The moral message of the *Disciplina* was essentially that men should use their intelligence and be vigilant in order to avoid being fooled by their wayward wives, and to contain the uncontrollable drives of the female body. The *Heptaméron* inverts this premise, substituting male violence for female waywardness, and transposing the roles assigned to men and women. The first stage of this inversion is thus the moral interpretation of tale 5, which rejects the exemplarity that is at the service of male representational violence, and which is essentially inappropriate for the moral education of women. The tale's narrator, Géburon, concludes the story with the following commentary:

> Je vous prie, mes dames, pensez, si ceste pauvre bastelliere a eu l'esperit de tromper l'esperit de deux si malitieux

---

[15] See Patricia Francis Cholakian, *Rape and Writing in the* Heptaméron *of Marguerite de Navarre* (Carbondale and Edwardsville: Southern Illinois University Press, 1991), and Carla Freccero, "Rape's Disfiguring Figures: Marguerite de Navarre's *Heptaméron*, Day 1:10," in *Rape and Representation*, ed. Lynn Higgins and Brenda Silver (New York: Columbia University Press, 1990), 227–47.

> hommes, que doyvent faire celles qui ont tant leu et veu de beaulx exemples, quant il n'y auroit que la bonté des vertueuses dames qui ont passé devant leurs œilz, en la sorte que la vertu des femmes bien nourryes seroit autant appelée coustume que vertu? Mais de celles qui ne sçavent rien, qui n'oyent quasi en tout l'an deux bons sermons, qui n'ont le loisir que de penser à gaingner leurs pauvres vyes, et qui, si fort pressées, gardent soingneusement leur chasteté, c'est là où on congnoist la vertu qui est naïfvement dedans le cueur, car où le sens et la force de l'homme est estimée moindre, c'est où l'esperit de Dieu faict de plus grandes oeuvres. (736)

Here Navarre is evidently writing within a long-established narrative tradition, using the technique that was typical of didactic discourse for centuries (an exemplary story followed by a moral). Nevertheless, the text makes the revolutionary claim that exemplarity by itself is not sufficient for the moral education of women, especially given their vilification in countless *exempla*. In contrast, Navarre's narrator asserts that feminine virtue is as much the product of divine inspiration as it is of moral instruction, questioning the authority and the efficacy of the narrative tradition modeled on the Bible and disseminated via the *Disciplina clericalis*. The narrator also proclaims the validity of individual judgment in matters of conscience. In other words, Geburon's comment clearly reflects Navarre's sympathy for Humanist ideals that favored a personal and intelligent consideration of ethical problems over the ready-made solutions to be found in Scholastic lessons and sermons. Rather than illustrating the appropriateness of *exempla* for the education of young men, Marguerite's work seems to examine the inadequacy of the *exemplum* as a medium of moral instruction for women, especially given the genre's misogynist origins. Or, it may be that this sequence of *nouvelles* addresses the crucially important notion that traditionally masculinist genres and narrative techniques must be revisited and revised in order to serve the moral purposes of women, which Marguerite repeatedly claims to have been far more demanding than those of men.

If the boatwoman of tale 5 serves paradoxically as an example of a woman who learned to be virtuous without the aid of exemplary literature, the following tale 6 offers perhaps a counter-example of what virtuous women had to avoid. While both positive and negative *exempla* were used for centuries in the moral education of men, the overwhelming majority of female figures in didactic discourse were negative, leaving women writers with the choice between learning without examples and creating new ones.

For this reason, traditional exemplary tales had to be revised, supplemented, and even rediscovered for the sake of educating women, as Christine de Pisan understood a century before Marguerite de Navarre in her *Livre de la cité des dames*. The narrator of tale 6, Nomerfide, emphasizes the need to rectify the abuses of this literary tradition in her prefatory remarks: "pour ce que nous avons juré de dire verité, je ne la veulx celer; car, tout ainsy que la vertu de la batteliere ne honnore poinct les aultres femmes si elles ne l'ensuyvent, aussi le vice d'une aultre ne les peut deshonorer" (737). Nomerfide's remark implies that women are not the only ones responsible for the evil that is attributed to them in exemplary discourse, and that this type of narrative itself is a kind of seduction that is perhaps far removed from the needs and necessities of the real world. Her insistence on the truth of what she is about to recount, in accordance with the goal of the *devisants* announced in the prologue to the work, signals the fundamentally different perspective adopted in this later text: that is, the true and the real are diverse and multifarious, and cannot be reduced to the level of standardized, exemplary cases that will apply to all individuals. Thus the conventional fantasy figures of the female that populate the male imaginary are simply not varied enough to be of any use to real women. With this distinction between the real world and its various representations, Navarre takes a step well beyond her literary models. In doing so, she attempts to extract the fantasy figure of woman from the realm of the male imaginary, where she is inevitably bad, and to judge her by the criteria of the actual world, where women are seduced by both evil and good.

The irony of this transfer of the anecdote to the domain of the real is, of course, that Nomerfide's story is not at all true, as she claims, and as historic details attempt to verify. This is the second major difference between the preceding versions of this story and Navarre's: in the *Heptaméron*, there is at least the semblance of a concern for verisimilitude. For example, the tale's first male protagonist is described as "ung viel varlet de chambre de Charles, dernier duc d'Alençon, lequel avoit perdu ung œil" (737). The name of Marguerite's real and historically verifiable first husband, Charles d'Alençon, is meant to authenticate a story that readers of *nouvelle* collections would recognize as a retelling of earlier tales. This intrusion of "the real" into a conventional and contrived plot invites the reader to evaluate the artificial ruse that is the heart both of this story and of didactic, misogynist tales in general. While the impossibility of this trick is never questioned in the earlier versions of the story, Navarre makes its lack of verisimilitude the crux of her implicit argument against its utility as an exemplary image. The husband's reaction to his wife's trickery unmasks its factitious nature, since, in the "real" world, such a maneuver would never go unrecognized:

> En ce temps, pendant qu'il ne veoyt goutte, [la femme] feit sortir son amy dehors, dont le mary se doubta incontinant, et luy dist: «Par dieu, ma femme, je ne feray jamais le guet sur vous; car, en vous cuydant tromper, je receu la plus fine tromperie qui fut oncques inventée. Dieu vous veulle amender; car il n'est en la puissance d'homme du monde de donner ordre en la malice d'une femme, qui du tout ne la tuera. Mais, puis que le bon traictement que je vous ay faict n'a rien servy à vostre amendement, peult-estre que le despris que doresnavant j'en feray vous chastira.» (738)

The severity of the husband's commentary on his wife's ruse forcefully underlines the moral message that this re-written and re-contextualized anecdote conveys in this dramatically different narrative frame. While Navarre's tale includes the standard misogynist dictum that a woman would have to be killed in order to be virtuous, which is echoed in hundreds of texts, it is clear here that the moral message of her revision is quite different. Simply put, it implies that the inculcation of virtue in women is beyond the capacity of men, if women do not first wish to become virtuous by themselves. Moreover, this reading of the anecdote suggests that male violence against women is fruitless, and can lead only to dire consequences for men and women alike. In her moral to the tale, Nomerfide places the responsibility for virtuous conduct squarely on the shoulders of women, especially given the stereotypically malicious intelligence that is ascribed to them in all of the versions of this tale, as Nomerfide continues: "si, pour couvrir ung mal, son esperit [celui de la femme] a promtement trouvé remede, je pense que, pour en eviter ung ou pour faire quelque bien, son esperit seroit encores plus subtil; car le bon esperit, comme j'ay tousjours oy dire, est le plus fort" (738–39). This insistence that a woman must use her legendary intelligence in order to do good works is a positive inversion of a narrative practice that condemned too-intelligent women for centuries, through the generation of a series of female fantasy figures who existed only within a certain male-dominated imaginary.

In conclusion, I have traced successive developments and revisions of a specific anecdote in diverse narrative frames in order to determine the relationship of the story itself to the configurations of power that are characteristic of narrative framing devices in general. The telling of the originating *exemplum* from the *Disciplina clericalis* was part of a technique or even a "technology" of power, in which the figurative exchange of women among men, both within discourse and as fantasy images, was the basis of a moralizing male authority, passed on from generation to generation via exemplary literature as a medium. In the second example, *Les Cent nouvelles nouvelles* 16, the essential interdiction of extramarital sex was overturned by the transgressive procedures of comedy, which celebrated the excesses of adultery as the material basis of an alternative, yet still male-dominated economy. The celebratory aspects of this tale were shadowed, however, by two types of institutionalized violence: that of war and the skills of war, which served as metaphors for sex; and that of religious intolerance and the crusades. This comic variant of the tale thus contains within itself the officially-sanctioned violence that was inflicted on women via the medium of widely disseminated literary forms. In *Les Cent nouvelles nouvelles* 87, this violence turned somewhat against the male characters of the story, who suffered from the paranoia and dread of feminine wiles that were typical of this anecdote from its beginnings. In this case, the exchange among men functioned as an antidote for the fear of castration, which was overcome by the institutionalization of relations among men, based on the trading of the female body. The nature of power in these examples required the circulation of stories within a group that was restricted on the basis of gender. Access to power was granted in the male-dominated frames by the telling of a certain story of women, and these stories were inevitably about a system of power relations based on the trading of women among men, or the parallel trading of stories about women among men.

Finally, Marguerite de Navarre's response to the weight of this narrative tradition was a re-evaluation of the didactic efficacy of the *exemplum*, especially for women, in light of the genre's evident artificiality. In the face of countless moralizing and comic examples claiming that women used their intelligence for malicious ends, Navarre proposed simply that in the actual world beyond narrative, real women should develop their minds in order to use them for virtuous purposes. Her description of exemplarity's inadequacy involved a rejection of male representational violence against women, which is evident in the frames of tales 5 and 6, and throughout the *Heptaméron*'s interrogation of rape. Moreover, Navarre frames this conventional and fictional tale of feminine wiles within the "reality" of male violence, since the author's actual husbands, Charles d'Alençon and Henri de Navarre, are named at the beginning and end of the story, with marriage being a kind of "violence" to which she was subjected twice in her own life. Henri's representative, the singularly violent Hircan, overpowers the other *devisants* in the commentary on tale 6, and is the narrator of tale 7, which describes the way in which male vehemence can overcome feminine intelligence. This text thus questions the accuracy of its models and their obsession with female duplicity, highlighting the representational violence that this narrative tradition inflicted on images of women, and ultimately on women themselves. The narrative frame of Navarre's revision problematized the power hierarchies in which it was inscribed in a much more sophisticated manner than its prototypes, which seemed merely to subtend and participate in the maintenance of a male homosocial status quo. As such, the *Heptaméron* represents the culmination of ancient literary practices, which it irrevocably transforms in its transcription of an authentically feminist voice, speaking softly but in a compelling manner against a torrent of masculinist discourse.

Jacques Yver's *Le Printemps d'Yver* and Trans-Gender Phantasmagoria

Deborah N. Losse

Human potential for recreating the self, adapting to new circumstances, and undergoing multiple transformations in the course of a lifetime is central to the thought and writings of Renaissance humanists from Pico della Mirandola to Montaigne, including Vives, Erasmus, and Rabelais. In his recent work, *Perpetuum mobile*, Michel Jeanneret establishes the evolution of this concept of self-transformation and metamorphosis through the major writers and artists of the Renaissance.[1]

Although early humanists such as Pico della Mirandola, Vives, and Rabelais locate man's uniqueness in the ability to change, and embrace this quality with unqualified enthusiasm, later humanists such as Montaigne approach such flexibility with reserve and look for a stable core in which the individual self is grounded—what Montaigne calls the "forme maistresse."[2] It is not surprising that Jacques Yver, whose *Printemps* (1572) was published at the time that Montaigne began composing his *Essais*, should build his work on the tension between the human penchant for adapting and adjusting to new forces and the will to remain consistent and constant amidst major social change or disturbance.

Fundamental to the individual's ability at once to adjust to the changes brought on by fortune and to remain faithful to certain principles growing out of an inner sense of integrity, conscience, and self, is the power of the

---

[1] Michel Jeanneret, *Perpetuum mobile* (Paris: Macula, 1997). Jeanneret quotes from Pico della Mirandola's *Oratio de hominis dignitate* (circa 1486), from Vives's *Fabula de homine* (1518), and from the correspondence of Erasmus (see 163–79).

[2] Michel de Montaigne, *Les Essais*, ed. Pierre Villey, 3 vols. (Paris: Quadrige/Presses Universitaires de France, 1992), 3: 2. 811. Subsequent references will be to this edition. Jeanneret cites other references in the *Essais* to this core which is the unique personality or pattern of the individual: "patron au dedans" (3: 2. 807); "qualitez originelles" (810); "forme sienne" (811).

imagination. The imagination can reflect events and images coming from outside the self—natural phenomena, learned texts, civil uprisings, other people—or generate from the self its own material. The mind serves either to accentuate the images received or to control them, to process them in such a way that they are set in a familiar context and no longer inspire fright. Phantasm, imagination, leisurely reflection give rise to a multitude of unformed images, but individual craft and industry are required to give them shape—"les mettre en rolle," as Montaigne says of his efforts in the *Essais* to record and give form to the chimera and monsters of his imagination (1: 8. 33).

The horror of France's civil and religious wars generates, in Yver's *Printemps*, the need among the people of Poitou to seek relief from the vicissitudes of external events in the greater stability of local custom. They retire collectively to a quiet spot for the purpose of engaging in recreative activity—games, dancing, eating, and storytelling: "conter et communiquer entre eux leurs pertes et se consoler par la pratique d'un devoir d'amitié en leur commune misère. Or, cette charité fut principalement pratiquée par la noblesse du pays, qui a bien cette bonne coutume de se rallier par étroites connoissances et cousinages, qui les font entretenir heureusement en leur grandeur et lustre ancien."[3]

The frame or *cornice* of *Le Printemps* embraces the tension between change and constancy, historic event and fictional cadre that extends to the entire work. Yver very precisely situates the generating moment of the tales: the peace of 1570 following the third civil war ("la troisième saignée" [521]). Yet the natural and artistic splendor and plenitude in which the storytellers recount their tales and pursue the leisurely activities of Poitevin nobility recall the rarefied settings of Boccaccio, Marguerite de Navarre, and other contemporary *conteurs*.[4]

Military strife is never far from the narrative surface, especially since the major theme of the stories—love's trials—is expressed in military terms. At the outset of the first day, the Sieur de Ferme-Foi describes love between men and women in terms of war:

---

[3] Jacques Yver, *Le Printemps d'Yver*, in *Les Vieux Conteurs français*, ed. P. L. Jacob [Paul La Croix] (Paris: Société du Panthéon Littéraire, 1841; repr. Geneva: Slatkine, 1970), 5. All subsequent references will be to this edition.

[4] Both Boccaccio's *Decameron* and Marguerite de Navarre's *Heptaméron* are set during events that one can trace to specific dates—the plague in Florence and the flood in the Pyrenees—yet Yver consistently returns to the disruption and violence of the religious wars in a manner that keeps the historic events close to the narrative surface.

> Mais, mon Dieu! maintenant le temps qui ne chante que paix; le nom des filles qui ne promet qu'amour et faveur; puis, la faute qu'avons de bons espions pour nous avertir, et de sûr rempart pour nous défendre, fait que tous désarmés nous tombions en la puissance superbe de ces cruelles amies, qui, se mettant en embuscade, nous surprennent à l'improuvu contre les trêves qu'elles nous promettent. (529)

The abundance of trees and fruit present in the setting ("laurier," "lierre," "jasmin," "houblon," "fraises," "salades," "noisettes," "cerises") lies perilously close to the pillage wrought by the warring parties in Poitou (524). The *trêve* from the devastation of civil war is indeed fragile and transitory, and mirrors the fragile peace between the sexes.

It is exactly the fragile and transitory nature of the peace that necessitates the retreat into phantasm and the fictional realm. Retreat into phantasm, even with the return of civil strife threatening at the very borders of the splendid castle, is exactly the remedy sought by the noble company gathered around the hospitable châtelaine. Echoes of war outside the gates inspire discussion, debate, and narration on internal battles between the heart and the mind, fantasy and reason, constancy and infidelity. Allegorical names encourage the separation between the historic context and the idyllic cadre of the work: "Parquoi, nommerons nos trois gentilshommes, qu'avons entreprins de faire jouer en ce théâtre d'amour, les sieurs de *Bel-Accueil*, de *Fleur-d'Amour* et de *Ferme-Foi*" (522).

All is not peaceful in this retreat to explore the ups and downs of human sentiment. A strong competition along gender lines shows itself between the three gentlemen and two young ladies, daughter Marie and niece Marguerite of the châtelaine. The two camps debate the relative constancy and frivolity of the male and female sex. It is not the case, as in the frame of the *Heptaméron*, that we see a varied spectrum of opinions, but rather two camps begin and end their storytelling with attacks on the virtue of the opposite sex or in praise of their own. The present study will examine the role which gender plays in exploring the phantasmic reflections of the male and female characters on the other sex. Errors in supposition occur because of misunderstandings about the way in which the female or male psyche operates. Gender alone is not the determinant factor, for individual personality and strength of purpose exert a powerful force on the outcome of the narrative.

The narration of *Le Printemps* is unique in its interruption of narrative action to recount not a probing of conscious reflection on events—

psychological deliberation, as we see in the *Heptaméron,* or less frequently in Bonaventure des Périers's *Nouvelles récréations et joyeux devis*—but rather an exploration of a mental image or an impression of the desired object. Inherent in the definition of phantasm is the notion that it is a mental image of the real: illusion, delusion, counterfeit, fancy, specter.[5]

The valiant Eraste ("Première Histoire") conjures up the dual image of Death and Fortune in his despair over losing the sacred chain given to him by his lover Perside as a reminder of their strong and unbreakable bond of affection. Like Poe's purloined letter, the chain, in Lacan's words, is "le symbole d'un pacte."[6] It is torn off Eraste's neck during the tourney and found by a third party who in turn gives it to his lover Lucine. The chain is then situated in a symbolic sequence foreign to the origin of the pact. Described as being abandoned by reason ("délaissé de sa raison") and guided only by blind furor ("aveugle fureur"), Eraste invokes death: "Hélas! dure mort, quel plaisir prends-tu à mon malaise? Seras-tu plus grasse quand tu m'auras mangé après être amaigri et asséché de tristesse?" (537). In his troubled state, he calls up Fortune along with Death: "Ah! aveugle, tu ne vois ce qui est bon de faire, non plus que Fortune, qui s'accorde fort bien avec toi pour me ruiner."

The inherent virtue and chastity that characterize Eraste restrict the play of phantasm in the narrative to reflection on his ill fortune, and the narrator, eager to illustrate masculine constancy and virtue, avoids passages in which he fantasizes on the physical attributes of his Perside. Instead, the gold chain becomes the object of pursuit—the purloined talisman the possession of which will return him to Perside's trust and good favor. Phantasm takes the form of summoning up the vision of the lost chain, and, as a consequence, becomes an object of peril. In his pursuit of the chain, Eraste puts his fidelity to Perside in doubt as he feigns interest in Lucine in order to gain access to her quarters and take back the chain, found by Lucine's lover and given to her.

In his right mind, Eraste would never have risked his reputation for constancy, but, despairing of recovering his beloved, he mortgages his reputation: "En quoi, il empira grandement sa condition, qu'il tâchait d'amender; car il se rendit d'autant plus suspect à sa jalouse Perside, qui faisoit bien son compte, qu'ores son Eraste étoit si bien convaincu, qu'il n'y avoit plus lieu d'aucune excuse pour couvrir sa déloyauté" (540).

---

[5] *Webster's Third International Dictionary of the English Language* (Springfield, MA: G. and C. Merriam, 1971), 1693.

[6] Jacques Lacan, "Séminaire sur 'La Lettre volée'," in idem, *Écrits I* (Paris: Editions du Seuil, 1966), 19–75, here 38.

The male narrator, the Sieur de Fleur-d'Amour, misses no opportunity to mention Perside's jealousy, her quickness to accuse the honest Eraste of infidelity: "Envie, haine et jalousie tenoient sa pauvre âme entre leurs mordantes tenailles" (538). Such is the strength of Perside's reaction, when she sees Lucine wearing the chain she had given to Eraste to celebrate their love and future marriage. Cruelty and harshness are two characteristics of feminine behavior that the male narrators in Yver's circle of storytelling repeatedly evoke. In failing to examine Eraste's long fidelity and his flawless virtue, Perside gives in too quickly to jealousy, opines the Sieur de Fleurd'Amour. That their love ends in tragedy is her responsibility: "toutes les plaintes, mécontentements et infortunes qui se trouvent en amour, viennent de la part des femmes" (548). Had she been more forgiving, less hasty to accuse Eraste for the loss of the chain, they might have lived a happy, fulfilling life together.

In the second day, the woman and not the chain is the object of pursuit and desire. Mademoiselle Marie narrates, seeking to restore woman's honor so reviled in the previous tale. She shows both her gender and class bias in depicting the phantasmic obsession of the clerk Ponifre in so boldly pursuing Fleurie, the daughter of a wealthy merchant, a woman well above his status. The imbalance in this pursuit is made all the more evident in that Fleurie is promised to Herman, a young man of equal age, wealth, and refinement ("les deux parties totalement égales en âge, en bien et bonté de mœurs" [557]). In contrast to the pair, the clerk and storekeeper is described as "ordinaire gardien de la boutique," with a penchant for phantasm, particularly in regard to young women: "n'avoit guère autre occupation qu'à regarder les passants, et remarquer d'entre les femmes quelle beauté gagneroit le premier lieu dans son jugement particulier" (557).

Ponifre's lecherous thoughts are expressed in culinary metaphors as he observes Fleurie's growing attachment for Herman. Her proximity and the attention she bestows upon Herman whet Ponifre's appetite: "lequel, après l'avoir, pour quelque temps, tenu aux abois, et repu de ses ordinaires entrées de table, qui sont regards muets, soupirs incertains, solitude mélancolique . . . lui fit venir l'appétit de plus solide pâture et de viande plus nourrissante" (557).

Part of the play of the narrative is the distance between the aristocratic background of the *devisants* in the idyllic setting and the common birth of Ponifre. Mademoiselle Marie describes his futile attempts to assume the trappings of gallantry to try to appeal to Fleurie: "il se fait brave et mignon; il se peigne, se fraise, se mire, et s'agence le plus soigneusement qu'Amour lui pouvoit enseigner" (557).⁷ The same female narrator takes every opportunity to point out his temerity, his "hardiesse" at daring to pursue a woman above his station. He is a "mal avisé," "un téméraire" who dares to play the "mignon," the gallant gentleman.

In spite of her youth, Fleurie stands up to the unwanted advances of her impertinent shopkeeper—as he is judged by the aristocratic narrator and her circle. Her courage and strength are obvious as she denounces his advances:

> De tels ou semblables propos ce jeune homme vouloit arraisonner sa nouvelle maîtresse, quand, d'un œil cruel, avec un visage tout embrasé de honte, de colère et dédain, lui ferma la bouche, et, après une rude menace, lui donna à ronger un repentir de sa trop précipitée hardiesse. (558)

Instead of attending to the clear and unequivocal distaste which Fleurie shows him, Ponifre listens only to his perception of what women want: hearsay. "Ouï-dire" has more power over him than the direct experience of Fleurie's antipathy. Phantasm prevails over reality. Ponifre subscribes to the widespread male belief that women prefer to have men force their affections on them:

> Ce qui donna bien à penser à notre poursuivant, qui avoit toutefois ouï dire que, quelque mine que fassent les filles, elles sont bien aises d'être aimées, s'estimant aimables, et néanmoins la vergogne, fondée sur je ne sais quelle opinion d'honneur, ne leur permet d'accorder ce que plus elles désirent; qui fait que volontiers elles voudroient qu'on les forçât, pour de là prendre couverture à leur consentement. (558)

---

⁷ Marguerite de Navarre has a remarkably similar passage in tale 4 of the *Heptaméron*, where the gentleman who has the temerity to desire and attack the sister of his noble guest stands admiring himself in the mirror: "et quant il eut prins la plus gorgiase et mieulx parfumée de toutes ses chemises, et ung bonnet de nuict tant bien accoustré qu'il n'y failloit rien, luy sembla bien, en soy mirant, qu'il n'y avoit dame en ce monde qui sceut refuser sa beauté et bonne grace": *Heptaméron*, ed. Michel François (Paris: Garnier, 1967), 29. The vanity, presumption, and temerity of the two men are equal, but Marguerite's lecher is of higher station.

The most striking use of phantasm in its meaning of specter, illusion, apparition occurs in a strange scene reminiscent of Rabelais's "sibylle de Panzoust" (*Tiers Livre*, Chapter 18), where, thanks to the powders and exorcisms of the magician, Ponifre ogles "d'un œil ententif la belle semblance de s'amie, admirant ores les beaux replis de son poil crépelu, ores sa face angélique, ores sa gorge d'albâtre, ores la rondeur de ses jumeaux tétins, ores ses bras ivoiriens, et tout ce dont une parfaite beauté se rend émerveillable" (560).[8] So convinced by his vision or fantasy is Ponifre that he throws his arms around the specter: "après avoir fait une anatomie superficielle de ce petit miracle, tout éperdu d'aise, voulut jeter ses bras lascifs au col de cette feinte beauté." His precipitous movement brings the fantasy to an end, "laissant ce pauvre insensé" in a state of ecstatic unconsciousness.

From his ecstasy he awakes to plot the downfall of Fleurie. Desire motivates his crime as he abandons reason to immoderate sexual appetite. Mademoiselle Marie finds such excess to be a particularly masculine attribute: "Mais, comme il n'y a rien si malicieux et dénaturé qui ne trouve lieu au cœur de l'homme, principalement de celui qui s'abandonne à son appétit déréglé, il s'avisa, pour le sixième moyen, de s'aider d'une méchanceté si monstrueuse et horrible, que les diables mêmes ne l'eussent osé penser" (561).

Bribing her servants, Ponifre serves Fleurie wine in her mother's absence. Ponifre throws himself on her unconscious body: "Et ne faut point s'étonner si ce malheureux print plaisir à souiller cette chair aliénée de sentiment, puisque la sensualité en a bien rendu quelquefois de si enragés, qu'ils ont bien osé assouvir leur affamée lubricité sur un corps mort, qui vif avoit si vivement résisté à leur lâcheté" (561). Ponifre's obsessive phantasm is one step away from necrophilia, as the commentary points out. Mademoiselle Marguerite attributes the resulting pregnancy to the bestial appetite of Ponifre: "Parquoi la soif forcenée de ce brutal amant fut cause qu'il trouva l'eau trouble si bonne, que de cette conjonction s'ensuivit un engrossement d'enfant" (561). Marie is relentless in leading up to her conclusion that "tout le malheur qui survient en amour procède toujours de la faute de l'homme" (568).

Women and men are equally subject to the suggestive power of phantasm in the fifth story recounted by the Sieur de Ferme-Foi. Two students from France, Claribel of Poitiers and Floradin of Xaintes, enjoy the leisure of travel in Italy until they are called back to France by their families. Following a remarkable series of coincidences, each man has a passionate encounter with

---

[8] Randle Cotgrave's *Dictionarie of the French and English Tongues* gives *fantasme* as a variant of *fantosme* or *phantosme* (Columbia, SC: University of South Carolina Press, 1950; reprint of the 1611 edition).

the other's present or future wife. On a visit to Poitiers, Floradin chances upon Marguerite, the recent bride of Claribel, while Claribel is in Paris. Marguerite's passion for Floradin takes her by surprise, since her marriage to Claribel had been arranged by her parents: "car, encore que ses parents l'eussent mariée de corps, si n'avoit-elle point été mariée d'esprit et volonté; et encore n'avoit apprins que c'étoit d'amour" (632).

Marguerite explores the depth of the violent emotion that grips her, particularly at bedtime: "tellement que, se tournant çà et là par son lit veuf, comme si elle eût été couchée sur des ardents charbons, ou sur des poignants chardons . . ." (632). She wonders why she was so drawn in by Floradin's physical attributes: "ces beaux cheveux," "cette face libre et ouverte" (633). Her phantasm takes her on an inventory of the "corps masculin," in much the same way as male poets such as Marot and Scève had fantasized on the beauty of the "corps féminin." She has reason to regret that she did not meet Floradin first: "Ah! que plût à Dieu, ami, que tu fusses venu plus tôt, ou jamais! mais hélas! tu es venu trop tard, et un autre a moissonné ton espérance." Her affection responds to the languorous lute playing of Floradin: "Et ne faut douter que le tendre cœur de la damoiselle ne fût extêmement combattu de pitié, car un rocher en devoit être amolli; mais elle se contraignoit tant, qu'elle n'osoit montrer à son impatient ami le bien qu'elle lui vouloit, et ne sais si elle avoit plus de peine à supporter son amour, ou à le bien cacher" (634). Following an exchange of poems and letters, their love moves from the realm of fantasy to reality.

Phantasm turns to appreciation of the moment stolen in the garden: "car le courageux amant, par une douce force, étendit le corps de sa belle sur le gazon fleuri, et, pour usuraire récompense des peines endurées, ravit d'un impatient désir la fleur, dont Amour couronne ceux qui ont bien servi" (639). It is here that the châtelaine intervenes to warn the Sieur de Ferme-Foi that his discourse has gone beyond the bounds of discretion: "Lors, la dame du château fit signe de vouloir réprimer la gaillardise de ce beau conteur qui parloit un peu trop librement . . ."

In the case of Floradin and Marguerite, the conflict between friendship and love, betrayal and desire feeds the phantasm, explored amply within the textual space. In contrast, when Claribel, Floradin's good friend and spouse of Marguerite, unwittingly sleeps with the future wife of Floradin, the narrator does not dwell on the power of fantasy to augment passion, but describes the consummation of desire in a few brief paragraphs. The absence of conscious conflictive emotions diminishes the role of phantasm in the relationship. The contemplation of forbidden pleasure nourishes sexual fantasy. Pain and delight are intertwined.

The power of art to instill passion and then to augment it through phantasm is the focus of the fourth story. King William of England falls in love with the portrait of the Princess of Denmark and Zeeland adorning the shield of his jousting opponent, the Marquis of Lubets, the flower of Danish chivalry. The portrait not only instills passion in William, but leads to reflection on the power of art. His senses overpowered by the beauty of the woman in the portrait, William retires to his chambers to contemplate the image:

> tout son plaisir n'étoit qu'à se dérober en la solitude de son cabinet, pour nourrir ses affections en l'admiration des grâces et perfections, desquelles sa nouvelle maîtresse enrichissoit l'écu que lui avoit laissé le marquis; lequel tenant un jour entre ses mains, après l'avoir attentivement regardé et baisé, commença à dire en soupirant . . . (605)

William blames the artist's talent for entrapping him in desire: "Ha! malheureux peintre, qui, d'un pinceau ennemi de l'humaine liberté, as si avarement ramassé, comme un trésor, toutes les perfections requises pour forcer les plus rebelles, et tourmenter les plus paisibles, las!"

The subject—the genesis and growth of desire—allows the king to reflect upon artistic license and the limitations of art. In his revery, it occurs to William that perhaps the painter has exaggerated the beauty of the princess: "Toutefois, si comme les sages nous apprennent, il ne faut témérairement croire à toute parole, combien moins à toute peinture? Vu que les peintres sont en possession immémoriale d'une liberté de faire tout à plaisir, selon leur fantaisie" (606). Art has its limitations in that it cannot capture the soul: "car les peintres, en représentant les traits et linéaments corporels, si ne peuvent-ils imiter ni assujettir à leur pinceau les façons, les grâces, mœurs et complexions spirituelles, qui, ou louables ou vicieuses, éclaircissent ou obscurcissent la beauté" (606). The only way to judge the verisimilitude of the painting is to go to Denmark to compare the painting with the princess herself.

Phantasm and the contemplation of a facsimile of his beloved lead him to betray his political instincts and to commit a foolish act—to leave his kingdom so newly acquired: "Or, il s'en va, cuidant bien avoir assuré toutes choses, guidé d'un impatient amour, qui, aveugle, l'empêchoit de voir quelle folie c'étoit de laisser ainsi son royaume, nouvellement acquis, en proie" (607). Love diminishes the king's political acumen—a fatal flaw from the humanist viewpoint of the monarch's responsibility to the body politic.

The king's love for the princess is short-lived, for en route to Denmark he drinks by mistake from the spring of hate, and so his passion for the princess turns to distaste. The narrator, Mademoiselle Marguerite, follows the transformation of his love to antipathy, and then describes a transferral of his passion to a new object of desire, as he takes in the beauty of Parthénie (or Viergine, as the narrator prefers to call her). Mademoiselle Marguerite lingers on the emergence of William's awareness of Viergine's beauty. The *coup de foudre* takes place during dinner, and the setting furnishes culinary metaphors for the growing passion of the king:

> Durant le souper, le chevalier déguisé regarda d'un si bon œil une damoiselle assise vis-à-vis de lui, qu'elle sembla plutôt quelque angelette faite de Dieu miraculeusement, que non pas une fille née de femme mortelle; laquelle reput ses langoureux esprits d'une viande qui lui fut bien malaisée à digérer. Et, après avoir sucé, avec les yeux goulus, le doux venin qui distilloit de cette beauté . . . (609)

Disguised as the chevalier de Messi so as not to attract undue attention, William yields easily to the charm of Parthénie/Viergine. In fact, Mademoiselle Marguerite comments on the vulnerability of the male sex to woman's beauty: "Ha! que la puissance d'Amour est merveilleuse et étrange! assujettissant tellement les hommes à son volage plaisir, que la cire molle ne se manie point plus aisément . . . comme les cœurs humains sont disposés à tout changement, selon que veut cette folle puissance, qui se joue ores de ce pauvre chevalier" (609). Yet she seems to suggest that all human hearts are at risk to the effects of love. Marguerite has commented several times on the folly that accompanies this unstable desire, a folly that seems to come from a lack of conscious reflection on love's consequences. It is as if William's reason and common sense have been snatched away: "Partant, ce prince, destiné (quoi qu'il fût) à aimer, après s'être baigné aux merveilles d'un si bel objet, il se sentit ravi jusques au tiers ciel, où logent les Amours, et pensoit bien être au paradis de beauté, puisqu'il en avoit trouvé la déesse" (609).

In his rapture, his reason gives way to fantasy: "Il se pâme, regardant ses cheveux, son front, sa bouche et son sein; mais il meurt quand elle parle, quand elle rit, quand son œil glissant l'aperçoit, ou quand elle fait parler les gestes de sa blanche main." The narrator depicts sensory overload, where the prince allows his gaze to take in each part of the woman just as he had done with the portrait earlier. Like Prince Adilon in the third story, the king, still in the guise of the chevalier de Messi, experiences an increase in torment and turbulence as he retires to bed: "mais las! c'étoit un lit d'angoisse et travaux pour le chevalier de Messi, qui, comme un feu est plus ardent quand plus il est couvert, aussi d'autant plus étoit-il maltraité de sa passion, qu'il ne l'osoit plaindre ne communiquer à ses compagnons, de peur d'être non-seulement estimé léger et volage, ayant si tôt changé d'affection . . ." (612).

If the king's love is depicted as somewhat inconstant, Marguerite portrays the steadfast virtue of Parthénie/Viergine. Although she is without fortune, brought by force to the court of Denmark, she is of royal birth and strong moral fibre. She, like Clarinde in the third story, holds her own against the prince's desire:

> Monsieur, si vous pensiez, pour être grand, et moi, pauvre princesse déshéritee, que j'eusse le cœur si mal logé que de consentir à quelque vilenie, vous seriez bien trompé; car j'aimerois mieux passer le reste de mes ans . . . avec mes semblables, voire être accompagnée jusques au tombeau d'une importune misère . . . que vivre en la pleine jouissance du malheureux bonheur qu'ont celles qui repoussent leur pauvreté avec la perte de leur renommée. (617)

She would, however, consent to marriage and an honest bond of love: "Mais, s'il vous plaît m'honorer de votre sainte amitié et me lier à vous par un chaste mariage, je veux désormais vivre et mourir en votre loyal service" (617).

As William promises his honest intentions, their bond is sealed by a discreet squeeze of the hand: "A quoi la pucelle répondit, lui serrant la main étroitement." Reflection following the initial turbulence of passion and phantasm allows them to consecrate their love and to plot their return to England.

The third story depicts the positive and negative effects of phantasm. Negative in inspiring to wrong action is the case of Prince Adilon, possessed of an overreaching and unrequited desire for Clarinde, who feels nothing but distaste for him. In contrast, the bond between the Seigneur d'Alègre and Clarinde inspires discreet love. Prince Adilon is first portrayed as felled by his passion for Clarinde. He foolishly retires to bed to seek rest, but desire has transformed the feather mattress into a harsh anvil where "il forgeoit mille projets fantastiques, qui, aussitôt qu'ils étaient étoffés, s'évanouissaient et perdoient en l'air" (581). We recognize the phantasm of Ponifre. Set off by immoderate desire and remaining unrequited, it is a figment of one person's imagination.

Like Ponifre, Adilon puts his faith in male folklore concerning female passion. He seeks male counsel in a gentleman of the court, Lucidan, on how to pursue his lady. Once again, male perceptions of female sentiment prove faulty. Lucidan advises him to pursue Clarinde's mother in order to gain access to the daughter:

> Les fleurs meurent tous les ans et renaissent tous les ans, mais l'amour des filles naît et meurt tous les jours, sans qu'on y puisse rien voir de certain, fors cette règle infaillible que toujours le dernier chasse le premier, comme l'on voit une onde pousser l'autre, tant la nouveauté plaît à un esprit volage. (583)

Adilon accepts the myth of the fickle nature of young women's love and fails to anticipate the firm and solid love that Clarinde awards Adilon's rival, the Seigneur d'Alègre.

For loving faithfully, Clarinde is not less vulnerable to fantasy and dreaming about the Seigneur d'Alègre: "tellement qu'ayant à part elle ententivement remarqué un nombre infini de grâces et vertus en son gentilhomme françois, et, en faisant secrète comparaison, ne savoit laquelle elle devoit plus admirer; mais elle savoit bien qu'on ne lui eût pu rien désirer pour l'accomplissment d'une humaine perfection" (585).

Clarinde and Alègre communicate their love discreetly with a look or a gesture, so that each is certain that the affection is reciprocal. In contrast, Adilon keeps his passion hidden, feigns affection for Clarinde's mother, and clandestinely visits the private quarters of Clarinde as she is combing her hair. His only direct communication with her comes at the moment she mistakes him for Alègre and then hastens to cover her mistake.

Clarinde's virtue, paralleled in Alègre, lies in her ability to express herself directly and without guile. Fearing that her French lover may share the French flaw for fickle passion, she warns him that if he shows himself to be "léger," or "volage," in the French way, she will respond in the manner of teasing Italian women, "qui vous tiendra le bec en l'eau, et ne vous abreuvera que de moquerie" (588). As a pledge of her love and fidelity, she gives the Seigneur d'Alègre a ring, engraved with the saying "foi et secret." True love is based on trust, honest communication between lovers, and discretion. Prince Adilon has none of these attributes and shows his love to be counterfeit, a phantom of genuine sentiment. His attempt to kill the Seigneur d'Alègre with a poisoned apple, unwittingly eaten by Clarinde, sets the stage for the full declaration of love between Clarinde and Alègre on her deathbed. Furious at his rival's treachery, Alègre impales Adilon's "cœur . . . méchant et dissimulé" (591).

The third day reveals that phantasm in itself is not impure or misguided. It is a companion to desire. Yet, depending upon whether it is directed toward a discreet and faithful passion or distorted, dissimulated desire, it inspires virtue or vice. Unchecked and uncontrolled it leads to wrong action, social transgression, and even murder.

Yver's *devisant*, the Sieur de Bel-Accueil, illustrates the later humanist's concept of self-reflection on human action and desire. Clarinde and Alègre engage in self-reflective love: desire that stops to test the waters, to confirm with the partner, to set ground rules of trust and discretion. Prince Adilon's passion has more in common with the "chimeres et monstres fantasques" that are the fruit of leisure and consume themselves without self-reflection and control. Montaigne warns of the dangers of such aimless phantasm and seeks to "les mettre en rolle" (*Essais*, 1: 8. 33). Zachary S. Schiffman characterizes the later humanists by their focus on the "mind's self-conscious experience of the cognitive moment."[9]

The "forme maistresse" of thought, fantasy, desire, and imagination is the active process of self-reflection. Yver practices Montaigne's habit of recording his daydreams: "J'escoute à mes resveries parce que j'ay à les enroller" (*Essais*, 2: 18. 665). He also shares Montaigne's uneasiness with unchecked transformation. His stories highlight again and again the feverish instability of human nature struck by desire. It is "cette inconnue frénésie" (581) which leads one to misjudge oneself: "il se voit tellement changé sans savoir comment, qu'il se méconnoît soi-même" (580). Cupid's unpredictable darts were the greatest menace to the humanist's quest for self-knowledge. Cognitive awareness of desire and reflection on the power of love do not ensure a happy ending to love's narrative, but they add to the store of self-knowledge, that core of humanist thought and endeavor.

The châtelaine, in fact, recalls Plato in positing a concept of love which has nothing to do with the common concept of sensuality or passion, but embraces the concept of a love born of reflection. Love, according to the châtelaine, should be classed among the comtemplative virtues: "Il le faut donc mettre entre les vertus contemplatives . . . pource que c'est la vraie queux pour aiguiser les cogitations spirituelles, et les ériger en haut pour chercher vérité; car, je vous prie, qu'est-ce qui élève l'âme à la contemplation, sinon l'amour de vérité?" (652).

Thus the author of *Le Printemps* appears more intent on exploring the human capacity for imagination and self-reflection than on mirroring the

---

[9] Zachary S. Schiffman, "Humanism and the Problem of Relativism," in *Humanism in Crisis: The Decline of the French Renaissance*, ed. Philippe Desan (Ann Arbor: University of Michigan Press, 1991), 69–83, here 80.

details of the physical world about him. Love within the context of the stories of the five days can lead to deception and delusion, as we see in several of the stories, or it can be a path to self-knowledge. The authoritative figure of the châtelaine intervenes at the end to reinforce a concept already developed in the preceding stories—that contemplative love leads to moral virtue: "amour n'est autre chose qu'un désir de ce qui est bon." It ultimately inspires to the love of God: "et ce bon-là n'est autre chose qu'une influence de cette grande bonté qui est Dieu: ce qui a ému quelques-uns de dire que l'amour est une petite scintille de ce grand et parfait amour qui est Dieu" (632). Without contemplation, love never leaves the commonplace, "le vulgaire." It is only through self-reflection that love reaches beyond the self to the other and consequently to divine love. Phantasm misdirected leads to the "herbes sauvages et inutiles" of which Montaigne speaks in "De l'oisiveté" (*Essais*, 1: 8. 32). The lovers who go beyond the phantasm that is guided by sensuality in Yver's work to communicate with their beloved in an open and discreet manner come closer to experiencing the contemplative love described and praised at the end of *Le Printemps* by the châtelaine. It is a love that leads to self-knowledge and to the love of God. As the Sieur de Ferme-Foi concludes in Day Five, love is not good or bad in itself, but depends on the virtue of the self who loves: "il ne faut chercher plus loin ce qui est en nous-mêmes, qui sommes et la cause d'amour et la cause de ce qui s'ensuit; comme étant amour une compassion indifférente qui prend sa qualité bonne ou mauvaise, selon l'habitude et disposition du sujet qu'il rencontre et par lequel il fait son opération organique" (628). The right disposition of the self is at the root of love. Those who have not achieved self-awareness and self-mastery will be at a disadvantage in the game of love. Panurge's self-absorption and self-doubt in Rabelais's *Tiers Livre* prevent his successful pursuit of a viable companion. The gaze which contemplates the other must turn back on the self, for it is the understanding of the self and the other which leads us to the love of God.

Bibliography

Alcripe, Philippe d'. *La Nouvelle Fabrique des excellens traits de vérité*. Paris: Librairie Jannet, 1853.

Alfonsi, Petrus. *Disciplina clericalis*. Ed. and trans. Angel Gonzalez Palencia. Madrid: Consejo Superior de Investigaciones Científicas Patronato Menéndez y Pelayo, 1948.

———. *Disciplina clericalis*. Ed. and trans. Eberhard Hermes and P. R. Quarrie. Berkeley: University of California Press, 1977.

Aneau, Barthélemy. *Les Trois Premiers Livres de la Métamorphose d'Ovide*. Lyons: G. Roville, 1556. Ed. Jean-Claude Moisan with the collaboration of Marie-Claude Malenfant. Paris: H. Champion, 1997.

Arbour, Roméo. *Les Femmes et les métiers du livre (1600–1650)*. Chicago: Garamond Press, 1997.

Arnould, Jean-Claude. "L'«Auteur» invisible: Les *Nouvelles récréations et joyeux devis de feu Bonaventure des Périers*, de Robert Granjon." In *Conteurs et romanciers de la Renaissance: Mélanges offerts à Gabriel-André Pérouse*, ed. James Dauphiné and Béatrice Périgot, 27–37. Paris: Honoré Champion, 1997.

Auerbach, Erich. *Mimesis: The Representation of Reality in Western Literature*. Trans. Willard R. Trask. Princeton: Princeton University Press, 1953.

Baddeley, Susan. *L'Orthographe française au temps de la réforme*. Geneva : Droz, 1993.

Bakhtin, Mikhail. *The Dialogic Imagination*. Trans. Caryl Emerson and Michael Holquist. Ed. Michael Holquist. Austin: University of Texas Press, 1981.

———. *Rabelais and His World*. Trans. Hélène Iswolsky. Bloomington: Indiana University Press, 1984.

Barnett, Mary Jane. "Erasmus and the Hermeneutics of Linguistic Praxis." *Renaissance Quarterly* 49 (1996): 542–72.

Bédier, Joseph. *Les Fabliaux: Etudes de littérature populaire et d'histoire littéraire du Moyen Age*. 6th ed. Paris: Champion, 1969.

Benjamin, Walter. "The Storyteller." In idem, *Illuminations*, trans. Harry Zohn, ed. Hannah Arendt, 83–109. New York: Schocken Books, 1968.

Béroul. *Le Roman de Tristan*. Ed. Ernest Muret. 4th ed. rev. L. M. Defourques. Paris: Champion, 1982.

Bideaux, Michel. "Figures, thèmes, motifs et configurations: Propositions pour une sémantique narrative de l'*Heptaméron*." In *La Nouvelle: Définitions, transformations*, ed. Bernard Alluin and François Suard, 73–88. Collection UL3. Lille: Presses Universitaires de Lille, 1991.

Billon, François de. *Le Fort inexpugnable de l'honneur du sexe femenin*. Intro. M. A. Screech. Wakefield: S. R. Publishers; New York: Johnson Reprint; Paris and The Hague: Mouton, 1970.

Binford, Roberta Kay. "The *Comptes amoureux* of Jeanne Flore: A Critical Study." Ph.D. diss., University of Iowa, 1972.

Boccaccio, Giovanni. *Decameron*. Milan: Arnoldo Mondadori, 1985.

Bodin, Jean. *Les Six Livres de la republique*. Paris: Jacques du Puys, 1580.

Bouchet, Guillaume. *Les Serees*. Lyons: Rigaud, 1614.

Bourassin, Emmanuel. *Philippe le Bon: Le Grand Lion des Flandres*. Paris: Editions Tallandier, 1983.

Bourdigné, Charles. *La Légende joyeuse de maistre Pierre Faifeu*. Ed. Francis Valette. Geneva: Droz, 1972.

Bovelles, Charles de. *Liber de differentia vulgarium linguarum et gallici sermonis varietate*. Paris: Robert Estienne, 1533.

Boyle, Marjorie O'Rourke. *Erasmus on Language and Method in Theology*. Toronto: University of Toronto Press, 1977.

Brantôme, Pierre de Bourdeilles, seigneur de. *Les Dames galantes*. Ed. P. Pia. Paris: Gallimard, 1981.

———. *Recueil des dames*. Ed. E. Vaucheret. Paris: Gallimard, 1991.

Bray, Alan. "Homosexuality and the Signs of Male Friendship in Elizabethan England." In *Queering the Renaissance*, ed. Jonathan Goldberg, 40–61. Durham and London: Duke University Press, 1994.

———. *Homosexuality in Renaissance England*. London: Gay Men's Press, 1982.

Brenkman, John. "Narcissus in the Text." *Georgia Review* 30 (1976): 293–327.

Bright, Francis T. "Phantasm and (Women's) Storytelling in *Heptaméron* 12." Unpublished paper.

Brinker, Menachem. "Farce and the Poetics of the *Vraisemblable*." *Critical Inquiry* 9 (1983): 565–77.

Broc, Numa. *La Géographie de la Renaissance (1420–1620)*. Paris: Bibliothèque Nationale, 1980.

Bromfield, Joyce G. *De Lorenzino de Médicis à Lorenzaccio: Etude d'un thème historique*. Paris: Marcel Didier, 1972.

Cardano, Girolamo. *De Sapientia*. Nuremberg: J. Petreium, 1544.

Castiglione, Baldassare. *Il Libro del cortegiano*. Ed. Ghino Ghinassi. Florence: Sansoni, 1968.

Cave, Terence. "Travelers and Others: Cultural Connections in the Works of Rabelais." In *François Rabelais: Critical Assessments*, ed. Jean-Claude Carron, 39–56. Baltimore: Johns Hopkins University Press, 1995.

———, Michel Jeanneret, and François Rigolot. "Sur la prétendue transparence de Rabelais." *Revue d'Histoire Littéraire de la France* 86 (1986): 709–16.

Cazauran, Nicole. "La Première Manière de Noël Du Fail." In *Noël du Fail, Ecrivain*, ed. Magnien-Simonin, 35–47.

Céard, Jean, and Jean-Claude Margolin. *Rébus de la Renaissance: Des Images qui parlent*. 2 vols. Paris: Maisonneuve et Larose, 1986.

Cent nouvelles nouvelles, Les. In *Conteurs français du XVIe siècle*.

Certeau, Michel de. *L'Ecriture de l'histoire*. Paris: Gallimard, 1975.

———, Dominique Julia, and Jacques Revel. "La Beauté du mort." In *La Culture au pluriel*, ed. Luce Giard, 46–68. Paris: Seuil, 1994.

———. *Une Politique de la langue: Enquête sur le rapport de l'Abbé Grégoire*. Paris: Gallimard, 1975.

Chevallier, Pierre. *Henri III, roi shakespearien*. Paris: Fayard, 1985.

Cholakian, Patricia Francis. *Rape and Writing in the* Heptaméron *of Marguerite de Navarre*. Carbondale and Edwardsville: Southern Illinois University Press, 1991.

Chrétien de Troyes. *Le Chevalier de la charrete*. Ed. Mario Roques. Paris: Champion, 1983.

Cicero, Marcus Tullius. *De inventione. De optimo genere oratorum*. Trans. H. M. Hubbell. Loeb Classical Library. Cambridge, MA: Harvard University Press, 1949.

Conteurs français du XVIe siècle. Ed. Pierre Jourda. Paris: Gallimard, 1965.

Coras, Jean de. *Memorabilium Senatus Consultorum Summae*. Lyons: B. Vincentius, 1599.

———. *Resolutions de droict*. Paris: Jean Houzé, 1610. (Trans. by Jacques Baron of *Memorabilium Senatus Consultorum Summae*.)

Cotgrave, Randle. *A Dictionarie of the French and English Tongues* (1611). Columbia, SC: University of South Carolina Press, 1950.

———. *A Dictionarie of the French and English Tongues*. Amsterdam: Theatrum Orbis Terrarum; New York: Da Capo Press, 1971.

Culler, Jonathan. *On Deconstruction: Theory and Criticism after Structuralism*. Ithaca: Cornell University Press, 1982.

Cullière, Alain. "De la controverse à la nouvelle: Alexandre van den Bussche, lecteur de Sénèque." In *La Nouvelle de langue française*, ed. Engel and Guissard, 40–52.

Curtius, Ernst Robert. *European Literature and the Latin Middle Ages*. Trans. W. Trask. New York: Harper and Row, 1953.

Davis, Natalie Zemon. *Fiction in the Archives: Pardon Tales and their Tellers in Sixteenth-Century France*. Stanford: Stanford University Press, 1987.

———. "1526, July: Life-Saving Stories." In *A New History of French Literature*, ed. Denis Hollier, 139–45. Cambridge, MA: Harvard University Press, 1994.

———. *Women on the Margins: Three Seventeenth-Century Lives*. Cambridge, MA: Harvard University Press, 1995.

Defaux, Gérard. "Sur la prétendue pluralité du prologue de 'Gargantua'." *Revue d'Histoire Littéraire de la France* 86 (1986): 716–22.

Derrida, Jacques. *Mémoirs d'aveugle: L'Autoportrait et autres ruines*. Paris: Editions de la Réunion des musées nationaux, 1990.

Des Périers, Bonaventure. *Contes ou Nouvelles récréations et joyeux devis, suivis du Cymbalum mundi*. Ed. P. L. Jacob. Paris: Garnier, n. d.

———. *Nouvelles récréations et joyeux devis*. Ed. Krystyna Kasprzyk. Paris: Champion, 1980.

[Des Périers, Bonaventure?]. *Discours non plus melancoliques que divers, de choses mesmement qui appartiennent à nostre France: & a la fin La maniere de bien & justement entoucher les Lucs & Guiternes*. Poitiers: Enguilbert de Marnef, 1557.

Dictionnaire du moyen français. Ed. A. J. Greimas and T. M. Keane. Paris: Larousse, 1992.

Dictionnaire historique de la langue française. Paris: Dictionnaires Le Robert, 1992.

Diefendorf, Barbara. "Widowhood and Remarriage in Sixteenth-Century Paris." *Journal of Family History* 7 (1982): 379–95.

Di Stefano, Giuseppe. *Dictionnaire des locutions en moyen français*. Montréal: Editions CERES, 1991.

Dubuis, Roger. *Les Cent nouvelles nouvelles et la tradition de la nouvelle en France au Moyen Age*. Grenoble: Presses Universitaires de Grenoble, 1973.

——— "Réalité et réalisme dans les «Cent nouvelles nouvelles»." In *La Nouvelle française à la Renaissance*, ed. Sozzi, 91–119.

Du Fail, Noël. *Propos rustiques*. Ed. Gabriel-André Pérouse and Roger Dubuis. Geneva: Droz, 1994.

Duffy, Eamon. *Saints and Sinners: A History of the Popes*. New Haven: Yale University Press, 1997.

Engel, Vincent, and Michel Guissard, eds. *La Nouvelle de langue française aux frontières des autres genres, du Moyen Age à nos jours*. Ottignies, Belgium: Editions Quorum, 1997.

Erasmus, Desiderius. *Colloquia*. Ed. L.-E. Halkin et al. In *Opera omnia Desiderii Erasmi Roterodami*, Part 1, Vol. 3. Amsterdam: North Holland Publishing Company, 1972.

Fabri, Pierre. *Grand et vrai art de pleine rhetorique*. Rouen: A. Héron, 1521.

Ferguson, Gary. "Pedestrian Chivalry: Novella 50 and the Unsaddling of Courtly Tradition in the *Heptaméron*." In *Heroic Virtue, Comic Infidelity: Reassessing Marguerite de Navarre's* Heptaméron, ed. Dora E. Polachek, 118–31. Amherst: Hestia Press, 1993.

———. "Symbolic Sexual Inversion and the Construction of Courtly Manhood in Two French Romances." *The Arthurian Yearbook* 3 (1993): 203–13.

Ferrai, Luigi Alberto. *Lorenzino de' Medici e la società cortigiana del cinquecento*. Milan: Ulrico Hoepli, 1891.

Ferrier, Janet M. *Forerunners of the French Novel: An Essay on the Development of the Nouvelle in the Late Middle Ages*. Manchester: Manchester University Press, 1954.

Flore, Jeanne. *Contes amoureux*. Ed. Le Centre Lyonnais d'Etude de l'Humanisme, sous la direction de Gabriel-A. Pérouse. Lyon: Presses Universitaires de Lyon, 1980.

Fontaine, Marie-Madeleine. "Les Enjeux de pouvoir dans l'*Heptaméron*." In L'Heptaméron *de Marguerite de Navarre: Actes de la journée d'étude Marguerite de Navarre, 19 octobre 1991*, ed. Simone Perrier, 133–49 and 155–60. Cahiers textuel 10. Paris: L'U. F. R. «Sciences des textes et documents» avec le concours du Conseil Scientifique de l'Université de Paris VII, 1992.

Freccero, Carla. "Margaret of Navarre." In *A New History of French Literature*, ed. Denis Hollier, 145–48. Cambridge, MA: Harvard University Press, 1994.

———. "Marguerite de Navarre and the Politics of Maternal Sovereignty." *Cosmos* 7 (*Women and Sovereignty*, ed. Louise Olga Fradenburg) (1992): 132–49.

———. "Patriarchy and the Maternal Text: The Case of Marguerite de Navarre." In *Renaissance Women Writers: French Texts/American Contexts*, ed. Anne R. Larsen and Colette H. Winn, 130–40. Detroit: Wayne State University Press, 1994.

———. "Rape's Disfiguring Figures: Marguerite de Navarre's *Heptaméron*, Day 1:10." In *Rape and Representation*, ed. Lynn Higgins and Brenda Silver, 227–47. New York: Columbia University Press, 1990.

Freud, Sigmund. "The Uncanny." In *The Standard Edition of the Complete Psychological Works of Sigmund Freud*. Ed. and trans. James Strachey. Vol. 17: 217–52. London: Hogarth Press, 1955.

Gauthiez, Pierre. *Lorenzaccio (Lorenzino de Médicis) 1514–1548*. Paris: Albert Fontemoing, 1904.

Genette, Gérard. *Palimpsestes: La Littérature au second degré*. Paris: Seuil, 1982.

Girard, René. *Mensonge romantique et vérité romanesque*. Paris: Bernard Grasset, 1961. Trans. Yvonne Freccero. *Deceit, Desire, and the Novel: Self and Other in Literary Structure*. Baltimore and London: Johns Hopkins University Press, 1966.

Glidden, Hope. "Gender, Essence, and the Feminine (*Heptaméron* 43)." In *Critical Tales*, ed. Lyons and McKinley, 25–40.

Greenberg, David F. *The Construction of Homosexuality*. Chicago and London: University of Chicago Press, 1988.

Hartmann, Heidi. "The Unhappy Marriage of Marxism and Feminism: Towards a More Progressive Union." In *Women and Revolution: A Discussion of the Unhappy Marriage of Marxism and Feminism*, ed. Lydia Sargent, 1–41. Boston: South End Press, 1981.

Hassell, James Woodrow, Jr. *Sources and Analogues of the* Nouvelles récréations et joyeux devis *of Bonaventure des Périers*. 2 vols. Athens, GA: University of Georgia Press, 1969.

Huguet, Edmond. *Dictionnaire de la langue française du seizième siècle*. 7 vols. Paris: Didier, 1925–1967.

Hutcheon, Linda. *A Theory of Parody*. New York: Methuen, 1985.

Irigaray, Luce. *Ce sexe qui n'en est pas un*. Paris: Editions de Minuit, 1977.

———. "When the Goods Get Together." In *New French Feminisms*, ed. Elaine Marks and Isabelle de Courtivron, 107–10. Amherst: University of Massachusetts Press, 1980.

Jeanneret, Michel. *Des Mets et des mots*. Paris: J. Corti, 1987.

———. *Perpetuum mobile*. Paris: Macula, 1997.

Jordan, Constance. *Renaissance Feminism: Literary Texts and Political Models*. Ithaca and London: Cornell University Press, 1990.

Jouanna, Arlette. "Faveur et favoris: L'Exemple des mignons de Henri III." In *Henri III et son temps: Actes du colloque international du Centre de la Renaissance de Tours, octobre 1989*, ed. Robert Sauzet, 155–65. Paris: Vrin, 1992.

Jourda, Pierre. *Marguerite d'Angoulême, duchesse d'Alençon, reine de Navarre (1492–1549): Etude biographique et littéraire*. 2 vols. Bibliothèque littéraire de la Renaissance, nouv. sér. 19 and 20. Paris: Champion, 1930; repr. Geneva: Slatkine, 1978.

Karrow, Robert, Jr. *Sixteenth Century Mapmakers and their Maps*. Chicago: The Speculum Press for the Newberry Library, 1993.

Kelley, Donald. *Faces of History: Historical Inquiry from Herodotus to Herder*. New Haven: Yale University Press, 1998.

Kelso, Ruth. *Doctrine for the Lady of the Renaissance*. Urbana and Chicago: University of Illinois Press, 1958.

Knox, Dilwyn. *Ironia: Medieval and Renaissance Ideas on Irony*. Leiden: Brill, 1989.

Kuhn, David. *La Poétique de François Villon*. Paris: Armand Colin, 1967.

Labé, Louise. *Œuvres complètes*. Ed. François Rigolot. Paris: Garnier-Flammarion, 1986.

Lacan, Jacques. "Séminaire sur 'La lettre volée'." In idem, *Ecrits I*, 19–75. Paris: Editions du Seuil, 1966.

LaGuardia, David. *The Iconography of Power: The French Nouvelle at the End of the Middle Ages*. Newark, DE: University of Delaware Press, 1999.

Lajarte, Philippe de. "La Nouvelle aux frontières du commentaire et du dialogue dans *L'Heptaméron* de Marguerite de Navarre." In *La Nouvelle de langue française*, ed. Engel and Guissard, 77–113.

Langer, Ullrich. *Perfect Friendship: Studies in Literature and Moral Philosophy from Boccaccio to Corneille*. Geneva: Droz, 1994.

Leclercq-Magnien, A. "*Propos rustiques*: Caractérisation des devisants et statut du texte." In *Noël du Fail, Ecrivain*, ed. Magnien-Simonin, 49–61.

Lefebvre, Henri. *La Production de l'espace*. Paris: Anthropos, 1971.

———. *Rabelais*. Paris: Les Editeurs Français Réunis, 1955.

Lemaire de Belges, Jean. *Œuvres*. Ed. J. Stecher. 4 vols. Geneva: Slatkine Reprints, 1969.

Le Roux, Nicolas. *La Faveur du roi: Mignons et courtisans au temps des derniers Valois (vers 1547–vers 1589)*. Seyssel: Champ Vallon, 2001.

Léry, Jean de. *Histoire d'un voyage faict en la terre du Bresil*. Ed. Frank Lestringant. Paris: Livre de poche, 1994.

L'Estoile, Pierre de. *Journal de L'Estoile pour le règne de Henri III (1574–1589)*. Ed. Louis Raymond Lefèvre. Paris: Gallimard, 1943.

———. *Registre-Journal du règne de Henri III*. Ed. Madeleine Lazard and Gilbert Schrenck. Vol. 2 (1576–1578). Geneva: Droz, 1996.

Lestringant, Frank. "Rabelais et le récit toponymique." In idem, *Ecrire le monde à la Renaissance*, 109–28. Caen: Editions Paradigme, 1993.

Liébault, Jean. *Thresor des remedes secrets pour les maladies des femmes*. Paris: Jacques du Puys, 1585.

Longeon, Claude. "Du nouveau sur les *Comptes Amoureux de Madame Jeanne Flore*." In idem, *Hommes et livres de la Renaissance*, 259–67. Saint-Etienne: Institut Claude Longeon, 1990.

———. *Les Premiers Combats pour la langue française*. Paris: Livre de Poche Classique, 1989.

Lorris, Guillaume de, and Jean de Meung. *Le Roman de la rose*. Ed. Ernest Langlois. 5 vols. Paris: Firmin-Didot, 1914–1924.

Lyons, John D. *Exemplum: The Rhetoric of Example in Early Modern France and Italy*. Princeton: Princeton University Press, 1989.

———, and Mary McKinley, eds. *Critical Tales: New Studies of the* Heptameron *and Early Modern Culture*. Philadelphia: University of Pennsylvania Press, 1993.

Machiavelli, Niccolò. *Il Principe e altre opere politiche*. Ed. Stefano Andretta. Milan: Garzanti, 1976.

Magnien-Simonin, C., ed. *Noël du Fail, Ecrivain*. Paris: J. Vrin, 1991.

Marguerite de Navarre. *L'Heptaméron*. In *Conteurs français du XVIe siècle*.

———. *L'Heptaméron*. Ed. Michel François. Paris: Garnier, 1967.

———. *Heptaméron*. Ed. Renja Salminen. Geneva: Droz, 1999.

———. *Le Miroir de l'âme pécheresse*. Ed. Renja Salminen. Helsinki: Suomalainen Tiedeakatemia, 1979.

Marie de France. *Les Lais*. Ed. Jean Rychner. Paris: Champion, 1983.

Marmontel, Jean-François. *Œuvres complètes*. 7 vols. Geneva: Slatkine, 1968.

Marot, Clément. *Œuvres complètes*. Ed. B. Saint-Marc. 2 vols. Paris: Garnier, [1911].

Mathieu-Castellani, Gisèle. *La Conversation conteuse: Les Nouvelles de Marguerite de Navarre*. Paris: Presses Universitaires de France, 1992.

———. "Pour une poétique de la nouvelle." *Canadian Review of Comparative Literature* 18 (1991): 167–78.

Matthieu, Pierre. *Histoire de France, & des Choses Memorables aduenues aux Prouinces estrangeres durant sept annees de Paix, du regne du roy Henry IIII. Roy de France & de Nauarre*. Cologny: Porret, 1613.

Medici, Lorenzo de'. *Apologia*. Trans. in Gauthiez, *Lorenzaccio*, 305–23.

Mignet, M. *La Rivalité de François Ier et de Charles-Quint*. 2 vols. Paris: Librairie Académique Didier, 1886.

Mignolo, Walter. *The Darker Side of the Renaissance: Literacy, Territoriality, and Colonization.* Ann Arbor: University of Michigan Press, 1995.

Montaigne, Michel de. *Les Essais.* Ed. Pierre Villey. 3 vols. Paris: Quadrige/Presses Universitaires de France, 1992.

———. *Œuvres complètes.* Ed. Albert Thibaudet and Maurice Rat. Bibliothèque de la Pléiade. Paris: Gallimard, 1962.

Musset, Alfred de. *Lorenzaccio.* Paris: Larousse, 1991.

Nabokov, Vladimir. *Lolita.* New York: Vintage International, 1997.

Nodier, Charles. *Des Auteurs du seizième siècle qu'il convient de réimprimer.* Paris: Techener, 1835.

Oresko, Robert. "Homosexuality and the Court Elites of Early Modern France: Some Problems, Some Suggestions, and an Example." In *The Pursuit of Sodomy: Male Homosexuality in Renaissance and Enlightenment Europe,* ed. Kent Gerard and Gert Hekma, 105–28. New York and London: Harrington Park/Haworth Press, 1988. Published simultaneously as a special issue of the *Journal of Homosexuality* 16, nos. 1 and 2.

Orgel, Stephen. *Impersonations: The Performance of Gender in Shakespeare's England.* Cambridge: Cambridge University Press, 1996.

Ovid. *Metamorphoses.* Ed. and trans. Frank Justus Miller. 2 vols. Loeb Classical Library. Cambridge, MA: Harvard University Press; London: William Heinemann, 1984.

Oxford Dictionary of the Christian Church, The. 2nd edition. Ed. F. L. Cross and E. A. Livingstone. Oxford: Oxford University Press, 1974.

Oxford English Dictionary, The. Compact Edition. 2 vols. New York: Oxford University Press, 1971.

Paradin, Guillaume. *Histoire de notre tems.* Lyons: Jean de Tournes and Guillaume Gazeau, 1558.

———. *Memoriae nostrae libri quatuor.* Lyons: Jean de Tournes, 1548.

Paris, Gaston. "Les Contes orientaux dans la littérature française du moyen âge." In *La Poésie du Moyen Age.* Deuxième série, 75–108. Paris: Hachette, 1895.

———. "Le Lai de l'épervier." *Romania* 7 (1878): 1–21.

Pérouse, Gabriel-A. "Le Dessein des *Propos rustiques*." In *Études seiziémistes offertes à Monsieur le Professeur V.-L. Saulnier par plusieurs de ses anciens doctorants*, intro. Robert Aulotte, 137–50. Geneva: Droz, 1980.

———. *Nouvelles françaises du XVIᵉ siècle: Images de la vie du temps*. Geneva: Droz, 1977.

Philipot, E. *La Vie et l'œuvre littéraire de Noël Du Fail*. Paris: Champion, 1914.

Poirier, Guy. *L'Homosexualité dans l'imaginaire de la Renaissance*. Confluences-Champion 7. Paris: Champion, 1996.

Rabelais, François. *Gargantua*. Ed. Jacques Boulenger. Paris: Gallimard, 1955.

———. *Œuvres complètes*. Ed. Mireille Huchon. Paris: Gallimard, 1994.

———. *Le Tiers Livre*. Ed. Michael Screech. Geneva: Droz, 1964.

Rally, Alexandre. "Commentaire de la XIIᵉ nouvelle de l'«Heptaméron»." *Revue du seizième siècle* 11 (1924): 208–21.

Reynolds-Cornell, Régine. "Madame Jeanne Flore and the *Contes amoureux*: A Pseudondym [*sic*] and a Paradox." *Bibliothèque d'Humanisme et Renaissance* 51 (1989): 123–33.

Robin, Gilbert. *L'Enigme sexuelle d'Henri III (Etude psycho-sexuelle du transsexualisme)*. Paris: Wesmael-Charlier, 1964.

Rocke, Michael. *Forbidden Friendships: Homosexuality and Male Culture in Renaissance Florence*. New York and Oxford: Oxford University Press, 1996.

Roman de Renart, Le. Ed. Mario Roques. 6 vols. Paris: Champion, 1955–1966.

Ronsard, Pierre de. *Œuvres complètes*. Ed. Paul Laumonier with I. Silver and R. Lebègue. 20 vols. Paris: Société des Textes Français Modernes, 1914–1975.

———. *Œuvres complètes*. Ed. Jean Céard, Daniel Ménager, and Michel Simonin. 2 vols. Bibliothèque de la Pléiade. Paris: Gallimard, 1993–1994.

Rose, Margaret. *Parody: Ancient, Modern, and Post-modern.* Cambridge: Cambridge University Press, 1993.

Rossi, Luciano. "Entre fabliau et facétie: La Nouvelle en France au XVe siècle." In *La Nouvelle de langue française*, ed. Engel and Guissard, 28–39.

Rubin, Gayle. "The Traffic in Women: Notes on the 'Political Economy' of Sex." In *Toward an Anthropology of Women*, ed. Rayna R. Reiter, 157–210. New York: Monthly Review Press, 1975.

Russell, Daniel. "Some Ways of Structuring Character in the *Heptameron*." In *Critical Tales*, ed. Lyons and McKinley, 203–17.

Saslow, James M. *Ganymede in the Renaissance: Homosexuality in Art and Society.* New Haven and London: Yale University Press, 1986.

Schenck, Mary Jane Stearns. "Narrative Structure in the Exemplum, Fabliau, and the Nouvelle." *Romanic Review* 72 (1981): 367–82.

Schiffman, Zachary S. "Humanism and the Problem of Relativism." In *Humanism in Crisis: The Decline of the French Renaissance*, ed. Philippe Desan, 69–83. Ann Arbor: University of Michigan Press, 1991.

Sedgwick, Eve Kosofsky. *Between Men: English Literature and Male Homosocial Desire.* New York: Columbia University Press, 1985.

Le Singe à la porte: Vers une théorie de la parodie, textes rassemblés et édités par Groupar. New York: Peter Lang, 1984.

Smith, Bruce R. *Homosexual Desire in Shakespeare's England: A Cultural Poetics.* Chicago and London: University of Chicago Press, 1991.

Smith, Catherine Delano. *Maps in Bibles.* Geneva: Droz, 1992.

Snyder, Susan. "Guilty Sisters: Marguerite de Navarre, Elizabeth of England, and the *Miroir de l'âme pécheresse*." *Renaissance Quarterly* 50 (1997): 443–58.

Söderhjelm, Werner. *La Nouvelle française au XVe siècle.* Paris: Champion, 1910; repr. Geneva: Slatkine, 1973.

Sozzi, Lionello. *Les Contes de Bonaventure des Périers: Contribution à l'étude de la nouvelle française de la Renaissance.* Turin: Giappichelli, 1965.

———. "L'Intention du conteur: Des textes introductifs aux recueils de nouvelles." In *L'Ecrivain face à son public en France et en Italie à la Renaissance*, ed. C. A. Fiorato and Jean-Claude Margolin, 71–83. Paris: Vrin, 1989.

———, ed. *La Nouvelle française à la Renaissance*. Geneva and Paris: Slatkine, 1981.

———, ed. *La Nouvelle française de la Renaissance*. 2 vols. Turin: G. Giappichelli, 1973–1977.

Stendhal. *Le Rouge et le noir*. In *Romans et nouvelles*. Paris: Gallimard, 1952.

Swearingen, C. Jan. *Rhetoric and Irony: Western Literacy and Western Lies*. New York: Oxford University Press, 1991.

Tabourot, Etienne. *Les Bigarrures et touches*. Paris: Jean Richer, 1603.

Tetel, Marcel. *Marguerite de Navarre's* Heptaméron: *Themes, Language, and Structure*. Durham, NC: Duke University Press, 1973.

Todorov, Tzvetan. *Poétique de la prose*. Paris: Seuil, 1971.

Tory, Geofroy. *Champ fleury*. Paris: G. Tory and G. de Gourmont 1529.

———. *Itinerarium provinciarum omnium Antonini Augusti*. Paris: Henri Estienne, 1512.

Tournier, Michel. *Le Coq de bruyère*. Paris: Gallimard, 1978.

Tournon, André. "Conte véritable, véritable conte." In *Conteurs et romanciers de la Renaissance: Mélanges offerts à Gabriel-André Pérouse*, ed. James Dauphiné and Béatrice Périgot, 379–93. Paris: Champion, 1997.

Troyes, Nicolas de. *Le Grand Parangon des nouvelles nouvelles* (choix). Ed. Krystyna Kasprzyk. Paris: Librairie Nizet, 1970.

Varchi, Benedetto. *Storia fiorentina*, extract trans. by Paul de Musset. In Alfred de Musset, *Lorenzaccio*.

Vaughan, Herbert M. *The Medici Popes (Leo X and Clement VII)*. London: Methuen, 1908.

Vigneulles, Philippe de. *Les Cent nouvelles nouvelles*. Ed. Charles H. Livingston. Geneva: Droz, 1972.

Vinge, Louise. *The Narcissus Theme in Western European Literature up to the Early 19th Century*. Lund: Skånska Centraltryckeriet, 1967.

Virgil. *Aeneid*. Trans. and ed. H. R. Fairclough, rev. G. P. Goold. 2 vols. Loeb Classical Library. Cambridge, MA and London: Harvard University Press, 1999–2001.

Vives, Juan Luis. *De Institutione Feminae Christianae*. Ed. C. Fantazzi and C. Matheeussen. Trans. C. Fantazzi. 2 vols. Leiden: Brill, 1998.

———. *The Education of a Christian Woman*. Trans. C. Fantazzi. Chicago: University of Chicago Press, 2000.

Weber, Henri. "La Facétie et le bon mot du Pogge à Des Périers." In *Humanism in France at the End of the Middle Ages and in the Early Renaissance*, ed. A. H. T. Levi, 82–105. Manchester: Manchester University Press, 1970.

Webster's Third International Dictionary of the English Language. Springfield, MA: G. and C. Merriam, 1971.

Wiesner, Merry E. *Women and Gender in Early Modern Europe*. 2nd. Ed. Cambridge: Cambridge University Press, 2000.

Yver, Jacques. *Le Printemps d'Yver*. In *Les Vieux Conteurs français*, ed. P. L. Jacob [Paul La Croix]. Paris : Société du Panthéon Littéraire, 1841; repr. Geneva: Slatkine, 1970.

Zerner, Henri. *L'Art français du XVIe siècle: L'Invention du classicisme*. Paris: Flammarion, 1996.

CONTRIBUTORS

Tom Conley, author of *The Self-Made Map: Cartographic Writing in Early Modern France* (1996) and *L'Inconscient graphique* (2000), has completed *A Map in a Movie* (University of Minnesota Press, forthcoming 2005).

Gary Ferguson is Professor of French at the University of Delaware. He is the author of *Mirroring Belief: Marguerite de Navarre's Devotional Poetry* (Edinburgh University Press, 1992) and of articles on medieval and early modern French literature and culture dealing in particular with religious history, women's writing, and questions of gender and sexuality. He has also published a critical edition of Anne de Marquets's *Sonets spirituels* (Droz, 1997).

Floyd Gray, Professor Emeritus at the University of Michigan (Ann Arbor), has a B.A. from Syracuse University, and an M.A. and Ph.D. from the University of Wisconsin (Madison). He is the author of various articles and books on French literature of the sixteenth and seventeenth centuries, notably: *Le Style de Montaigne* (1958), *Rabelais et l'écriture* (1974), *La Poétique de Du Bellay* (1978), *La Balance de Montaigne: Exagium/essai* (1982), *La Bruyère amateur de caractères* (1986), *Montaigne bilingue: Le Latin des Essais* (1991), *Rabelais et le comique du discontinu* (1994), and *Gender, Rhetoric, and Print Culture in French Renaissance Writing* (2000). In addition, he edited Albert Thibaudet's *Montaigne* (1963), an *Anthologie de la poésie française du XVIe siècle* (1967), and Rabelais's *Gargantua* (1995) and *Pantagruel* (1997). He has taught at Michigan State University and the University of Wisconsin and was Distinguished Visiting Professor at the University of California, Santa Barbara.

David LaGuardia is Associate Professor at Dartmouth College, where he teaches French and Comparative Literature. His book, *The Iconography of Power: The French Nouvelle at the End of the Middle Ages* (1999), examines the ways in which narrative structures gender and power relations in three *nouvelle* collections. He is currently working on a study of masculinity in Rabelais, Brantôme, and the *Cent nouvelles nouvelles*. He has also written on Blaise de Monluc, the *Heptaméron*, and American popular culture.

Deborah N. Losse is Professor of French and Divisional Dean of Humanities at Arizona State University. She has also served three years as chair of the Department of Languages and Literatures and six years as Associate Dean of the Graduate College. With a B.A. in French from Connecticut College and an M.A. and Ph.D. from the University of North Carolina at

Chapel Hill, Losse has published *Rhetoric at Play: Rabelais and Satirical Eulogy* and *Sampling the Book: Renaissance Prologues of the French Conteurs*. She has also published articles on Rabelais, Montaigne, Marguerite de Navarre, and the *conteurs* of the Renaissance for such journals as *Poetics Today, MLN, Romanic Review, Neophilologus, Medievalia et Humanistica*, and *Renaissance and Reformation/Renaissance et Réforme*. She contributed articles on Bonaventure des Périers, Guy Le Fèvre de La Boderie, and Béroalde de Verville to the *Encyclopedia of the Renaissance*.

John O'Brien is Professor of French at Royal Holloway College, University of London. His publications range from the classical tradition (*Anacreon redivivus* and *Les Odes d'Anacréon de Remy Belleau*, both 1995) to literary and cultural theory (*(Ré)Interprétations* [1995] and *Distant Voices Still Heard* [2000]), with a particular source of interest in Montaigne: he is the editor of *La Familia de Montaigne* (2001) and a contributor to the forthcoming *Cambridge Companion to Montaigne* (Cambridge University Press) and the *Dictionnaire de Montaigne* (Champion, 2004). He is currently working on a monograph entitled *The Third Eye: Imagination's Sight in the French Renaissance* and plans a book on the Martin Guerre narratives under the title *La Chaleur de la narration*.

Richard L. Regosin is Professor of French at the University of California, Irvine. His publications include books on D'Aubigné and Montaigne, including *Montaigne's Unruly Brood: Textual Engendering and the Challenge to Paternal Authority* (1996). He has also published recent articles on such French Renaissance writers as Marguerite de Navarre, D'Aubigné, La Boétie, and Du Bellay.

Emily Thompson is Associate Professor of French at Webster University in Saint Louis. Her research interests include gender, truth claims, and intertextuality in the *nouvelle*. She is currently working on a book entitled *Alternative Discourses in the French Nouvelle*.

Index of People and Works

Aesop, *Fables*, 32, 37
Alcripe, Philippe d'
   La Nouvelle Fabrique, 21
Alfonsi, Petrus
   Disciplina clericalis, 13, 139–49, 152, 153, 154, 156
Aneau, Barthélemy
   Les Trois Premiers Livres de la Métamor-phose d'Ovide, 29n. 29
Apian, Peter, 40n. 8
Arbour, Roméo, 125n. 7
Aretino, Pietro, 100n. 10
Aristotle, 107
Arnould, Jean-Claude, 47n. 18
Auerbach, Erich, 1, 5, 17n. 3, 19, 19n. 9
Augereau, Antoine, 36n. 1

Baddeley, Susan, 36n. 1
Bakhtin, Mikhail, 1, 63n. 6, 148n. 10
Bandello, Matteo, 139n. 1
Barnett, Mary Jane, 27n. 24
Baron, Jacques, 115n. 51, 118n. 63
Bédier, Joseph, 1, 3
Belleforest, François de, 57
Bello, Francesco
   Menbriano, 77n. 1
Benjamin, Walter, 69–70
Béroul
   Roman de Tristan, 111
Bible, 9, 35, 39–40n. 7, 144, 154
Bideaux, Michel, 107n. 27
Billon, François de
   Le Fort inexpugnable, 82n. 2
Binford, Roberta Kay, 88n. 15
Boccaccio, Giovanni, 160
   Decameron, 5n. 10, 17, 19, 25, 29, 61, 68, 77n. 1, 78–79, 122n. 71, 152, 160n. 4
   Genealogia Deorum, 29n. 29
Bodel, Jean, 37
Bodin, Jean, 108
   Les Six Livres de la republique, 108

Boemus, Joannes, 56n. 25
Boiardo, Matteo Maria
   Orlando innamorato, 77n. 1
Bouchet, Guillaume, 125n. 8
Bourassin, Emmanuel, 145n. 8
Bourdigné, Charles
   La Légende joyeuse de maistre Pierre Faifeu, 47n. 17
Bovelles, Charles de, 37n. 3
Boyle, Marjorie O'Rourke, 27n. 24
Brantôme, Pierre de Bourdeilles, seigneur de, 113, 115, 125
Bray, Alan, 113, 114nn. 48–49, 118, 119n. 66
Brenkman, John, 90n. 17
Bright, Francis T., 103, 103n. 22, 104n. 23, 105, 121
Brinker, Menachem, 33n. 32
Broc, Numa, 56n. 25
Bromfield, Joyce, 99n. 8, 112n. 41
Bussche, Alexandre van den
   Premier Livre des procès tragiques, 4

Cabei, Giulio Cesare, 125
Cardano, Girolamo, 98, 98n. 5, 110
   De Sapientia, 98
Castiglione, Baldassare
   Il Libro del cortegiano, 28–29
Cave, Terence, 26n. 23, 38n. 5
Cazauran, Nicole, 66n. 8
Céard, Jean, 42–43n. 12
Cent nouvelles nouvelles, 1, 3n. 6, 5n. 10, 6, 6n. 15, 8, 13, 17, 25, 36, 139n. 1, 140–41, 144–51, 157
Certeau, Michel de, 39n. 6, 123n. 3, 137
Charles V, Holy Roman Emperor, 101n. 15
Charles d'Alençon, 155, 157
Charles the Bold, Duke of Burgundy, 37, 144n. 8
Chevallier, Pierre, 116n. 54, 119n. 67

Cholakian, Patricia Francis, 104n. 23, 153n. 15
Chrétien de Troyes
   Chevalier de la charrete, 111
Christine de Pisan, 81n. 7, 155
Cicero, Marcus Tullius, 27
Collerye, Roger de, 50n. 20
Colonna, Francisco
   Hypnerotomachia Poliphili, 77n. 1
Conley, Tom, 9–10
Coras, Jean de, 115, 118n. 63
Cotgrave, Randle, 48, 42n. 11, 50n. 20, 64–65, 111n. 38, 165n. 8
Crenne, Hélisenne de, 78n. 2
Culler, Jonathan, 91n. 17
Cullière, Alain, 4
Curtius, Ernst-Robert, 81n. 7

Davis, Natalie Zemon, 123, 137
Defaux, Gérard, 26n. 23
Denisot, Nicolas, 56n. 24
Derrida, Jacques, 137–38
Des Périers, Bonaventure, 17–18, 26n. 22
   Cymbalum mundi, 42n. 10, 56n. 24
   Discours non plus melancoliques que divers, 9–10, 37–41, 55–59
   Nouvelles récréations et joyeux devis, 8–9, 14, 17–34, 35–55, 162
   Les Poésies du feu Bonaventure Des Périers, 35
Diderot, Denis, 64
Diefendorf, Barbara, 124n. 4
Di Stefano, Giuseppe, 111n. 37
Dolet, Etienne, 78n. 2
Du Bourg, Marguerite, 78n. 2
Dubuis, Roger, 3, 6, 18–19, 60
Du Fail, Noël
   Les Propos rustiques, 9, 10–11, 59–77
Duffy, Eamon, 120n. 68
Du Guillet, Pernette, 78n. 2

Edward II, King of England, 119n. 67

Erasmus, Desiderius, 35, 37, 125, 159
   Adages, 35
   Colloquia, 35, 84n. 11

Fabri, Pierre
   Grand et vrai art de pleine rhetorique, 20, 27n. 26
Ferguson, Gary, 12, 111n. 39
Ferrai, Luigi Alberto, 99–100n. 10
Ferrier, Janet, 3, 5, 7, 18n. 4
Flore, Jeanne
   Les Comptes amoureux, 9, 11, 77–96
Fontaine, Marie-Madeleine, 12, 98nn. 3–4, 100–101, 103, 109, 110
François I, King of France, 40, 97, 102n. 18
Freccero, Carla, 101, 101n17, 104n. 24, 153n. 15
Freud, Sigmund, 13, 101n. 17, 142, 150
Fusco, Horatio, 126

Gaillarde, Jeanne, 78n. 2
Gauthiez, Pierre, 100n. 10, 120n. 68
Gaveston, Piers, 119n. 67
Genette, Gérard, 63n. 6
Gesta romanorum, 139n. 1
Girard, René, 12, 101–2
Glidden, Hope, 129n. 13
Granjon, Robert, 36, 47n. 18
Gray, Floyd, 11
Greenberg, David F., 114n. 48
Grégoire, Henri (L'Abbé), 39n. 6

Hartmann, Heidi, 104–5n. 25
Hassell, James Woodrow, 25
Henri, King of Navarre, 157
Henri III, King of France, 112n. 41, 116–9
Henri IV, King of France and Navarre, 136
Herodotus, 137
Hollier, Denis, 123n. 1

Huguet, Edmond, 149n. 12
Hutcheon, Linda, 63n. 6

Irigaray, Luce, 105n. 25, 149

Jeanneret, Michel, 26n. 23, 66–67n. 9, 159
Jerome, Saint, 57, 124n. 5
Jordan, Constance, 124n. 5, 125n. 7, 125n. 9
Jouanna, Arlette, 119n. 67
Jourda, Pierre, 23n. 19, 99n. 9
Julia, Dominique, 39n. 6
Justin (Marcus Junianus Justinus), 57
Justinian
  Novellae constitutiones, 4

Karrow, Robert, Jr., 40n. 8
Kaufman, Andy, 64
Kelley, Donald, 136n. 20, 137nn. 21–22
Kelso, Ruth, 124, 125n. 9
Knox, Dilwyn, 85–86n. 13
Kuhn, David, 49n. 20

Labé, Louise
  Débat de Folie et d'Amour, 85, 94
La Borderie, Arthur de, 75
Lacan, Jacques, 162
LaGuardia, David, 2n. 3, 13–14
Lajarte, Philippe de, 3n. 5
Langer, Ullrich, 107n. 30, 109n. 34
Leclercq-Magnien, A., 71n. 14
Lefebvre, Henri, 40n. 9
Lemaire de Belges, Jean, 11, 82, 83n. 9, 86
  Illustrations de Gaule, 82, 83n. 9
Leonardo da Vinci, 40n. 9
Le Roux, Nicolas, 119n. 67
Léry, Jean de, 123n. 3
L'Estoile, Pierre de, 116–17, 119n. 67
Lestringant, Frank, 37n. 3
Liébault, Jean, 113n. 44
Longeon, Claude, 38n. 4, 78n. 2

Lorris, Guillaume de and Jean de Meung
  Roman de la rose, 94n. 21
Losse, Deborah N., 14–15
Louis XI, King of France, 144–45n. 8
Lucian, 36n. 2
Lyons, John D., 7n. 17, 72n. 15, 129n. 13, 151–52n. 13

Machiavelli, Nicolo, 108, 120
Magnien-Simonin, C., 61n. 3
Margolin, Jean-Claude, 43n. 12
Marguerite de Navarre, 22, 26n. 22, 35, 157, 160
  Heptaméron, 1, 3n. 5, 4, 5, 7, 9, 12–14, 17, 22, 25, 32, 68, 72n. 15, 78, 81, 97–122, 123–38, 141, 144n. 7, 151–58, 161, 162, 164n. 7
  Miroir de l'âme pécheresse, 81, 81n. 7, 102n. 18
Marie de France, 111
Marlowe, Christopher, 119n. 67
Marmontel, Jean-François, 77n. 1
Marnef, Enguilbert de, 37, 54
Marot, Clément, 35, 45–46, 46n. 16, 49, 51, 166
  Adolescence clémentine, 45–46
Mathieu-Castellani, Gisèle, 9, 17, 20–21, 72n. 15, 128n. 12
Matthieu, Pierre, 136–37
Maugin, Jean, 75n. 16
McKinley, Mary B., 7n. 17, 129n. 13
Medici, Alessandro de', 97–99, 100n. 12, 109–10, 112n. 41, 120
Medici, Catherine de', 97, 100n. 13
Medici, Francesco de', 120n. 68
Medici, Giulio de' (Pope Clement VII), 97n. 1, 120n. 68
Medici, Laudomia de', 112n. 42
Medici, Lorenzo de', 97–112, 97n. 1, 99n. 8, 120n. 68
Medici, Lorenzo de', Duke of Urbino, 97n. 1

Mignet, M., 144n. 8
Mignolo, Walter, 138n. 26
Montaigne, Michel Eyquem de, 1, 14, 159
   Essais, 14, 55n. 24, 112n. 40, 118n. 64, 159–60, 171, 172
Montreuil, Jean de, 81n. 7
Münster, Sebastian, 56n. 25, 57
Musset, Alfred de, 12, 97

Nabokov, Vladimir, 6–7n. 16
Nisard, Charles, 39n. 6
Nodier, Charles, 55, 55n. 24

O'Brien, John, 12–13
Olivétan (Pierre Robert), 36n. 1
Oresko, Robert, 114n. 50
Orgel, Stephen, 116–17
Ovid, 11, 82, 90–94
   Metamorphoses, 77n. 1, 83, 90–94

Paradin, Guillaume
   Histoire de notre tems, 98n. 6, 99n. 8
   Memoriae nostrae libri quatuor, 98
Paris, Gaston, 1, 3
Pasquier, Etienne, 10, 59–63
Patrizi, Francesco
   Della historia diece dialoghi, 138n. 26
Paul, Saint, 38, 40, 57
Pelletier du Mans, Jacques, 55n. 24
Pérouse, Gabriel-A., 5–6, 7, 59n. 1, 60, 61n. 3, 62n. 4, 67
Petrarch, Francesco
   Trionfi, 77n. 1
Philipot, E., 61n. 3, 62n. 4, 66, 75
Philippe the Good, Duke of Burgundy, 144–45
Picart, Bernard, 55n. 24
Pico della Mirandola, Giovanni, 159
Plato, 60, 171
Poe, Edgar Allan, 162
Poggio Bracciolini, Gian Francesco, 17, 36n. 2
Poirier, Guy, 113n. 44, 114 nn. 48–49, 115n. 51, 118n. 62, 119n. 67

Rabelais, François, 1, 10, 15, 35, 37n. 3, 38, 40, 43n. 13, 50, 55n. 24, 59–67, 74, 75, 77, 159
   [*Cinquiesme Livre*], 43n. 13
   Gargantua, 10, 21n. 16, 26, 35, 47, 59, 61, 66
   Pantagruel, 10, 35, 50, 59, 61, 77
   Tiers Livre, 165, 172
Rally, Alexandre, 99n. 10, 100nn. 11–12, 110n. 35, 112nn. 41–42
Regosin, Richard L., 10–11
Reynolds-Cornell, Régine, 80n. 5
Revel, Jacques, 39n. 6
Rigolot, François, 26n. 23
Robin, Gilbert, 116n. 54
Rocke, Michael, 114n. 48, 117–18
Ronsard, Pierre de, 67, 92n. 19, 116n. 52
   La Franciade, 30n. 29
   Roman de Renart, 121
Rose, Margaret, 63n. 6
Rossi, Luciano, 2–3, 4, 6
Rothstein, Marian, 112n. 40
Rubin, Gayle, 104n. 25
Russell, Daniel, 7–8, 132n. 14

Salminen, Renja, 97n. 3, 99n. 8, 100n. 13
Saslow, James M., 114n. 47
Saulnier, V. L., 1n. 2
Savonarola, Girolamo, 125n. 9
Scève, Claudine, 78n. 2
Scève, Jeanne, 78n. 2
Scève, Maurice, 166
Schenck, Mary Jane Stearns, 20
Schiffman, Zachary S., 171n. 9
Sedgwick, Eve Kosofsky, 12, 102
Seneca the Elder, 115
   Controversiae, 4
Smith, Bruce, 114, 119n. 67
Smith, Catherine Delano, 40n. 7
Snyder, Susan, 102n. 18
Socrates, 47, 60
Söderhjelm, Werner, 1, 5, 17n. 3, 18, 19n. 8

Sozzi, Lionello, 1n. 2, 6, 9, 20–21, 36n. 2
Stendhal (Marie Henri Beyle), 10
Strabo, 57
Strozzi family, 100n. 13, 101n. 15
Strozzi, Filipo, 100n. 12
Strozzi, Pierre, 112n. 42
Strozzi, Robert, 112n. 42
Swearingen, C. Jan, 85–86n. 13

Tabourot, Etienne, 43n. 13
Tetel, Marcel, 127n. 11
Thompson, Emily, 9
 Thousand and One Nights, 68
Todorov, Tzvetan, 19
Tory, Geofroy, 37, 42–43n. 12
Tournes, Jean de, 35
Tournier, Michel, 8
Tournon, André, 121–22n. 71
Trissino, Gian Giorgio, 124n. 5
Trotto, Bernardo, 125
Troyes, Nicolas de
 Le Grand Parangon des nouvelles nouvelles, 18n. 5, 32

Valois, Marguerite de, 115
Varchi, Benedetto, 98, 99n. 8, 107n. 28
 Storia fiorentina, 98, 99n. 8, 107n. 28
Vaughan, Herbert M., 120n. 68
Vauzelles, Jean de, 100n. 10
Vigneulles, Philippe de, 21–22
 Cent nouvelles nouvelles, 21–22, 25
Villon, François, 46, 49
 Le Grant Testament, 49, 51
Vincent of Beauvais, 139n. 1
Vinge, Louise, 93n. 20
Virgil, Polydore, 11, 82
 Aeneid, 82, 83n. 9, 132n. 14
Vitruvius, 36
Vives, Juan Luis, 125n. 9, 159

Weber, Henri, 51n. 22
Wiesner, Merry E., 124n. 4

Yver, Jacques
 Le Printemps, 8, 14, 159–72

Zerner, Henri, 36n. 2